FRANCE

Guernica
San Sebastián
Irún
CONGADAS

PYRENEES
NAVARRA

Perpignan
Vernet
Andorra
Port - Bou
Olot   Figueras
Gerona   La Bisbal
Huesca   Palafrugell
Tardienta   Casa de la Selva
Zuera   Balaguer   La Garriga
Ebro   Mataró
ZARAGOZA   Lerida   Mollerusa   Granollers
Fuentes   Igualada
Mediana   Pina   CATALUÑA   BARCELONA
AN MTS   Belchite   Quinto   Flix
Azaila   Caspe   Falset   Tarragona
RAMA   Siguenza   Albalate   Corbera   Mora de Elbro
Almadrones   Alcañiz   Gandesa
Mirabueno   Morella   Tortosa
Brihuega   Vinaroz
adala jara   NUEVA   Teruel   San Mateo
ón   Tarancón   Benicasim
z   LA   Onda   Castellón de la Plana
cañas   Sagunto
ázar   VALENCIA
Mahora   Casas Ibañez   Palma   Mallorca
zanares   Albacete   Gandía
    LEVANTE   Almansa   Denia   Ibiza   Ibiza
    MURCIA   Alcoy
EÑA   Alicante
    Archena
    Murcia
    Cartagena
A
ERRA NEVADA
    Almería
Adra   ALGIERS

Mahón

Oran

ALGERIA

CONNOLLY COLUMN

CONNOLLY COLUMN

The story of the Irishmen who fought
in the ranks of the International Brigades
in the national-revolutionary war of the Spanish people,
1936– 1939

by
Michael O'Riordan

1979   New Books Dublin

Published by
New Books Publications
James Connolly House
43 East Essex Street
Dublin 2 Ireland

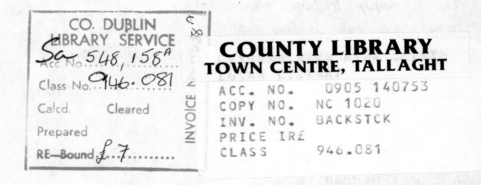

The author specially wishes to thank the following
for their help in writing this book:

John Peet,   fellow International Brigader, Berlin,
                  capital of the German Democratic Republic
Peter O'Connor, Waterford
Sean Nolan,   Dublin

Author's Note

Most chapters of this book are prefaced
by a short quotation.
Further information on these quotations
will be found in Appendix 1 at the end of the book.

TO THE MEMORY OF MY FATHER,
WHO, BECAUSE OF THE PROPAGANDA AGAINST
THE SPANISH REPUBLIC IN IRELAND,
DID NOT AGREE WITH MY GOING TO SPAIN,
BUT WHO DISAGREED MORE WITH OUR
"COMING BACK AND LEAVING YOUR COMMANDER,
FRANK RYAN, BEHIND."

Appendix

Maps

(Sources:

Maps 1, 3, 6a, 6b, 7, 8 from "Pasaremos", Berlin, German Democratic Republic, 1966

Maps 2, 4, 5 from "The Book of the XV Brigade", Madrid, 1938)

Illustrations

The illustrations follow page 64 and page 128

THE REVOLT OF GENERALS

... "Los Cuatro Generales,
    Los Cuatro Generales,
    Los Cuatro Generales,
    Mamita mia,
    Que se han alzado" ...

"ORPHANAGE BLOWN UP IN SPAIN!"
"NUNS AND CHILDREN KILLED!"

> "In the mining district of Barruelo near Leon, it is reported that insurgents blew up an orphanage for miners' children conducted by nuns." *(1)

It was with such headlines and atrocity stories that the struggle of the opposing forces in Spain, in the 'thirties, was presented to the Irish people. It provoked an understandable reaction from a people who themselves had suffered religious penalisation in the process of the British imperialist attempt to conquer Ireland.

There was very little redress to the balance of reports from Spain except in the smaller-circulation journals of the Irish Socialist and republican organisations.

"THEY LIED ABOUT SPAIN" was a little-read answering headline in "An Phoblacht", the organ of the Irish Republican Movement.*(2)

The contrasting headlines did not refer to the Spanish War of 1936–39. They dealt with an earlier armed struggle which occurred in the province of Asturias in October 1934. That struggle formed the immediate background to the later war which engulfed all of Spain, and in which roles were reversed with the insurgents becoming the lawfully elected Government.

In October 1934, the miners of Asturias had transformed a general strike into an armed revolt. The strike had been called to halt the imposition by right-wing political forces of the first phase of a Fascist dictatorship. For two weeks the insurgent workers fought fiercely and courageously, but were eventually crushed by the superior forces of the Spanish Foreign Legion and

Moorish troops. The latter for the first time since 1492 were reintroduced into Spain by the direction of General Franco at the War Ministry.

These forces machine-gunned men, women and children. The dead numbered 2,500. Sixty thousand were arrested and sentenced to terms ranging from one year to life imprisonment.

October 1934 was more than a preview of the events of 1936–39. As the headlines quoted above indicated it was to shape different reactions in Ireland to subsequent events in Spain.

In its story about Spain, the Irish Republican weekly said that: "Tribute is due to the gallant fight of the Basque, Catalan and Spanish workers who have perhaps failed, but at least fought."*(3)

The reference to the Catalans was occasioned by the fact that the Asturian Rising was accompanied by a revolt in Catalonia, the "Ireland of Spain" *(4), on the issue of national independence and long overdue agrarian reform. The Irish republican reference was understandable. In another October, that of 1920, there had taken place in Barcelona a demonstration of solidarity, which clashed with the police, during the 74-day hunger strike of the Mayor of Cork, Terence McSwiney. There were other Irish-Catalan bonds.*(5)

The October 1934 events were the outcome of developments in Spain that began in the period of 1923–29 under the military dictatorship of Primo de Rivera who had suppressed the "Cortes" (Parliament) and set out, influenced by his personal friend Mussolini, to replace it with a "Corporative Chamber."

There was intense popular opposition both to de Rivera and the Monarchy. This culminated in sweeping Left victories in the 1931 local elections. On April 14th, a Republic was proclaimed and the King, Alfonso XIII, had to flee the country in a British warship — a facility that was no doubt provided because his Queen, Victoria Eugenia, was the grand-daughter of another Victoria—the one of Irish Famine fame.*(6)

Because of the popular victory, the right wing forces reorganised themselves in the "Spanish Confederation of Autonomous Right Parties" (Confederación Española de Derechas Autonomas)—the CEDA. It was the rise of this front and its threat of imposing a fascist dictatorship which sparked off the Rising of 1934.

What sort of country was Spain in those days? It possessed a semi-feudal form of economy with three powerful institutions — the Grandee landowning class; a Church which was medieval, and an Army which was the instrument of the nobility.

The land was divided thus:

20,000	Grandees owned	51.1 per cent.
700,000	Wealthy Farmers	35.2 per cent.
1,000,000	Small Farmers	11.1 per cent.
1,250,000	Very Poor Peasants	2.2 per cent.

Among the Grandee class, the Duke of Alba—whose family's boast was that it could ride from the Atlantic to the Mediterrean without once leaving its own land—possessed over 86,000 acres; the Duke of Medinaceli owned over 197,000 acres.

There were 2 million farm-labourers who only worked half of the year.
In 1931 the rate of unemployment amongst them was 60 per cent.

The Church had riches estimated at a third of the national wealth. It was also a great landowner existing on, in, and as part of the feudal structure of Spanish society. It had a powerful influence in all spheres of the country's life, particularly in education. In the census of 1931, 46 per cent of the population could neither read nor write. Only in the Basque provinces was the Church in any way close to the people.

The Army was the relic of the "Conquistadores" that had once, in Latin America, created an empire with fire and blood. Despite the loss of its once big colonial empire the Army was maintained at full strength of 200,000 men and 20,000 officers (an extraordinary ratio of one officer to 10 men). It was a necessary internal force because of the ever insecure political situation arising from the reactionary economic and social structure.

The Governments of the Republic that had reigned since 1931 were far from radical. They never applied themselves to a solution of Spain's problems as, for instance, the crying need for a wholesale agrarian reform. The Establishment, despite the change of form of Government, still maintained its influence in the ruling of the country.

After 1934, Spain like many other parts of the world, experienced an economic crisis. This was particularly sharp because of the nature of the economy. The remedy was sought in big reductions in the already inadequate wages of the urban workers and the agricultural labourers. Whilst the rest of the world recovered somewhat by 1935 the Spanish economic decline continued. The 'conservative-centre' Government lead by Chapaprieta underwent a crisis. The Cortes was dissolved on January 7th, 1936 and a General Election was set for February of that year.

The country poised itself for a vital election struggle. The parties of the Left came together and formed a united electoral alliance known as the Peoples Front, which consisted of the Republican Union (a moderate party); the Republican Left (a party for democratic social reform); the Socialist Party (equivalent of the British Labour Party); the Socialist Youth; the Communist Party; the U.G.T. (Unión General de Trabajadores—Trade Union); and the Catalan Left Party, which had policies similar to the Republican Left but with the added objective of an independent Catalonian Republic.

It was a coming together of parties that were even antagonistic to each other but who, in the face of the common danger of a right-wing success, had temporarily sunk their differences.*(7)

Their platform of unity was based on eight points: —

1. An amnesty for the political prisoners who had been incarcerated since 1934, and who were estimated to number 30,000, and the reinstatement of workers who had been dismissed for political reasons.
2. Reforms to reinforce the constitutional guarantees of the Republic, and an enquiry into the deaths, tortures and jailings that followed the Asturian rising.
3. Reductions in taxes and excessive rents or leases for the peasants, with an increase in farm credits, and a new tenancy law.

4. Protection for small industry and trading.

5. A major programme of public works to relieve unemployment.

6. A modification of the system of direct taxation and the reform of credit through the Bank of Spain.

7. The reestablishment of labour legislation, of minimum wages, and the State direction and unification of private charities.

8. Educational reform with an increased number of schools and greater opportunities of secondary education for working class students.

On February 16th, 1936 the people of Spain gave a verdict through the ballot box. Of the 480 seats in the Cortes, the parties of the People's Front won 269.

A new Republican Government was elected. It included neither Socialists nor Communists but these two nevertheless gave it full support in carrying out the programme agreed to by the People's Front.

By June 1936 the new Government had made considerable progress. It had given land to 87,000 peasants; it had restored the semiautonomous status of Catalonia.

Toward the well-known right-wing Generals like Mola, Franco, Goded, and others, it had however displayed an amazing weakness. It 'exiled' them to key military posts, Franco to the Canary Islands, and Goded to the Balearic Islands. In such vital positions the Generals began to implement their plans for an armed overthrow of the lawfully elected Government and to set the clock back in Spain.

On July 18th, 1936 they began to carry out their rebellion. First, with the use of the Foreign Legion and the Moorish troops again, they took over Morocco. Franco had flown there in a British plane on July 11th accompanied by Commander Hugh C. B. Pollard of Scotland Yard.*(8)

Though successful in Morocco, the General's army mutiny failed in the main centres like Madrid, Barcelona, Valencia, Bilbao, and Albacete where the workers—as in hundreds of other smaller towns, armed only with sticks and improvised weapons, but with the superior force of numbers—had attacked the revolting garrisons and quelled the rising. Only in Burgos, Cadiz, Seville, and Salamanca had the rebellious generals been triumphant.

The revolt was doomed to failure—but then German Nazi aircraft ferried over the Moors and Foreign Legion from Morocco. There arrived Italian fascist tanks und more German planes, and an abundance of war material from the two sources. This showed a long and well prepared plan.*(9)

The revolt was carried over to the mainland of Spain as, concentrating their forces, the mutinous Generals moved forward under Italian and German air protection to take the capital, Madrid.

The revolt was to set off a war which lasted 986 days and which claimed one million lives.

Chapter 1 Notes

*(1) "Irish Independent," daily newspaper, October 9th, 1934.
*(2) "An Phoblacht" (The Republic), October 13th, 1934.

*(3) Ibid.

*(4) "March of Time," Series, No. 12. Pilot Press, London, 1943.

*(5). (i) In 1932, Juan Fabregas (in 1936 to be Catalan Councillor for Economics) wrote a book titled "Irlanda i Catalunya." On its publication he obtained from Eamon de Valera a message which stated: "Tell the Catalan people, comrade, that although I do not know the whole origin of their national problem, as far as I can judge it, their desire for liberty and independence has the warmest sympathy of the Irish people and their President." (ii) John Langdon-Davies recounted, in his book, how in 1921 he had lectured in the Catalan language in the town of Vich on the "Irish Sinn Fein Movement." See "Behind Spanish Barricades," Martin Secker and Warburg, London, 1936.

*(6) In 1845—46—47, during the reign of the British Queen Victoria, the Irish potato crop was destroyed by the blight disease. Living standards were so low that the potato was the main food. With the failure of this crop there occured the Great Irish Famine. With the deaths from starvation and enforced emigration the population dropped from 8 to 4 million. That this was no natural disaster is aptly described in the Irish folk-saying: "God sent the Blight, but the British sent the Famine." The amount of corn and cattle exported to Britain during the Famine would have fed, twice over, all those who died from hunger, but the imperial economy demanded these foodstuffs, and the English landlords demanded the continued payments of their rents. The role of Queen Victoria has been bitterly remembered in the legend that the subscription she gave the Famine Relief Fund amounted to £5, and that on the same day she gave a similar amount to a dog-show. The accuracy of the amount she subscribed to the Relief Fund has been contested, but what is unchallengable is the direct responsibility of her government for the horrors of the Irish Famine.

*(7) This development had a precedent in Irish history in the Irish Mansion House Convention in 1918 against the treat to impose Conscription on the Irish people. There united were such different parties and personalities as the Irish Parliamentary Party (Devlin & Dillon), Sinn Fein (Griffiths & de Valera), Irish Labour Party (Johnson & O'Brien), and the All-For-Ireland Party (Healy & O'Brien).

*(8) Vid. "News Chronicle," November 7th, 1936 for an article by the pilot of this plane, the British airman Captain Bebb.

*(9) "In March 1936, following the victory of the People's Front General Sanjurjo and Jose Antonio Primo de Rivera, fascist leader of the Spanish Falange (and son of the dictator of 1923—29) went to Berlin to finalise the details of foreign armed intervention against the Republic."—Page 17, "Spain, 1936—1939" by Jose Sandoval and Manuel Azcarate. Lawrence & Wishart, Ltd. London, 1966.

AN EARLIER
REVOLT
AND CIVIL WAR —
IN IRELAND

...."The Citizen Army is out today and
    if you wonder why,
Go ask the lords of the tram-lined way
    if their cash returns be high.
'Tisn't the bosses who bear the brunt,
    'tisn't you or I,
But the women and kids whose tears
    are hid as the strikers go stumbling by.
The docker loads two hundred tons in
    his master's ship per day.
At night the docker's daughter bends
    'her weary limbs to pray.
From the old North Wall to Liberty Hall
    was a deadline of unskilled,
They heaved and hauled when the bosses called
    and stopped when the bosses willed."

"The Citizen Army is out today and
    if you wonder why,
Go ask the men in the grey and green
    why the Plough and the Stars flag flies,
'Tisn't only the bosses we challenge
    now, 'tis Connolly has cast the die,
For the women and kids whose tears
    are hid as the soldiers go marching by.
Four hundred bosses planned to break
    that deadline of unskilled;
Four hundred bosses drink tonight
    for Connolly is killed.
But dead or alive, there are those
    who strive a glorious thing to do,
For Connolly built that union up,
    for the likes of me and you ..."

It was not by chance that the title of "James Connolly Unit" was taken by Irish men to designate their section from the others of the International Brigades that went to Spain to defend the Republican Government in 1936.

Twenty-one years before "Asturias" Ireland had its own fierce version of a class war in the form of the 1913 Lock-Out; this was followed three years later with the Easter Week Revolt of 1916 when the working class united with nationalists in a bid for Irish National Independence.

In those two great events the name and work of Connolly were predominant.

It is also another coincidence that, 15 years before the revolt of the Generals in Spain, Ireland also had a Civil War in which the forces involved were later to play a different part in presenting the issues of Spain's struggle to the mass of the Irish people.

James Connolly*(1) was born in Edinburgh, Scotland, in 1868, the son of Irish working class parents. Coming to Ireland he formed the Irish Socialist Republican Party, published a paper "The Workers' Republic" and wrote a classical historical study, "Labour in Irish History" and many pamphlets, including "Labour, Nationality and Religion", which was his reply to a series of Lenten Sermons against Socialism by Father Kane, S.J., in Gardiner Street Jesuit Church in 1910.

A leading organiser of the newly formed Irish Transport & General Workers' Union, he was deeply involved with Jim Larkin in the gigantic task of organising the Irish workers into trade unions, in Dublin, Belfast, Cork, Wexford and elsewhere.

His main work was to be in Dublin of the 1900's; it was then a city of poverty, gross exploitation, squalor and slums dominated by an iron-faced Employers' Federation, which looked with unconcealed hatred upon the activity of Larkin, Connolly and the Transport Union.

The masters were determined to smash the new workers' organisation. They were led by William Martin Lombard Murphy, the proprietor of the city's public transport, the Dublin United Tramway Company, owner of the morning daily newspaper, the "Irish Independent" and its "Evening Herald," a hotel, and a string of other concerns, (including the religious weekly the "Irish Catholic").

Martin Murphy fired the first salvo in the war against the workers by locking-out his workers who refused to sign a pledge that they would leave the Transport Union. The other members of the Dublin Employers Federation followed his example. The I.T. & G.W.U. hit back with a walk-out of the tramway workers on August 26th, 1913, the day of the annual event of the Royal Dublin Society's Horse Show. At 10 a.m. the crews left every tram where it stopped on the streets of Dublin and took the driving-handles with them. Scabs, under police and military protection, with rachets as driving handles, eventually took the tram-cars back to their depots.

The worker-employer conflict became a fierce one that involved all of the city's labour force. Meetings and demonstrations of workers were brutally batoned; two workers, James Nolan and James Byrne, were clubbed to death. The strikers set up their own defence corps which consisted of stewards, armed with hurley-sticks, flanking their meeting and parades. This was the nucleus of what later developed into the first workers's army in western Europe in this century—the Irish Citizen Army.*(2)

For eight long months of hunger and violence the workers fought a cold and grey struggle, illuminated only by profound feelings of solidarity, by the inspiring oratory of Larkin and the peristent organising work of Connolly. Faced with the combined might of the employers, the British-controlled police and the Church*(3), the workers eventually went back to work, but the document demanding their disassociation from the Transport Union was never enforced.

Dublin's 1913 struggle left a great imprint on the Irish working class. After the battle, Connolly wrote:

> "When that story is written ... by a man or woman with honesty in their hearts, and with a sympathetic insight into the travail of the poor, it will be a record of which Ireland may well be proud. It will tell of how old women and young girls, long crushed and enslaved, dared to risk all, even life itself, in the struggle to make life more tolerable, more free of the grinding tyranny of the soul-less Dublin employers ... and it will tell how that spectacle of the slave of the underworld, looking his masters in the face without terror, and proudly proclaiming the kinship and unity of all with each and each with all, how that spectacle caught the imagination of all unselfish souls so that the skilled artisan took his place also in the place of conflict and danger, and the men and women of genius, the artistic and the literati, hastened to honour and serve those humble workers whom all had hitherto despised and scorned."*(4)

"Big Jim" Larkin roared at the Employers Federation: "You'll crucify Christ no longer in this town."

The Dublin employers were revealed, not as they depicted themselves as "gentlemen of integrity and culture" but as savage, ruthless and vindictive protagonists in the war of classes. Mr. Dennehy, the Editor of the "Irish Catholic" did not bother to disguise his desire to shoot down the strikers: "Volleys fired over the heads of mobs," he maintained, "has always been a useless performance."*(5)

What was also revealed was the basic hostility to the workers' struggle of a conservative section of the National Movement. "Sinn Fein," the paper of Arthur Griffith, later the leading advocate of the Anglo-Irish Treaty of 1921, called Larkin a "Communist" and an Anarchist," and demanded that the British military and police force should be used to break a strike of railwaymen.*(6)

Three years after the strike, Connolly led the Irish Citizen Army into an alliance with the radical wing of the National Movement for joint participation in the Easter Week revolt. For Connolly it was to be a twin blow against the Imperialist War and for National Liberation.

It was his knowledge of Ireland's past history, of which he regarded the working class as the "only incorruptible inheritors," and his foresight about the future, that no doubt inspired his statement to the parade of the Irish Citizen Army, preparatory to taking up combat positions, "Being the lesser party," he said "we join in this fight with our comrades of the Irish Volunteers. But, hold your arms. If we succeed, those who are our comrades to-day we may be compelled to fight to-morrow." Later events in 1922–23 proved how correct he was.

The story of the 1916 revolt has been well documented and recorded*(7). The Volunteers, led by the radical patriot Padraig Pearse, and the Citizen Army commanded by Connolly, fused their forces into an army of the Irish Republic. It proclaimed Ireland's independence, and in doing so took on the might of the British Empire in a brave and unequal battle that lasted one week.

The native men of property were aghast at this display of disloyalty. They rushed to condemn it and to pledge again *their* loyalty to the British Crown. In such a favourable atmosphere the British set out to execute the leaders. A normal imperialist practice after disloyal insurrections was helped by the anti-rising prejudices generated by the employers' press.

Even though the overwhelming majority of those who fought in the Rising were Catholics, many of them devout ones, the Church leaders, with one exception, joined in castigating them.*(8)

Connolly had been seriously wounded in the fighting and he lay in the military hospital with gangrene having set in. He therefore was not amongst the leaders who were taken out daily and executed. These executions were to become counter-productive for the British. Feelings of disquiet amongst the populace grew to reactions of nausea and horror at the British Government's methodical and ruthless way of dealing with its opponents. Perturbed by this feeling, there were indications that it was hesitant about executing Connolly. He was a grievously wounded prisoner and they were also concerned with his links with the Labour Movement in Britain.

William Martin Murphy's daily "Irish Independent" was also perturbed but only about the British hesitancy. In its first issue after the Rising it made clear what should be done with all those involved. Its leader writer wrote:

> "No terms of denunciation that pen could write would be too strong to apply to those responsible for the insane and criminal Rising of last week. Around us, in the centre of Ireland's Capital, is a scene of ruin which is heart rending to behold ... Irishmen have been agents for the commission of this crime from the consequences of which it will take many years to recover ... The men who took the initiative in disturbing the peace of the country have not, and had not, a shred of public sympathy. Whilst they held certain strongholds the Military were being catered for and longed for by the citizens. These men are now held prisoners in England, and the leaders who organised, and the prominently active spirits *deserve little consideration or compassion.* So far as we are concerned when we think of the many valuable lives lost ... the enormous material damage which has already been done, and the huge loss of trade and employment which must be the consequence, *we confess that we care little what is to become of the leaders* who are morally responsible for this terrible mischief." *(9)

17

On May 10th, after a break in the executions, and when it was felt that Connolly would not be executed, the "Irish Independent" published his photo with the caption: *"Still lies in Dublin Castle slowly recovering from his wounds."* Then in unmistakeable terms it editorally demanded that he should be executed:

> "The rank and file and all those who filled only minor parts in the tragedy might be dealt with leniently; also those who came under a misconception. When, however, we come to some of the ring-leaders, instigators and fomenters, not yet dealt with, we must make exceptions. If these men are treated with too great leniency they will take it as an indication of weakness on the part of the Government, and the consequences may not be satisfactory. They may be more truculent than ever and it is therefore neces-sary that society should be protected against their activity. *Some of the leaders are more guilty and played a more sinister part in the campaign than those already punished with severity, and it would be hardly fair to treat these leniently because the cry for clemency has been raised, while those no more guilty than they have been severely punished. Weakness to such men at this stage may be fatal ... Let the worst of the ringleaders be singled out and dealt with as they deserve."* *(10)

The British acceded to the call. On May 12th, Connolly was brought on a stretcher to the execution-yard in Kilmainham Prison. The gangrene in his wounds would not allow him to stand. The firing squad strapped him to the stretcher which they propped up against the wall, and shot him.

On the morning of his ghoulish execution, the "Independent" still deman-ding his execution and having gone to press before its repeated clamour had been satisfied, wrote:

> "We cannot agree with those who insist that all the Insurgents no matter how sinister or abominable the part they played in the Rebellion should be treated with leniency. *Certain of the leaders remain undealt with,* and the part they played was worse than that of some of those who have paid the extreme penalty. *Are they because of the indiscriminate demand for clemency to get off lightly, while others* who were no more prominent *have been executed?* If so, leniency will be interpreted as a sign of weakness. *We are no advocates of undue severity but undue leniency to some of the worst fire brands would be just as bad.* We hear a lot about the fate of the insurgents, but little of the tragedy of the hundreds of victims; the widows, the orphans, the ruin and the havoc, all of which must be laid at the doors of the Insurgent leaders who for months planned and arranged the Rebellion. We think, in a word, that no *special leniency should be extended to some of the worst of the leaders whose cases have not yet been disposed of."* *(11)

Next day when it was satisfied that it had succeeded in its task of getting Connolly executed, it adopted in its editorial a much more conciliatory tone:

"With the executions of James Connolly and John McDermott, all the leaders in the Rebellion who signed the Proclamation of a Provisional Government have suffered the extreme penalty. The total executions to date number 15, and the penalty of Capital Punishment should not, we think, be inflicted in any other case ..." *(12)

In view of the special role played by the "Irish Independent" in its coverage and presentation of the later war in Spain it is not surprising how effective it was, given the way it reported and commented on the very events of Ireland's Rising to a people who were direct eye-witnesses.

Martin Murphy was also the proprietor of the religious weekly, "The Irish Catholic." In its coverage of the 1916 Rising (which is now honoured as *the Great* national occasion by the Government and by *all* the political parties in the Irish state), it wrote on April 29th, of the revolt:

"The movement which has culminated in deeds of unparalleled bloodshed and destruction of property in the capital was as criminal, as it was insane."

On May 3rd, Padraig Pearse (the devout Catholic whose picture now hangs in many Irish Catholic schools) of whom many laudatory articles are written in the contemporary issues of the "Irish Catholic" was executed. The religious weekly commented:

"Pearse was a man of illbalanced mind, if not actually insane, and the idea of selecting him as chief magistrate of an Irish Republic is quite enough to create serious doubts as to the sanity of those who approved of it ... Only the other day when the so-called Republic of Ireland was proclaimed ... no better President could be proposed ... than a crazy and insolent schoolmaster. This extraordinary combination of rogues and fools ... To find anything like a parallel for what occurred it is necessary to have recourse to the bloodstained annals of the Paris Commune."

After the 15 executions had taken place, the "Irish Catholic" summed up the outcome:

"What was attempted was an act of brigandage pure and simple, and there is no reason to lament that its perpetrators have met the fate which from the very dawn of history has been universally reserved for traitors ... We need say no more, but to say less would be traitorous to the highest and holiest interests of Ireland." *(13)

On this note the press of the men of capital and property pulled down the curtain on what it thought was to be the final act of a dangerous national drama.*(14)

But from the lime-pits where the bodies of the executed lay there arose a flame that ignited the country. Four years of militant rural and urban guerrilla struggle and mass resistance followed. Another new chapter in the old fight of the Irish people was written. The British sent in punitive detachments of "Black and Tans" (so-called from the uniforms which consisted of black police trousers and khaki soldiers' jackets) to try to terrorise the population into submission, but the people remained staunch.

That national struggle, however, had within it antagonistic pressures of those (who unfortunately dominated the leadership) of less rich property than William Martin Murphy but with a conscious potential and ambition for the same; and the rank-and-file who were sometimes torn between pure nationalism and the realisation that Ireland's problem of national freedom was, as Connolly pointed out, "a social question." *(15)

The struggle was broken by the British, not by the force of arms but by the tempting offer of a peace settlement, which would not give the country its national freedom, but would give to the potentially propertied sections within the national movement the opportunities to develop their class interests. A 'Pax Brittanica' which safeguarded Britain's imperial interests in Ireland. This was done by partitioning the island into two states—a colonial one in the North-East, and a neo-colonial one in the remaining major part of the country.

In the early hours of December 6th, 1921, an Anglo-Irish Treaty was signed by representatives of the Irish national movement in London.

The movement was split on the terms of the Treaty, and "the reactionary middle class and their allies, the feudal remnant ... came bawling out now from behind the demesne walls in whose shelter they had sulked all through the Independence struggle, to support the Treaty, not for the measure of political freedom it gave but for the fetters it imposed." *(16)

Civil War began between the pro-Treatyites ("Free Staters") and the anti-Treatyites ("Republicans") when with British-lent artillery the former launched an attack on the Four Courts Buildings, the Republican headquarters, on July 28th 1922.

On Sunday, October 22nd, the Irish Catholic Hierarchy issued a Pastoral Letter, which was read at all masses, condemning the Republicans (or Irregulars as the Bishops called them).*(17)

Less than seven weeks later, on December 8th (the Feast of the Immaculate Conception), Liam Mellowes*(18), Rory O'Connor, Dick Barrett and Joe McKelvey—the commanders of the Four Courts—were executed, without trial and at short notice, in Mountjoy Jail. In the months that followed, 73 other Republicans were to die in front of the firing squads before the Civil War ended in victory for the "Free Staters."

It was a war that was characterised by a large number of atrocities on the part of the pro-Treaty forces. In Dublin, the political section of their newly established police force maintained an 'Interrogation Centre' at Oriel House (now the head-office of a semi-state company, Gaeltarra Eireann, Ltd.). In the countryside many dark deeds were perpetrated.

In Ballyseedy, Country Kerry, there occurred one such act of horror. The writer Dorothy Macardle told that one morning a shattering explosion was heard. Later in the day a great rent was discovered in the roadside along with "hideous evidence of bloodshed." A short time later, "nine coffins containing the mutilated remains of prisoners were sent out from the barracks and for days afterwards the birds were eating the flesh off the trees at Ballyseedy Cross." *(19)

Nine Republican prisoners had been taken to Ballymullen Barracks in Tralee for interrogation. Each of them was first blind-folded, his arms tied to his sides and a hammer used to beat him around the head. Refusing to talk they were sentenced to death. The execution took the form of tying them to a land-mine and blowing them to pieces. One of the prisoners, Stephen Fuller, miraculously escaped death and crawled away to safety. The Free State forces shovelled the scattered remains of the other eight into nine coffins, one of which bore the name of Stephan Fuller.

> "There was madness among the people of Tralee. What prisoners were in those coffins? No one could tell. The people opened them in the streets. The frenzy that followed was terrible; the women seemed demented; Free State soldiers were stoned; the funerals of these Republicans kindled a fire through Kerry that it would be difficult to subdue." *(20)

In the daily newspapers of March 21st, 1923 the Free State Government issued a new army regulation which stated that "Prisoners who die while in military custody in the Kerry Command shall be interred by the troops in the area in which the death has taken place."

The Kerry Command was part of the South West Divisional Area of the Free State Army. The Divisional Officer in Charge was General Eoin O'Duffy*(21) who in 1936 was to lead an Irish contingent to aid Franco in his overthrow of the Spanish Republic.

Chapter 2 Notes

*(1) vid. "Life and Times of James Connolly." C. Desmond Greaves. Lawrence & Wishart, London, 1961.

*(2) The first workers' army in Europe as a whole in the 1900's, was of course, that of the participants in the Moscow 1905 Uprising. In his development of the Irish Citizen Army as an armed force, after 1913, Connolly wrote a brilliant series of articles for them, entitled "Insurrectionary Warfare" in his paper the "Workers' Republic" in 1915. They have been republished by New Books Publications, 14, Parliament Street, Dublin. See Appendix II

*(3) The Irish Bishops and priests were antagonistic to the strikers. In the Lenten Pastorals of 1912 they opposed Connolly and Larkin: "The evil is spreading; every year is adding new recruits to this professedly anti-Christian body; the false flag of a 'heaven here below' is being waved before our Irish people by the paid agents of Socialism." After the strike began the "Irish Catholic" warned the workers to listen to their priests, and it denounced Larkin as that "Moloch of iniquity." The heading of the editorial (27th September, 1913) was "Satanism and Socialism."

*(4) "Irish Worker" November 28th, 1914.

*(5) "Labour and the Republican Movement" by George Gilmore, Republican Publications, Dublin, 1966, p. 12.

*(6) Ibid. p. 12.

*(7) vid. "Life and Times of James Connolly," by C. Desmond Greaves, Lawrence & Wishart, London, 1961, and Appendix III

*(8) The one exception was Rev. Dr. Dwyer, Bishop of Limerick.

*(9) Irish Independent, May 4th, 1916.

*(10) Ibid. May 10th, 1916.

*(11) Ibid. May 12th, 1916.

*(12) Ibid. May 13th, 1916.

*(13) "Irish Catholic," May 20th, 1916.

*(14) There was complete unity between Catholic and Protestant employers. The latter would have formed the main bulk at that time. When the Commission of Enquiry into the Rising took place, the Protestant employer Dockrell maintained that the cause of the Rising was that the Government was to blame "for its feeble handling of the 1913 strike. He did not think that the police were active enough then" (!)

*(15) "Labour in Irish History" by James Connolly, Chapter 16.

Chapter 2   *(16) "The Gates Flew Open," by Peadar O'Donnell, Jonathan Cape, London, 1932.
*(17) vid. Appendix IV for the Bishop's 1922 Pastoral.
*(18) Mellowes, whilst in jail after the fall of the Four Courts, wrote a memorandum on the reason for the defeat of the Republicans. Known as "Notes from Mountjoy" it was captured by the Government, and published as a "red smear" in the "Irish Independent," September 21st, 1922. Relevant excerpts are in Appendix V of this book. For fuller information see "Liam Mellowes and the Irish Revolution" by C. Desmond Greaves, Lawrence & Wishart, London 1971.
*(19) "Tragedies of Kerry" by Dorothy Macardle, Irish Book Bureau, O'Donavan Rd., Dublin 8.
*(20) Ibid.
*(21) Vid. "Irish Republic." Dorothy Macardle, p. 701. Corgi Edition, London, 1968.

IRELAND IN THE THIRTIES

... "Our masters all, a godly crew,
    Whose hearts throb for the poor,
    Their sympathies assure us, too,
    If our demands were fewer.
    Most generous souls! But please observe,
    What they enjoy from birth
    Is all we ever had the nerve
    To ask, that is, THE EARTH" ...

The Irish Civil War, which began when the Free State forces attacked the Four Courts on July 18th, 1922, came to an end when de Valera, the spokesman of the Anti-Treatyites, issued "a ceasefire order" on May 24th, 1923. All during that Civil War, the British had supplied arms and material to the Pro-Treaty forces, accompanied by insistence upon more vigorous suppression of the Republican resistance. Lloyd George, the British Prime Minister, saw the military operations of the Pro-Treaty Provisional Government as the way of perpetuating British domination in Ireland with "an economy of British lives."

The means by which the Civil War was won were attested to by General Sir Nevil Macready, the General Officer Commanding-in-Chief of the British forces in Ireland, 1918–20, who said that the Treaty forces won, "by means far more drastic than any which the British Government dared to impose during the worst period of the Rebellion." Though the British claimed hundreds of Irish lives through military operations, assassinations, on the spot executions, shooting of prisoners "trying to escape" etc., their total of judical executions in the period of 1916–21 amounted to 40. In the ten months of the Civil War, the Free State courts martial executed 77 fellow-Irishmen.

After the "cease-fire," the Government, based on the support of the most conservative elements in Irish society—the big ranchers, the commercial and industrial interests that were bound up with the British regime—proceeded to consolidate their power. By July 1923 the jails and prison-camps held 11,316 opponents, of whom 250 were women. It imposed "loyalty tests" on teachers, municipal and state employees, which no Republican in all conscience could accept. Consequently many of them had to leave the country and emigrate abroad, particularly to the U.S.A.

An uneasy peace characterised the life of the Government led by Cosgrave. Coercion Acts were promulgated which established Military Tribunals for the hearing of charges against political opponents of the regime.

Popular opposition to the pro-Treaty Government developed to the point that it was defeated in the General Election of February, 1932.

In contrast to the conservative forces that supported Cumann na nGaedheal*(1) (the pro-Treaty party), the new government led by de Valera drew its support from large sections of the workers, the unemployed, small farmers, small employers, self-employed, and some of the middle farmers engaged in milk production.

The issues in the Election were the easement of the grip of the Anglo-Irish Treaty on political and economic development; the payment of the Land Annuities*(2); the Cosgrave policy of "cattle for export" rather than industrial development; cuts in social services (the Cosgrave administration actually reduced the Old Age Pensions)*(3) and the release of the Republicans in the military prisons (among those imprisoned was the then 30 year-old, Frank Ryan, leading Left Republican personality and later the Commander of the James Connolly Section of the International Brigades in the Spanish War).

In the period before the election, General O'Duffy, (then Chief of Police) had visited the Bishops of the various dioceses and showed them files that purported to show that "Communism was making rapid headway" in Ireland.*(4). Four months before the polling day, the Bishops issued another Pastoral Letter.*(5)

In February 1933, General O'Duffy was relieved of his post as Chief of Police by the de Valera (Fianna Fail) Government. This action was to spur the pro-Treaty party into all sorts of serious political obstruction. Already in early 1931 in an attempt to curb the popular opposition that later triumphed in the 1932 Election it had formed an organisation of ex-members of the Free State Army. This was known as the A.C.A. (Army Comrades Association). Two months after his dismissal it adopted O'Duffy as its Leader and the "blueshirt" as its uniform, thus patterning itself on the rising Fascist movements in Europe.*(6)

The electoral defeat of the Cosgrave Government was a serious setback for Irish conservatism. Under the flag of "anti-communism" it set out to regain ground by fomenting a hysterical campaign. This was not only directed against left-wing Republicans and the newly emerging Irish Communist movement, but also against the Fianna Fail party led by de Valera.*(7)

All this occurred at a time when a dark night was falling on Europe. Hitler was gaining power. Mussolini was well entrenched in Italy. In Roumania and Hungary, the crooked creed of Fascism was going from strength to strength. In Portugal the Corporative state of Salazar was firmly established, and in Spain reaction was poised to inflict its blows on the workers and peasants.

The future seemed to be with those who wore fascist shirts of various colours and who preached of a "new order."

The sweep of European Fascism helped the "Blueshirts." In 1933 they claimed a membership of 100,000*(8). In December 1934 O'Duffy attended an International Fascist Conference in Montreux, Switzerland at which were representatives of 13 other countries: Austria, Belgium, Denmark, France,

Greece, Holland, Italy, Lithuania, Norway, Portugal, Roumania, Spain and Switzerland. The representative from Norway was none other than Major Quisling.

On February 28th, 1934 one of the Fine-Gael-Blueshirt Party's senior spokesmen, Deputy John A. Costello (later Prime Minister in 1948) said in the Dail (Parliament) that "the Blackshirts were victorious in Italy, the Brownshirte were victorious in Germany, as, assuredly the Blueshirts will be victorious in Ireland."*(9)

The Irish Fascist movement had a number of theoreticians: Ernest Blythe, (the ex-Minister for Finance who had reduced the Old Age Pensions); and the Professors, Michael Tierney of University College Dublin, and James Hogan and Alfred O'Rahilly who were attached to University College Cork.

Even the poet W. B. Yeats began to dream of new order grandeurs that inspired him to write a marching song for the Blueshirts.*(10)

Swollen with their own success and the triumphs of Fascism abroad, the Blueshirts planned a Mussolini-type march on Dublin in August 1933. This was opposed not only by the Government but also by the workers and Republicans who mobilised themselves to prevent it. In face of such opposition O'Duffy called off the march. From that capitulation began the eventual decline of the movement.

The economic base of the "Blueshirts" were the big merchants, big farmers and their hangers-on. The big farmers, the suppliers of live cattle to the British market had been hit by the economic sanctions imposed by the British. Instead of being anti-British they blamed the de Valera Government for the "loss of their British market." They consequently refused to pay rates and embarked on campaigns of violent resistance to enforced rate-collections by blocking roads and railway lines, tree-felling and telegraph-wire cutting.

They were not without powerful backing from Church personalities. Cardinal MacRory said that it was "a shame and a sin" to wage the Economic War and that a settlement should be negotiated with Britain.*(11)

In December 1933, the Bishop of Achonry, Dr. Morrisroe, sent a personal congratulatary telegram to O'Duffy. On some platforms priests wearing, not Blueshirts, but blue sashes appeared. This served the purpose of clearly manifesting their politics without having to obscure their Roman collars.

Opposition to Socialist ideas was forcibily manifested in March 1933, when Connolly House, the headquarters of the Irish Revolutionary Workers and Small Farmers Groups (the founding organisation of the Communist Party of Ireland) was attacked and sacked by an incited hymn-singing mob. Despite this terroristic atmosphere the Communist Party of Ireland was launched in June 1933. It was to become one of the participating organisations in the formation of the Irish Republican Congress, a united movement of Left Republicans, Tenants and Unemployed associations, Small Farmers and Irish Anti-Fascists that was set up in September 1934 under the leadership of Peadar O'Donnell, George Gilmore and Frank Ryan.

The fascist threat of the "Blueshirts" was not demolished by the de Valera Government. This was done by a powerful "anti-blueshirt" movement that developed in the streets and in the countryside. A fighting united front met them everywhere — led by such people as Frank Ryan, Peadar O'Donnell, George Gilmore, (of the Republican Congress) Tom Barry (of the Irish Republican Army) and Sean Murray and "Kit" Conway (of the Communist Party of Ireland). This front drove the "Blueshirts" off the streets in many violent encounters. Prominent in that campaign were many who later fought in the International Brigade.

The climate aroused by the successes of the Fascists abroad favoured the "Blueshirts." The same was true of the tremendous emotive propaganda of the Irish newspapers. The papers aimed a two-pronged attack on radical and progressive ideas at home and at the general revolutionary movement abroad. Side by side with support for the "Blueshirts" were such statements as that which appeared in the newspaper "Killkenny People" in September 1934 which when writing about the Soviet Union, described it as "that unhappy land which is the first and probably the only country in the world where the recognition of a Supreme Being is an offence punishable by death." *(12)

Yet despite the strong "anti-communist" feeling which the various journals and newspapers not only reflected but stimulated, there was no lack of courage in opposing such hysterical outpourings. In September 1934 when it was feared that the Nazis would execute Ernst Thaelmann*(13) a group of Irish writers and other public figures called for his release. They were Frank O'Connor, F.R. Higgins, Shelah Richards, Seamus O'Sullivan, Peadar O'Donnell, Mrs. Sheehy-Skeffington, Professor T.B. Rudmose Brown, Denis Johnston and Sean O'Faolain.*(14). Significantly enough, two refused to associate themselves with this call; Francis Stuart, who in the latter period of World War II broadcast for the Nazis, and Aodh de Blacam, who became an apologist for Franco in 1936.*(15)

There were other happenings of that period that merit mention. When the Nazi Ambassador Herr von Kuhlmann came to Ireland in October 1934 he was greeted with slogan placards that demanded in English, German and Gaelic—"The Release of Thaelmann"; "Freiheit für Thaelmann'"; and "Leig Amach E." Two 36-feet long scrolls fluttered down from the top of Nelson Pillar making the same demand.

Nevertheless, the campaign completely to discredit any progressive ideas and thought went on relentlessly and scurrilously. It reached a crescendo in, and after, February 1936 when the Spanish Popular Front Government was elected. Against a background of repetitive "atrocity" stories of nuns raped, priests murdered, churches desecrated—and more and more orphanages being blown up—the Spanish Republican Government was presented to the Irish people as a "group of bloodthirsty bolsheviks, persecutors of the Faith." *(16)

The "Martin Murphy" group of newspapers excelled themselves with banner headlines and "extra-special" horror stories. A deep feeling of revulsion against the Spanish Republican Government developed amongst an ever-increasing section of the Irish people.

An atmosphere was created which made it possible, for instance, for a combined group of "Blueshirts" and various other obscurantist elements to mount an attack on the Annual Commemoration Parade for the dead of 1916 which was held in April 1936. In it marched Captain Jack White, one of the

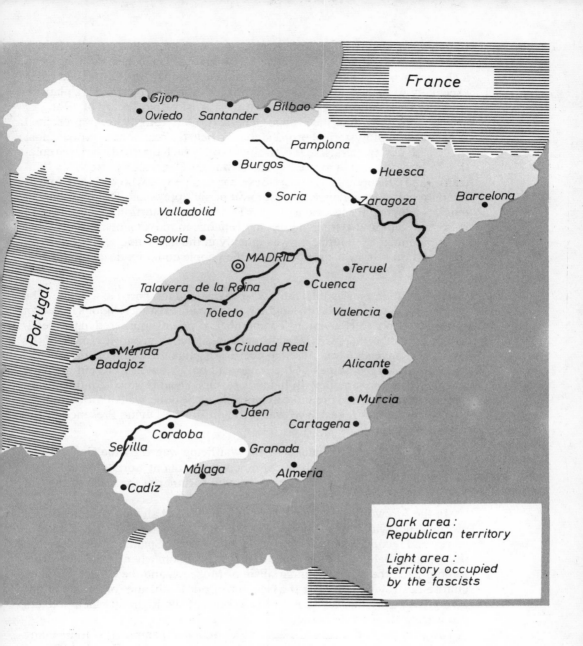

Spain, the front line, July 1936

founders of the Irish Citizen Army, and William Gallacher, the British Communist Member of the House of Commons. Gallacher had long been a champion of Ireland's struggle for national freedom. In 1921 he had come especially to Dublin to warn (in vain) of the British Government's plans to trick the Irish national movement with the Anglo-Irish Treaty of 1921.

The actual revolt of the Franco Generals on July 18th, 1936 was presented at a new pitch of hysterical propaganda. To help the reactionary propaganda, the British newspapers, like the "Daily Mail" (which then had a large circulation in Ireland), began to present the traitorous Generals as "Rebels," "Patriots" and "Insurgents" descriptions dear to a people who had long fought for national independence against an imperial oppressor. The Irish papers quickly adopted these designations. The all-out distortion even confused many workers in the Irish labour and republican movements.

A pamphlet by de Blacam was quickly in the newsagents, church bookstalls and on sale in the schools. In it the people could read statements like this:

> „Outrages against nuns were many, and too horrible to relate. The complete tale of slaughter of these unresisting religious is known only to Heaven ... The number of priests murdered in this festival of hate was 400 in Barcelona alone. A striking example of the savagery was this: the coffins of nuns were dug up and opened and the bodies of the long dead holy women were put on show in the streets with hideous results. Dead Carmelite monks were exposed in the same manner along the outer wall of the church ... Dreadful sacrilege was wrought on the Divine Presence of the altar."

Then, describing the course of the war being waged by the Generals, he painted a pious image of them: "Franco met Mola at Burgos. There, after Mass at the historic cathedral, they prayed together at the tomb of the Cid Campeador ..."

In the foreword the readers were enjoined: "Let all who read, read with awe and not with anger, praying for the victory of the good cause and for mercy and reconciliation among the people of noble Spain. Let all remember that Spain is fighting for the cause of all Christendom when its soldiers strive to hold back the atheistic materialism of Moscow, and the church-burning, culture-destroying fury. For the freedom of our Faith, and for the life of our own grave, Christian civilisation, the parties of the Right and their soldiers are waging the Last Crusade."

Towards the end of his 32-page mass-circulated pamphlet, with its many gory details, he issued the call: "Were we to stand neutral or indifferent, when this Last Crusade is being fought, we would deserve to go down to history as a shameless generation, helping by our silence and consent the new Crucificion."

In the ferment of organised prejudice and hysteria, O'Duffy, the discredited leader of the "Blueshirts", saw the opportunity to pose as a champion of religion. A few weeks after the Franco revolt he announced his intention to form an Irish Brigade to "fight for Christianity in Spain." It also gave him the prospects, on his return, of personal power in Ireland.*(17)

There was a rush of volunteers for O'Duffy's Irish Brigade. On September 3rd, the "Irish Independent" could report that they numbered 5,000. Three weeks later, O'Duffy went to Spain and there had talks with General Mola and Franco himself about his Brigade.

At the same time the "Irish Christian Front" was formed. At first it was composed of a heterogeneous collection of individuals; a Miss Aileen O'Brien, born in California, reared in South Africa and educated in the Germanic part of Switzerland from where she came to Ireland with a lavish anti-Soviet illustrated exhibition called "Pro-Deo" (this venture was subsequently discovered to have been financed by Vickers, the British machine-gun manufacturers); a Mr. F. Noone, an Englishman with the grandiloquent rank of head of the "League of Crusaders"; Lord ffrench (sic); Dr. Brennan, the Coroner for Dublin South County, and Mr. Paddy Belton (of whom more anon).

The "Christian Front" for the support of Franco quickly grew into a nationwide organisation. Long discredited politicans, many of whom lost their seats in the 1932 General Election, agilely jumped on the bandwagon of "saving Christianity." Huge rallies were held in various Irish centres. They were graced by clerical and lay dignitaries, including some from the Trade Union and Labour movement, such as Michael Keyes, Labour Deputy for Limerick and a prominent member of the National Union of Railwaymen.

At these mass rallies when the audiences were sufficiently aroused they would be asked to give a special salute—not the Blueshirt-Fascist one—but to *cross* their hands above the head and to chant in unison "Long Live Christ The King!"

At every meeting of almost every local, city and county council resolutions were passed praising Franco. It was truly the era of Salem, in which every native 'crawthumper' reigned supreme.*(18)

A typical example of the oratory at such council meetings was reported in the "Irish Independent" (September 1st, 1936):

> "Mr. H. McMorrow, N.T, P.C. speaking at the Leitrim County Council said, 'Paid agents of Russia were in every parish in the Free State at present. There were 40,000 Communists the Free State who were prepared to take up guns against God'."

Incredible as it may seem now, this succeeded in getting unanimous support for his resolution condemning the 'Irish Communist Society' (sic!) and the Republican Congress. In the course of his speech he also said:

> "'At a recent meeting in Dublin, ..., the establishment of a workers republic, which meant the establishment of a Soviet State was advocated. Under such a regime,' continued Mr. McMorrow, 'nuns and priests would be murdered, morality, freedom and independence would be at an end, the labouring classes would be treated as serfs as in Russia'."

Despite the hysterical support for the Spanish Generals the Irish Anti-Fascists stood firm. Credit for this must go to Sean Murray,*(19), the Secretary of the Communist Party of Ireland who in his weekly articles on international affairs in the columns of the duplicated "Worker" gave a clear analysis of what was happening in Spain.

A week after the Franco revolt there appeared from him the first of many articles on the Franco revolt:

"In Spain, as we write, a new and immortal page of working class history is being inscribed. The reports published by the capitalist press are like a cloud of dust obscuring the fighters as they strain in combat, but from the glimpses of the truth we can picture the rest; and the heart of working class Ireland goes out to our Spanish brothers and sisters in their life-and-death struggle with Fascism."

And then after detailing the programme of the People's Front and how neither the Socialist or Communist Parties were in the new Government, but had promised full support in carrying out that programme, the article recounted the week-old events of the Revolt and the peoples' fighting resistance and concluded with ... "Greetings to our heroic Spanish brothers and sisters in their glorious fight!" *(20)

Meanwhile, the Christian Front continued in its work of popularising the Franco cause. Its main spokesman now became Mr. Patrick Belton, Deputy of Dail Eireann and a member of the Dublin County Council to boot. Formerly a member of Fianna Fail, he had been expelled from that Party in 1927. He lost his parliamentary seat in the June election of that year; and then joinded the Cumann na nGaedheal (Pro-Treaty) Party and was successful in being returned once again to the Dail. He joined the "Blueshirts" with O'Duffy, and again was expelled from Fine Gael, (the party that arose from an amalgam of the "Blueshirts" and Cumann na nGaedheal). He set a still unbeaten Irish record for changing political parties!

He became the most vociferous of the "Front" spokesmen, calling everybody to task. On one occasion when Father Ryan of Queen's University, Belfast, was engaged in a debate about the war in Spain with the Northern Ireland M.P., Harry Midgely, the priest—who was pro-Franco—indicated that he did not necessarily agree with the wild exaggerated "atrocity" stories that were being peddled about by Paddy Belton. Whereupon the "Commander-in-Chief" of the Christian Front wrote to Father Ryan demanding to know when that clergyman had "joined the Communists!"

As the "Front" developed, Belton felt so secure in his position that not only did he act as a "lay pope" calling clergymen into line but he also began to treat trade unionism in a cavalier fashion. He was not alone a big farmer and a big shopkeeper, he was also a big builder. He had received a Government subsidy for the construction of a housing estate (which he called "Belton Park"!). To qualify for the subsidy he was bound to pay the trade union rate of 1s/3d per hour to his labourers. This he did not do, paying only 1s/— per hour, despite repeated protests from the Irish Transport & General Workers' Union*(21)

This situation, even if it did not set off a strike, certainly provoked a poem of mockery in the pages of an Irish anti-Franco journal*(22) ...

"Hail, glorious 'Saint' Patrick!
(The 'new', not the 'old')
With a nice shiny halo,

And Blueshirt, I'm told.
You were stuck up so high
On your platform of steel
That you nearly reached Heaven
So great was your zeal."

"In the fight for your Seat
You trade in the Faith
Just as did the Keogh-Sadliers*(23)
You now emulate.
But the pulse of devotion
That throbs in this land
Will never keep time
With Pat Belton's Brass-Band."

" 'This said you were building
A new 'Christian' state;
But the workers, the Bolshies!
Asked trade-union rate.
Fifteen whole pence an hour
For a labourer's job
Would endanger his soul
So you gave him a 'bob'."

"I'm thinking, now, Patrick,
That you're growing vain
And hoping to live
In a castle in Spain.
But, Pat, sure we'd miss you
If you lived afar
From sweet Donnycarney,
Your own Alcazar."

Whilst the Bishops of Ireland organised pro-Franco collections (that netted over £ 43,000!) in the emotive circumstances of Masses on the occasion of the Feast of Christ the King (October 25th, 1936*(24), the Christian Front was busily engaged in similar activities. Their collections were supposed to be for Medical Aid for the "Nationalist" Army in which they collected some £ 32,000. Some of this amount found its way to the Franco military forces, and later in the "Front" itself there was much controversy about its actual total disposal. No balance sheet was ever published!

The task of exposing the use of religion to cloud the real issues of the struggle in Spain was undertaken by people like Sean Murray, Peadar O'Donnell*(25) and the priest, Father Michael O'Flanagan.

Meetings were held to tell the truth about Spain. At one of these, in the Engineers Hall, Dawson Street, Dublin, Murray—an outstanding public speaker—told his listeners:

"I warn the workers of this country that this is not a rebellion of
the type of Easter, '16 in Dublin. It is the type of Lord Carson's
rebellion in Belfast, General Gough's mutiny at the Curragh. It

is a landlord's rebellion. It is a conspiracy of Fascist murderers against the decent people of Spain.

"I warn the workers not to be misled into believing that this a religious issue in Spain. It is no more a religious issue than was the Irish Land War, the struggle for Home Rule, the fight for complete independence, but what did the aristocracy of this country say the fight was about? Religion, of course! Home Rule is Rome Rule, roared the landed Ascendancy and their hirelings, the generals and lawyers. 'Were fighting for religious freedom!', shouted Carson, Craigavon and General Gough.*(26)

"Franco at the head of a Mohammedan army of coloured Moroccans and the cut-throats of every nation under the sun organised in the Spanish Foreign Legion is out to restore Christianity to Spain! O'Duffy and Lombard Murphy and other kindred spirits are calling for Irishmen to go and join this army of ruffians! Was there ever such a combination of hypocrites and traitors! But the Irish people who have seen these gentlemen at work in their own country, have seen their country partitioned by the introduction of religious issues into politics, and seen the Republic of Ireland betrayed by these supporters of Franco and his Riff army will not be deceived into throwing their lot against the Spanish people.

"The Spanish Government has the support of four-fifths of the Spanish people. It has the support of the trade unions, of the Socialist, Communist and Republican parties, AND, bear this in mind, it has the support of the Catholic masses and such Catholic Conservative parties as the Basque Nationalists. That's the reply to the lying press.

"The Fascist generals at the head of their Foreign Legion and Mohammedan army have the support of the Spanish aristocracy, all that is decayed and rotten in the life of Spain. They are backed by the two Fascist powers, Germany and Italy, who are trying to dictate to the Spanish people, and are prepared to plunge the world into a dreadful war in order to set up a Fascist dictatorship in Spain. British Imperialism, too, is playing a treacherous dirty part in this business. It is spreading the wildest lies against the Spanish Government and people. It is hampering the Spanish fleet in its operations against Franco, and encouraging the brazen policy of the two Fascist Powers. Thus we see arrayed against the lawful Government, against Spanish democracy and its heroic defenders, the imperialist forces of Europe. That is the position. The gallant Spanish people are not only fighting against the traitors within Spain but against the enemies of liberty throughout all Europe, Ireland included. This makes the Spanish question indeed a question for the friends of freedom in every land. Are we in Ireland to stand aside and allow this crime against the people of Spain to be carried out before our eyes? If we did, we would be traitors to the best traditions of our race, to the men who gave their lives for the cause of freedom in this country. What would Wolfe Tone, John Mitchell, or James Connolly and Pearse say if they could speak to us to-day! They would be behind their brother Republicans in the Spanish fight. They would be against the Murphys, the Churchills and O'Duffys. They would have nothing but contempt for the treason to Republicanism of de Valera and his newspaper, ('The Irish Press') who are also behind the criminal Fascist gang in Spain.

"The spirit of the dead and the voice of justice speak to us in this crisis and tell us plainly to do our duty by the heroic defenders of freedom in the Spanish Republic. It is a shame that no lead has yet come from the official Labour movement on this question. The Spanish workers are giving their lives in defence of liberty in every country. I ask every Irish man and woman to answer the question. What are you doing? Have you raised your voice on the side of the heroic Spanish people? Have you protested against the shameful attitude of de Valera's newspaper, against the foul campaign of Murphy's bloodstained 'Independent', against the criminal attempt of the Fascist O'Duffy to raise a brigade of Irishmen to attack the Spanish Republic? It is the sacred duty of every man and woman in their trade unions and political parties, to demand that their leaders give the people a lead in support of justice. We must demand that a United Front of Labour and Republicanism be formed in this country in support of the Spanish people, and that financial assistance be organised for the sufferers of this Fascist rebellion. By doing so we will be striking a blow to the enemies of Ireland and taking a step forward to the social and national emancipation of our own nation, to the smashing of coercion, the opening of the jails and the clearing away of would-be Fascists in both Northern and Southern Ireland."

This appeal was made on August 10th, 1936, three weeks after the outbreak of the Franco revolt. It did not receive the support that it should have got, because of the power and pressure of lay and religious press campaign and the thundering denunciations from the pulpits and the political-religious hustings. It did however have the effect of steadying many of those in the Republican and Labour movements who were vacillating under the pressure of the pro-Franco propaganda campaign.

The atmosphere of hysteria forced the leadership of the Irish Labour party and of the Irish Trade Union Congress to "forget" that in 1934 they had issued a Joint Manifesto*(27) condemning Fascism, the advocates of the Corporative State, the Fine Gael-Blueshirt movement and its leaders. When the Fine Gael leader, W.T. Cosgrave, moved in the Irish Parliament on November 27th, 1936 that Franco should be recognised as the head of a legal Spanish Government, the Labour Party deputies remained silent. The climate was so intimidating that even in the Workers' Union of Ireland—the militant trade union led by 'Big' Jim Larkin—there was a regulation forbidding one of its leading officials, Jack Carney, from adopting a public anti-Franco stand.*(28) Nevertheless, the courageous work of Murray, O'Donnell and Father O'Flanagan went on. O'Donnell, well known guerrilla fighter in the war against the British and the Civil War, and comrade of Liam Mellowes, played an outstanding part. Associated with him in the task of defending Republican Spain was another famous guerrilla leader, Ernie O'Malley, the author of one of the best books on the Irish war of independence, "On Another Man's Wounds" (which has been republished under the title "Army Without Banners".)

Peadar O'Donnell had actually been travelling in Spain when the revolt broke out. His first-hand accounts made an important contribution to making the truth known. In his book "Salud!" *(29) he recounted his experiences and observations of the early days of the war, and also of the hysterical reaction that was being fomented in Ireland.

He had planned to spend his holidays, July 1936, in the Highlands of Scotland, but the idea of a holiday in Spain "came roaring in at the last moment and I was swept along" ... "There was this touch of edging away from cross dogs in my search for a cottage in the Highlands; crowds had got into the habit of singing hymns at me and hurtling bottles" ... "I missed the turn for Scotland and took the road for Spain instead. I am not sure that this stumbling at the crossroads was bad luck, anymore than the chance that drew me to a cottage at Adull Island in an earlier attempt to work out my dream of a workshop among fishermen was bad luck. I walked into a Civil War in Achill just as I walked into one in Spain, and it was the same Civil War."

He also gave in his own inimitable style the picture of how the Christian Fronters mobilised the "lumpen-proletariat" elements in Dublin as an offensive force against any attempts to hold meetings in support of Republican Spain. There was a concentration to win the support of the "Animal Gang" of backward vicious criminal elements who specialised in bottlethrowing and of potatoes studded with razor blades against opponents. Despite their backwardness, the "Gang" in question was not too convinced about the righteousness of the Franco cause:—

> "The Animal Gang was not so sure they should regard us as enemies, so they were assembled in a hall to be told all about us. First, they were given religious emblems by a lay theologian who spoke briefly to them about the menace of Communism. They were then addressed by a very charming young woman who explained what was exactly on foot. She had it on good authority that I had taken a leading attack on churches, and she quoted from a magazine conducted by an order of priests in the City of Dublin to show that this was no new development for me. This article told how I had gone to Russia some years ago and studied church burning at the Lenin College in Moscow (the truth is, by chance, I have never been in Russia.) The fight in Spain was only a preliminary to a war against religion in Ireland, and the Churches in Dublin would be the first to suffer. She was in a position to reveal the plan the Reds had set out for themselves in this respect. The Pro-Cathedral would be turned into an anti-God museum.

Westland Row Church would be made into a dance-hall. University Church would become a public-house.

> She asked the meeting if they wanted to see their Pro-Cathedral turned into an Anti-God museum, and they thundered back angrily that they did not want their Pro-Cathedral turned into an Anti-God museum. So she told them the way to stop that was to obey the word of the Holy Father and promote Catholic Action by making war on the Reds. And asked them if they wished to dance and make love in Westland Row Church, and the crowd thundered angrily that they did not wish to dance and make love in Westland Row Church. So she told them to obey the Holy Father and make war on the Reds. And she asked the meeting if they wanted to make themselves drunk in a bar set up inside University Church, and they roared back angrily that they did not want to make themselves drunk in a bar inside University Church. So she asked them to cross their hands above their head and swear to fight to the death against the Reds."

In face of this type of propaganda about the issues in Spain many people believed that, with the outbreak and progress of the war there, attacks on priests and churches in Dublin were also imminent ...

> "Some children at play outside Gardiner Street Church chalked meaningless inscriptions on the footpath. Three old ladies on their way home from a convent where they had been given alms paused outside the chapel door, 'Mother of Jasus,' one exclaimed, 'see the Communist marks.' Others whom life had similarly wrecked rushed up and joined them, and in a few moments breathless speakers were proclaiming the news that the Communists had marked all the churches of the city so that the burning gangs might know where to start their work that night."

Peadar O'Donnell described other means by which the defenders of the Franco cause in Ireland went about their task ...

> "Catholic" employers were approached to sack Red workmen. The first victims to this drive were shop assistants, clerical workers, messengers, isolated workers not protected by trade unions—but doctors and solicitors came under fire too, and their earnings were endangered. The campaign extended to the lodging-houses in the villages where, if a landlady refused to order a 'Red' lodger to leave, the other lodgers would be induced to leave her ... Denunciations from the altar on Sundays swelled into a spate."

About the leader of the Christian Front he had this to say ...

> "Mr. Belton had one great advantage. He could give the new Movement some touch of a non-political appearance, as he had been in and out of so many parties that one had nearly as much right as another to claim him."

With every indication of attempts to win support for the anti-Franco struggle, the Irish capitalist and religious press stepped up their campaign of opposition. Despite the paucity of progressive papers and the continued existence of a pogrom-like atmosphere the work of the first Irish defenders of the Spanish Republic began to have some results.

A Committee was formed in Dublin and Belfast to organise an All-Ireland Ambulance Corps for the Spanish Republican forces. A Spanish Aid Committee was formed in Dublin with leading members like Mrs. Sheehy-Skeffington (well known public figure and widow of an Irish pacifist who had been murdered by a British officer during the 1916 Rising); Nora Connolly O'Brien (daughter of James Connolly); the writer Dorothy Macardle; Robin N. Tweedy and Mai Keating. Its Secretary was Aileen Walshe (later the wife of Frank Edwards, member of the Irish Section of the International Brigade). Likewise in Belfast a Committee was formed around Betty Sinclair, W.H. McCullough, Jack Magougan and Victor Halley. Harry Midgely, the Chairman of the Northern Ireland Labour Party, Member of the Stormont Parliament, and Alderman of the Belfast City Council declared his stand against Franco.

When the London Executive of the Amalgamated Transport & General Workers' Union granted £ 1,000 for humanitarian "Red Cross" help to the Spanish Government, there began a campaign of intimidation to force Irish members of that Union to repudiate that action. However, the Irish conference of the A.T. & G.W.U. meeting in September 1936 declared its approval of the Executive's decision.

Though, as pointed out, the Irish Catholic Church was violently pro-Franco with many of its leading figures playing a most vociferous part in the work of the "Christian Front" and otherwise, one outstanding Irish priest, the Reverend Michael O'Flanagan, fearlessly championed the cause of Republican Spain.*(30)

Father O'Flanagan was born in Castlerea, County Roscommon in 1886. He spent time in the service of the Church in the U.S.A. and Rome before he became curate at Cliffoney, County Sligo. When the people were denied access to their traditional turf-banks, he asked them to wait, one day in 1915, after he had celebrated Mass, and then addressing them in the chapel grounds, he said:—

> "What I advise the people to do is for every man who wants a turf bank and can work a turf spade is to go to the waste bog to-morrow and cut plenty of turf. You need not be in the least afraid. God put the bog there for the use of the people and if you are not as well fortified as if you were in a German trench, you will be a formidable opponent enough if anybody chances to come along and interfere with you. I'll go myself, and if anybody has a spare turf spade. I'll show you that I can cut turf too. Have we been quiet too long? Are we going to let poor little children shiver to death with cold next winter for want of a fire? I think that if we start to-morrow morning at nine o'clock it would be a good thing."

This was typical of the approach of Father O'Flanagan—he put people first. This was the clue to his attitude to the Spanish War.

Associated closely with the Irish National struggle, it was he who delivered the funeral speech at the lying-in-state of O'Donovan Rossa at Dublin's City Hall, on the day before Padraigh Pearse gave the final historic oration at Glasnevin Cemetery. He played a prominent part in the Sinn Fein Election of 1918, earning the tribute from Cathal Brugha as "the staunchest priest who ever lived in Ireland". He was invited to open the first meeting of Ireland's parliament, the First Dail Eireann.

Just before the signing of the Anglo-Irish Treaty of 1921 he was sent on a mission to America, and so was out of the country during the Irish Civil War. He went from America to Australia where he made contact with an old friend, Archbishop Mannix, who had played a leading part in that country in resisting conscription. The Archbishop presented him with a set of vestments and a chalice.

After several years abroad he returned to an Ireland of the post Civil War. He straight away flung himself in the Republican struggle once again. It was a period of defeat, of disillusionment and of bleak despair. For him it was a time of searching for what went wrong with the "Four Glorious Years." Speaking at an Easter Week Commemoration in 1926 he gave some of his conclusions in a speech in which he said:—

> "Pearse represented the new generation in the fight of Easter Week, 1916, and it serves to illustrate how quickly the waves of resurgent national life succeed each other in Ireland when we remember that side by side with Pearse was the old Fenian who had served so many years of imprisonment in the Jails of the Empire, Tom Clarke.

> "When these two men took their stand side by side, it was mainly as representatives of Irish Nationalism that they stood, but *there stood with them another great Irishmen who stood not merely for the right of Ireland to national independence, but who was in a more particular sense the representative of the workers of Ireland—James Connolly. He laid down his life for the Irish people to assert for them not only the right to be the political rulers of Ireland, but the economic owners of Ireland as well.*" (Author's emphasis).

To such a man the issue of the Franco revolt was no complex one. Speaking at a meeting of solidarity with Republican Spain in the Engineers Hall, Dublin on December 3rd, 1936, Father O'Flanagan said:—

> "The fight in Spain is a fight between the rich privileged classes against the rank-and-file of the poor oppressed people of Spain. The cause being fought for in Spain was nearer us than we realised. The Foreign Legion and Moorish troops were to Spain what the 'Black and Tans' were to Ireland. The Spaniards didn't send any people to join the 'Black and Tans' here and they didn't make any collections in their churches to help the 'Black and Tans' in Ireland.

"The Government of Spain was elected by the votes of the people and on the other side was a body of rebels, mostly the old Army. They were just the same type as our own General Goughs and Carsons at home. The people who were calling the Spanish rebels 'Patriots' had proved to be very bad judges of Patriots in Ireland.

"When we had real Patriots fighting in Dublin they were called looters and it was said they were in the pay of Germany. We had an editorial in one newspaper (an allusion to the 'Irish Independent') asking for the death of the noblest Patriots in the history of Ireland, James Connolly and Sean McDermott.

"It was in the Red Republic of Russia that nationalities similar to the Basques, got their fullest freedom.

"We have had the experience here," said Father O'Flanagan "of men being refused the rites of their Church because they were real Patriots. Even clergymen, who were true to their country, such as Father Murphy in '98 were spurned by the ecclesiastics of their time, who were hand and glove with the British Government. Now we have monuments erected to these Patriot priests. I hope that the Irish people will see through the hypocrisy and sham of their enemies and rally to the cause of justice." *(31)

Unfortunately few of the Irish people rallied to the cause of the Spanish people. An important factor for this failure was a Joint Irish Bishops' Statement on October 12th, 1936*(32) which supported Franco.

In November, the first batches of O'Duffy's volunteers went to Franco Spain via Portugal. The next month, 700 of them embarked from Galway on the Nazi Liner, "Urandi". In January another 500 assembled at the Waterford port of Passage East, but the promised transport ship never arrived. They, and the balance of the thousands who volunteered to take part in the O'Duffy Crusade never got to Spain. They were left behind, frustrated at being unable to participate in the "glorious task of defending the Faith".*(33)

So, a bare four months after the Generals' revolt, but after a period of hysterical indoctrination, Ireland was committed to their infamous ranks.

There was little then that Irish anti-Fascists could do, but there was, however, brought into play a traditional Irish weapon, which has so often been used in what seemed hopeless situations before—and that was the satirical ballad. There began to circulate, though in too limited circles, the "BALLAD OF O'DUFFY'S IRONSIDES."

"You've heard of Slattery's light dragoons,
Who fought at Waterloo,
And those who ran at Bunker's Hill
Or bunked at Timbucktoo?
There is still a page of history
Which may never be uncut
To tell the glorious story of
O'Duffy's mounted foot."

"In old Dublin town my name is tarred
  On pavement and slum wall.
  In thousands on its Christian Front
  The starving children call,
  But with my gallant Ironsides
  They call to us in vain,
  For we're off to slaughter workers
  In the sunny land of Spain."

"Let loose my fierce Crusaders,
  O'Duffy wildly cries.
  My grim and bold moss-troopers
  That poached by Shannon sides,
  Their shirts are blue, their backs are strong,
  They've cobwebs on the brain,
  If Franco's troops are beaten down
  My Irish troops remain."

"Fall in, fall in, O'Duffy cries,
  There's work in Spain to do,
  A martyr's crown we all will gain,
  And shoot the toiers through.
  In paradise an Irish Harp,
  A Moor to dance a jig,
  A traitors' hope, a hangman's rope
  An Irish peeler's pig."*(34)

"On Badajoz' red ramparts,
  The Spanish workers died,
  And Duffy's bellowing Animal Gang
  Sang hymns of hate with pride.
  The sleuths who called for Connolly's blood
  And Sean MacDiarmid's too,
  Are panting still for workers gore, from
  Spain to far Peru."

"Bring forth my war horse Rosinant,
  The bold O'Duffy cries,
  My squire Patsy Panza*(35)
  The man who never lies;
  My peeler's baton in my hand
  A gay knight-errant I,
  O, Allah guide our gallant band,
  And Hitler, guard the sky."

"Put on my suit of 'Daily Mail,'
  A crescent on my back,
  And hoist the 'Independent' Flag
  The Freeman's Castle-hack;*(36)
  My name is tarred in Dublin town,
  On pavement and slum wall,

But far away in distant Spain
Grandee and landlord call.
With Foreign Legion, Riff and Moor
We'll fight for Al-fon-so
And the fame of O'Duffy's Ironsides
Will down the ages go."

"On the village pump in Skibbereen*(37)
An eagle screams its woe,
As it hears the tramp of armed men
From the bogs of Timahoe,
The war drums roll in Dublin town
And from each lusty throat,
The Fascists sing the ancient hymn,
'The Peeler and the Goat'."

In a much more serious vein was the poem that was inspired by the news that came of the deeds of the Franco forces in the town of Badajoz. This was a part of Spain where the peasants had taken some land, for which they offered rent, from the huge tracts of an absentee landlord. When the fascists entered Badajoz they perpetrated a massacre by herding the people into the bullring and mowing them down with machine-guns. A short and horrible glimpse of the truth was revealed in an agency dispatch of Monday, August 17th, 1936:

"In each street there is a barricade, and each barricade is now almost a mountain of corpses. A red, blood-stained wall, the grim spot where some 2,000 men were executed by the insurgents.

"The ruined blood-stained streets are haunted by the pitiful figures of women and children dressed in the deepest mourning, who move furtively about looking for the bodies of their loved ones. I witnessed terribly pathetic scenes whenever a woman found the corpse of her husband or son among the bodies littering the abandoned barricades."

In contrast to this description, de Blacam in his pamphlet "For God and Spain" (p. 23) quoted:

"At Badajoz as soon as the insurgents entered the city the churches were immediately filled to offer thanks to God for delivery from tyranny and from extermination."

The association of the O'Duffy of the Irish Civil War with Franco evoked the bitter memories of the atrocities in Kerry. One under the pseudonym of "Somhairle MacAlstair"*(38) who had written many satirical ballads about O'Duffy's Brigade and the "Christian Front" now took another theme with the solemn note of muted horror:

"From Ballyseedy To Badajoz"

"O'Duffy's dupes are killing as their Fascist masters bid,
Gas bombs are falling on the mothers of Madrid

(The birds at Ballyseedy picked flesh from off the stones,
And Spanish suns at Badajoz are bleaching baby bones).
God, they claim is Fascist, the Voice that Pilate feared,
Is spitting streams of hellish hate from a Moorish soldier's beard;
They use the Cross of Calvary to veil their foul designs,
'Vivat Hispania' the voice of Hitler whines.

"Defend the Republic", cries out the sturdy Basque
'Tis the crescent, not the Cross, is looming over Spain,
But the servants of Mahommed will glut their lust in vain;
The hireling hordes of Italy that come with ev'ry tide,
Will conquer proud Iberia when all her sons have died.
O'Duffy calls his 'godly band' and leads them to the fray,
(They murdered Liam Mellowes upon Our Lady's Day).
God help you, Spanish Connollys, if Lombard Murphy's crew
Should blood their drunken hellhounds and send them after you,
Our lands are marked with crosses to trace their bloody trail
While others lie in quicklime pits in every Irish jail.
They cant of Salamanca, our Irish pharisees;
They hope to lure our Irish youth to learn their murder trade,
And bring them back to Ireland as a Fascist shock brigade,
They talk of Hearth and Altar as the things that they defend
(which means in Fascist lingo the sweater's dividend);
O'Duffy crowned dictator, 'midst the rolling of the drums,
And the dupes that listened to him still rotting in the slums."

The many references to the Moors in that poem were occasioned by the fact that they provided the main force to be given licence to carry out the atrocities in Badajoz. They were under the direct control of Franco at the line of Badajoz.

This cry from a soul was not heard to any great extent; O'Duffy's Brigade had gone off to cheers and blessings, and the religious and secular press carried on with its task of popularising the Franco forces.

Despite this, however, the Irish anti-Franco forces fought back. Although the Labour Party and the Trade Union movement leaders kept a quiet silence, with here and there some of its prominent members actually speaking on pro-Franco platforms, many individual trade union leaders made generous but anonymous personal subscriptions to the Irish Aid Committee for the Spanish Republic. One leading trade union personality who refused to be anonymous but instead forthright in raising financial aid from his fellow trade unionists was John Swift, now retired General Secretary of the Irish Bakers' Union and a leading figure in the International Union of Food Workers.

The work of the small group of people who comprised the Irish movement of solidarity with Republican Spain went on regardless of all opposition. On Sunday, January 17th, 1937 it was able to hold, despite organised opposition, a meeting in one of Dublin's largest halls, the Gaiety Theatre.

The main speaker at this meeting was a famous Basque priest, Father Ramon Laborda, who had been in Dublin five years previously for the 1932 International Eucharistic Congress.

"Many really think that General Franco is a defender of Christianity," said Father Laborde, "but already 13 Basque priests have been Put to death by Franco's forces. The war is not religious nor were the elections before it concerned with religion. The Left Wing had beaten the Right Wing with votes, and now the Rights were trying to beat them with guns." Father Laborda compared the treatment of both priests and people in the Basque Country by the Franço forces to ravages of the Hun Attila. "Without availing themselves of the law courts," he said "generally without even asking a question, they shot priests and workmen to the accompanying cries of 'Long Live Chirst the King' and 'Long Live Catholic Spain'. That was the religion in the name of which they talked in their broadcasts and newspapers."

"In no sense was it a religious war," added Father Laborda, "Neither was it a war for civilisation. In the Basque country, at least, it was frankly and indisputably an imperialist war—anti-autonomist and anti-Basque. Because they were General Franco's political opponents, thousands of peaceful and defenceless citizens had been dragged from their homes and shot, after they had been beaten and their bones disjointed as in the case of Senor Olarte, Attorney of Vittoria."

"In the regions of the Basque country at present dominated by Fascists the native language is forbidden. There are heavy penalties for talking it, and even the Basque salutation, 'Agur' had been prohibited. Basque music and dancing also had been suppressed. Poets, writers, orators and musicians had all been persecuted, many of them shot, and others of them imprisoned or exiled."

As to the statement that the Government in Spain was Communist, Fr. Laborda said that of the 480 deputies that composed the Spanish parliament only 15 seats were held by the Communists. "I will explain, but by no means justify, the burning of churches after the elections," he went on, "Before the elections came on, many of the churches were used by Fascist priests as an opportunity for political meeting." It was a crime to link Christianity with such a blood-thirsty brute as Franco, said Father Laborda.

"When I read recently that the Catholics of Ireland were offering men and money to Fascist Franco—the personification of the most brutal imperialism, I exclaimed, indignantly: 'It is impossible! Ireland could not do that unless she had been miserably deceived'."(39)

By then the Irish anti-fascist movement had moved a long step forward. Its struggle had now taken on a new dimension, Irishmen had gone to Spain not to fight for Franco but to take their place in the ranks of the International Brigades that had sprung up to fight and die side by side with the Spanish people in their resistance against the Fascist generals.

Already by the time of Father Laborda's meeting two Irishmen had died in the defence of Madrid, and nine others had fallen on the Cordova front. Unknown at that time to those present at the Gaiety Theatre meeting, the twelfth had already given his life in the fighting at Las Rosas. He was Denis Coady of Dublin, symbolically enough, the son of a Dublin worker who had fought, starved and suffered with Connolly and Larkin in the great lockout—the blood of "1913" was still being spilled, but not this time in Dublin's O'Connell Street, but on the battlefields of Spain, in defence of "the poor oppressed people" there.

*(1)   Cummann na nGaedheal later changed its name to Fine Gael (United Ireland Party—U.I.P.)

*(2)   The Land Annuities were an annual payment of over £ 3 million pounds to the British Government as compensation for bonds it had issued to the former British landlords in Ireland who, following a fierce "Land War," were forced to agree to let the tenants buy their farms. When in 1932, the de Valera government withheld payment, the British Government retaliated by declaring an "Economic War" by imposing heavy duties on Irish cattle exports.

*(3)   The Cosgrave Government, like the Bishops, were not keen on any form of direct state social services. It believed that the alleviation of poverty was a field for voluntary Church-run charities. When limited school meals were introduced, the Rev. Canon Hegarty of Belmullet denounced the "queueing up of children" as this was "engendering Communism." Vid. "Irish Times" daily newspaper, November 19th, 1935.

*(4)   Vid. statement by de Valera in the Dail (Irish Parliament), November 27th, 1933.

*(5)   See Appendix VI. for the 1931 Bishop's Pastoral.

*(6)   For more information, see "The Blueshirts" by Maurice Manning, Gill and Macmillan, Dublin, 1970, and a documentary Broadcast by Radio Eireann (Dublin) July 7, 1974.

*(7)   The "United Irishman" (organ of the Cumann na nGaedheal Party) in its editorial of December 10th, 1932 declared: "It had become all too apparent that Mr. de Valera is leading the country straight into Bolshevik servitude. We do not say that he had set out with the objective of creating a communist state ... but whatever his intention may have been, or may not be, he is proceeding along the Bolshevik path almost as precisely as if he was getting daily orders from Moscow. His government is unmistakably out to demoralise the police force, and render them incapable of dealing with armed terrorists. His financial policy is leading inevitably to despoilatory taxation, which, rounded off with a dose of inflation, may be trusted to dispose of our Irish Kulaks."

*(8)   "Irish Times," February 9th, 1934.

*(9)   Dail Debates (the Irish parliamentary Hansard), Vol. 50, col. 237.

*(10) The Blueshirts song "O'Duffy Abu" was sung to the old Irish marching air, "O'Donnell Abu". In his "Three Songs to the Same Tune," W.B. Yeats wrote ...

> "Down the fanatic, down the clown
> Down, down, hammer them down,
> Down to the tune of O'Donnell Abu,
> When nations are empty up there at the top,
> When order has weakened and faction is strong,
> Time for us all, boys, to hit on a tune, boys,
> Take to the roads and go marching along."

*(11) "Irish Times", August 16th, 1932.

*(12) The militant Irish lay-Catholic organisation, the "Legion of Mary" which played an active anti-socialist role in the 1930s, organised in 1969 a tour of the Soviet Union. It made no statements, on its return, attesting to the correctness, or otherwise, of the "Kilkenny People's" claim.

In connection with the U.S.S.R. it should be mentioned that in 1920 negotiations opened between it and the Irish Republic, and a Draft Treaty of Friendship was drawn up providing for mutual recognition, trade and joint activities for peace. Article 5 of the Draft Treaty read: –

"The Government of the Russian Socialist Federal Soviet Republic accords to all religious denominations represented in the Republic of Ireland every right accorded to religious sects by the Russian Constitution, and entrusts the accredited representative of the Republic of Ireland in Russia the interests of the Roman Catholic Church within the territory of the Russian Socialist Federal Soviet Republic."

Despite continued negotiations the Draft Treaty of Friendship was never signed. Because of the vacillating attitude of de Valera further contact was made impossible. (For fuller information see the book, "With de Valera in America" by Dr. Pat McCartan.)

Finally in September 1973 an agreement was reached for the establishment of diplomatic relations between Ireland and the U.S.S.R.

*(13) Ernst Thaelmann, leader of the Communist Party of Germany, was arrested by the Nazis in March 1933 on trumped-up charges. A world wide protest movement frustrated the Nazi aim to execute him. They held him in prison and murdered him in July 1944 in he infamous Buchenwald Concentration Camp.

*(14) In the Spanish War the majority of poets, writers and playwrights were on the side of the Republic. In 1937, the "Left Review" issued a questionaire as to where they stood. 100—among them Sean O'Casey— were for the Republic. 16 declared themselves neutral, including T.S. Elliot, Ezra Pound, Charles Morgan, Alec Waugh, H.G. Wells, Vita Sackville and Sean O'Faolain, who shifting his position from that of 1934 declared that the issue was "not the business of an artist." Mairin Mitchell, the author of "Storm over Spain" (Secker and Warburg. London, 1937) was pro-Republican Spain. Oliver St. John Gogarty was an "admirer of Hitler and Mussolini, close friend of Rothermere, Yeats and General O'Duffy and violent anti-semite" according to Grattan Freyer in an article in "Scrutiny," the Cambridge literary magazine, Vol. VI.

*(15) Aodh de Blacam, was a columnist for the "Irish Press" (the daily newspaper founded by de Valera) under the pen-name of "Roddy the Rover." In September 14th, 1936 ("The Feast of the Exaltation of the Cross" as he termed the date) he wrote a mass-circulation pamphlet which sold for twopence. It was titled "For God and Spain" and bore on its cover the crucified Christ and a vertical sword. It was published by the "Irish Messenger," a journal of the Irish Jesuit Fathers, 5, Great Denmark Street, Dublin, C. 16.

*(16) A propaganda "godsend" was the news item that appeared in the Irish newspapers in February 1936, telling of the organisation of an "International Godless Congress" in Moscow. The "Irish Independent" had even reported that Dimitrov (of the Reichstag Fire Trial) had spoken at this Congress—that never took place! The Soviet News Agency, Tass, had issued a quick denial that such a Congress had taken place or was even planned. Of all the Irish newspapers only the "Cork Examiner" published the Tass denial. Later it was revealed that the report had originated from Goebbel's Nazi Propaganda Ministry. This did not diminish its value later as opening text for many speeches calling for the defeat of Bolshevism and Republican Spain, and for the necessary victory of Franco. See, also appendix IX.

*(17) Peter Kemp, member of the pro-Franco Spanish Foreign Legion, in his book, "Mine Were of Trouble," Cassell, London, 1937, conceded that O'Duffy was using the Spanish War "to strengthen his own political position in Ireland."
A similar but belated admission was made 38 years later by the Blueshirt, ex-Minister, Ernest Blythe, ... "O'Duffy wanted to bring thousands of men to Spain to get military training, do a little fighting, them come back, put him in power here ... He was a wild man. He was full of pride and conceit and thought no man his equal ... ... Thousands of idiots would have gone to Spain to 'fight for Christ'. Dolts through the country would have thought that they were defending their faith." —— "An Irishwoman's Diary". Irish Times, April 22nd, 1974.

*(18) "Crawthumper" is an old Irish expression of contempt for those who display hypocritical and excessive piety. "Craw" is the Gaelic word for breast, hence a "thumper" is one who beats his in an outward display of "devotion."

*(19) Sean Murray (1898—1961) born the son of a small farmer in Cushendall, Co. Antrim. His grandfather had been a United Irishman in 1798, and the three generations of his family spanned the most tumultous years of Irish history, 1798, 1848, 1867, the Land League, and 1916—23. Although showing signs of being a brilliant pupil at Glenaon National School, he had to leave it at the age of 14 years to work on his father's and uncle's farms. However, his teacher, "Master" McNamee took a continuous interest in his education and introduced him to classical literature. As a youth he became interested in the national and labour movements. He joined the I.R.A., becoming Commandant of the Antrim Battalion which engaged in attacks on police barracks. Whilst on his way to join a Flying Column, with his Adjutant Malcolm McKeegan, in 1920, he was arrested by the British forces and brought to Crumlin Road Jail, Belfast, and later transferred to the Curragh Internment Camp, from which he was released on the declaration of the Truce that preceded the Anglo-Irish Treaty of 1921. In December 1922 he met Peadar O'Donnell for the first time; thereafter they became close friends and comrades-in-arms on the Republican Anti-Treaty side in the Civil War. Afterwards he emigrated to Britain becoming a delegate to the London Trades Council and Secretary, of the "Irish Worker League" which had been formed in Ireland by "Big Jim" Larkin. In 1928—31 he was a student at the Lenin International School in Moscow, and when he returned to Ireland he became Organiser of the Irish Workers' Revolutionary Groups. He was nearly burned alive when its headquarters, Connolly House at Great Strand Street, Dublin, was set alight by a religious-incited mob in March 1933. At the foundation of the Communist Party of Ireland, in June of that year, he was elected General Secretary. In October, he was served with an expulsion order from the territory of Northern Ireland which he refused to recognise. He continued to make many secret journeys there but was eventually arrested and jailed. A man of great intellect, he was an outstanding Marxist-Leninist scholar with the specific ability to apply his revolutionary knowledge to the Irish conditions. He was also a prolific journalist, editor and pamphleteer.

*(20) "The Worker," 32 Lower Ormond Quay, Dublin, July 27th, 1936.

*(21) Mentioned in the "Irish Democrat," Dublin, March 27th, 1937 as having appeared in "Labour News." an Irish Labour Party periodical.

*(22) "Irish Democrat", Dublin, April 24th, 1937.

*(23) John Sadlier and William Keogh, leaders of the Irish "Catholic Defence Association" were popularly known as "The Pope's Brass Band." They were so nicknamed because of their passionate and pious (and hypocritical) declarations of loyalty to the cause of the exploited Catholic tenant-farmers, and the fact that they always appeared in public surrounded by Bishops. Elected in the Westminister General Elections of 1852 they, with the support of Cardinal Cullen and the Irish Hierarchy, betrayed their election pledges. As a reward for their treachery, Keogh was appointed Solicitor-General, and later Lord Chief Justice of Ireland in which post he zealously sentenced many Fenians to long terms of imprisonment. Sadlier was made a Junior Lord of the British Treasury, and poisoned himself following the public scandal of the collapse of an Irish small depositors bank with which he was associated (For fuller information, vid: "Ireland Her Own," an outline history of the Irish struggle, by T.A. Jackson, published by Lawrence & Wishart, London, Chapters XIX and XX.)

*(24) Catholics form 94.9% of the population of the area known as the Republic of Ireland (in which the main events recorded in this book took place), and 34.9% in Northern Ireland. In the 1930s attendance at Sunday Mass would have been 100%. Even today, when there is a marked general decrease in Mass attendance in all Catholic countries, 94% attend in the Republic, according to a survey conducted in 1971 by the Market Research Bureau of Ireland.

*(25) It would be impossible in a footnote to give even an outline of the work of Peadar O'Donnell (February 28th, 1893 ——) as a writer, and of his remarkable record as a fighter in the Irish struggle for independence, and of his varied activities in the field of international solidarity. Readers are refered to "The Life and Times of Peadar O'Donnell," by Michael MacInerney due to be published by E. & T. O'Brien, Dublin.

*(26) *Sir Edward Carson* was Solicitor-General in the British Tory Cabinet, 1900—06. In 1912 he organised

the armed Ulster Volunteer Force which opposed the intention to grant Home Rule to Ireland by the then British Liberal Government. Lenin described Carson as "the British Purishkevich."

Lord Craigavon (Sir James Craig), representative of the landed gentry, as a leader of the Ulster Volunteer Force, who became first Prime Minister of Northern Ireland.

Brigadier-General Hubert Gough a leader of the 1914 "Curragh Mutiny" of British Army Officers, who refused because of the ties of class and tory politics to carry out a disarming of the Ulster Volunteer Force. (For Lenin's view of this Mutiny, vid; his Collected Works, Vol. 20, pp. 130–33, 205–08, 226–27, and "Lenin On Ireland" published by New Books Publications, Dublin, 1970.

*(27) Vid: Appendices VII and VIII.

*(28) Vid: "Jim Larkin" by Emmet Larkin, First Nel Menter Edition, London, 1968, p. 269.

*(29) "Salud!," by Peadar O'Donnell, published by Methuen, London, May 1937.

*(30) See; "Father Michael O'Flanagan—Republican Priest," by C. Desmond Graeves, Connolly Publications, London.

*(31) "The Worker," December 12th, 1936.

*(32) See Appendix XI

*(33) The atmosphere in which O'Duffy's men left can be seen in such a typical statement as that of Rt. Rev. Monsigner Ryan, Catholic Dean of Cashel: —

"The Irish Brigade have gone to fight the battle of Christianity against Communism. There are tremendous difficulties facing the men under General O'Duffy, and only heroes can fight such a battle. Those at home can help the cause in their prayers; the Rosary is more powerful than the weapons of war; in the presence of Our Lord Jesus Christ, let us promise that we will offer up a decade of the Family Rosary daily ... let us pray that the destruction of civilisation may be averted and that Christ may live again and reign, and that Communism, and the powers of darkness in it, can be brought to nought."

A description of their departure was given in a Documentary "There is a Valley in Spain called Jarama," broadcast by Radio Eireann (Dublin), May 26th, 1974: "As each group left Dublin crowds gathered to cheer them off, the flags of Ireland, Spain and the Pope were waved, religious emblems were distributed and the occasion took on the air of a medieval crusade. But perhaps the most dramatic departure of all was from Galway at the beginning of December when a German ship picked up a contingent waiting aboard the 'Dun Aengus' tender. Initially, they passed the time singing 'The Faith of Our Fathers' and 'The Soldiers Song', but they were in no mood for singing when they reached Spain." One of O'Duffy's Brigade whe had gone with the first batch through Portugal, described their arrival: "We were at Mass at a place called Caceres, 'tis a little town in the centre of Spain, seven or eight miles from Madrid, or somewhere, and when they arrived they were shabby looking, they had beards on them and we didn't know, we hardly recognised them, even the fellows we knew. They got a terrible time on the boat. They had to go out on a tender, 'twas a German ship, you see, that was taking them over, and they couldn't come inside the three mile limit, for they had to go out on a tender and they were there for two nights and for two days and when the boat did arrive beside the tender, they were some of them sick and cold, and they wouldn't volunteer to go up the ladder, climb up the rope ladder to get on to the ship. So, about half of them was all that volunteered to go up the ladder, the others returned home."

*(34) A reference to O'Duffy as ex-Chief of Police. "Peeler" is a traditional Irish derisive term for a police-man, after Sir Robert Peel, founder of the English Police Force.

*(35) A reference to Paddy Belton of the "Christian Front."

*(36) The "Freeman" was a newspaper taken over by William Martin Murphy and incorporated in his daily "Irish Independent." "Castle-hack" a term applied to Irishmen who collaborated with the British Government's centre of authority at Dublin Castle.

*(37) "Skibbereen Eagle"—the title of an Irish provincial weekly which became an object of fun for its ponderous leading articles on world affairs. Its most famous one was that which analysed Imperial Russia's foreign policy. It concluded with the warning to the Czar that "the Skibbereen Eagle" was keeping its eye on him."

*(38) The identity of "Somhairle MacAlstair" is still a well-kept secret, at his own request (even in 1978!). It is incorrectly given as Desmond Fitzgerald in "A Poet's War" by Hugh D. Ford, Oxford University Press, 1965.

*(39) "The Worker", January 23rd, 1937. Published at 32 Lower Ormond Quay, Dublin.

THE INTERNATIONAL BRIGADES

... "Die Heimat ist weit,
Doch wir sind bereit,
Wir kämpfen und siegen für dich:
Freiheit! ...

At the start of the rising in July 1936, mass resistance by the workers defeated the mutinous Generals in the main centres of Madrid, Barcelona, Valencia and Bilbao. But they had been successful in other parts of Spain; and in the autumn, with Moorish troops flown in from Morocco, covered by Italian Fascist and German Nazi planes, and with great supplies of tanks, artillery and other war material from both these sources, the Generals set out to take the capital, Madrid. This was an important objective for political, military, geographical and prestige reasons.

It was accepted, because of the overwhelming military forces that the Franco army had assembled, that this would be an easy task. But the Franco forces with their massive support from Hitler and Mussolini did not reckon with the heroic people of Madrid, who dug defence trenches, threw up fortifications and manned the barricades determined that the Fascists would not capture their city.

On November 4th, 1936 one of the mutinous Generals, Varela, summoned a special press conference of foreign correspondents at the captured town of Getafe to announce, "You may inform the world that Madrid will be captured this week." This reflected a confidence that seemed justified by the overwhelming armament of the besieging fascist forces and their progress to date. Toledo had fallen, Talavera had been taken, and everywhere in the path of the Fascist advance the ill-armed and untrained workers' militia had retreated before the long columns of Italian tanks, the clouds of foreign planes and the onrushing squadrons of Moorish cavalry.

The workers' militia resisted as best as it could, with an inadequate supply of rifles—the Republican Government, the legitimate one, being refused supplies of arms from the Western countries.

In anticipation of a quick Generals' victory, the Italian and German Foreign Ministers, Count Ciano and Von Neurath had on October 21st, drawn up their document of formal recognition of the illegal regime. They stood waiting for the capture of Madrid to give it a combined "de jure" and "de facto" semblance.

German and Italian planes were bombing the city, and because the inhabitant-defenders had no anti-aircraft defences, they swooped without any risk to machine-gun the citizens of Madrid in their streets. The Nazis used in this operation their latest plane, the Heinkel III K.

By November 7th, the Moors were in the suburbs, and the "Fifth Column" of rich and middle class elements inside the beleaguered city was poised to help the four fascist columns that had surrounded Madrid.

The same evening, Dolores Ibarruri*(1) the woman Communist deputy, known for the fiery character and integrity of her speeches as "La Pasionaria" went before the microphone of the Madrid Radio Station and spoke to the defenders, exhorting them not to surrender their city, crying that "it is better to die on your feet than to live for ever on your knees." The people fought back more fiercely. "NO PASARAN!" (They Shall Not Pass!) became the battle-cry of Madrid.

The scattered ill-armed militia units of the trade unions and of the various political organisations resisted with an unbelievable bravery. These units had been created spontaneously and lacked any overall command centre. To overcome this situation the Spanish Communist Party handed over the control of its militia to the Republican Government, thus setting the example for the unified and centralised organisation of the defence. This Communist Party unit of 70,000 became known as the "Fifth Regiment" because before the revolt there had been four regiments of the regular army always stationed in the capital.

"El Quinto Regimiento" (the Fifth Regiment) became the backbone of the defence and the prototype for the later development of a new regular army under the control and authority of the Republican Government.

On November 7th, the 19th anniversary of the Soviet workers' and peasants' revolution, the fascists prepared for their final assault with a thunderous artillery bombardment. The shells were intended to pave the way for a "triumphal" advance that was timed for a fascist marking—in reverse—of the historic commemorative date. However, instead of being subjugated the people rushed to the front lines of the defence of their city. Most of them were unarmed, but they took the guns from the hands of those who had fallen, and with grenades and petrol bombs they stopped the enemy tanks.

The foreign pressmen accompanying Franco's army considered that it was only a matter of days before the city would be overrun. They began to file their dispatches telling the world that Madrid had fallen. The people of Madrid had other ideas. Preparing for the next massive attacks they sang of the "Quinto Regimiento" which, by now, had four shock battalions of workers and intellectuals ...

"Venga, jaleo, jaleo—	Come and be happy, be happy
Sueño de una ametralladora,	Hear the avenging machinegun
Y Franco se va paseo—	It will be the end of Franco!
Y Franco se va paseo.	It will be the end of Franco!
Con Lister y Campesino,	With Lister and the 'Peasant',
Con Galan y Modesto,	With Galan and Modesto,

Con el comandante Carlos,   With Carlos the Comandante,
No hay miliciano con miedo."   No militiaman has fear.

"Con el quinto, quinto, quinto,   With the quinto, quinto, quinto
Con el Quinto Regimiento,   With the Quinto Regimiento,
Madre, yo me voy al frente   For the front, Mother, I'm
Porque quiero entrar en fuego."   leaving

"Son los cuatro batallones   For I, too wish to go under
                            fire.

Que a Madrid estan defendiendo,   With the four battalions
Va toda la flor de España   Which are defending Madrid,
Al flor mas roja del peublo" …*(2)   Goes the flower of Spain,
                            The reddest flower of the
                            people.

As Madrid prepared for the worst, aeroplanes suddenly appeared in the sky and the people gritted their teeth for another aerial assault. They were small fighter-planes that dipped their wings in salute to the now perplexed people. Their wing-tips bore the colours of the Republic: crimson, gold and violet. The people cheered. The planes were Russian, I—15 and I—16, and the pilots were volunteers who had come from the other end of Europe to fight with the people of Spain on the most significant anniversary date not only in their people's history but that of all mankind.*(3)

Early in the morning of November 8th, 1936 the Madrileños heard the sound of steady marching feet; at first they thought that the Fascists had broken through the city's defence, but then they heard the sound of a song that was now becoming more and more familiar to their ears, as the columns marched along the Gran Via, towards the front. The song they heard was a song of defiance, and *international solidarity and comradeship*. It was the "Internationale." The people listened and heard it sung not in Spanish, not in just another language but in a variety of languages. The first of the International Brigades had arrived. They had come from many lands, across many frontiers, sometimes in face of what seemed insuperable obstacles to fight with the heroic Spanish people in defence of Madrid. The marching men and the people shouted "Salud!" to each other and raised their clenched fists in greeting.

The people who up to now had proved capable of throwing back the mighty fascist offensives went wild with delight as they realised they no longer fought the battle of Spain, and of the world, alone. Across the waves of the ether from Radio Madrid there had gone that day from Fernando Valera, a Republican deputy, a call emphasising the universal character of the struggle of the Spanish people against the Fascist Generals;

    "Here in Madrid is the universal frontier that separates liberty and
    slavery. It is here in Madrid that two imcompatible civilisations
    undertake their great struggle: love against hate, peace against
    war, the fraternity of Christ against the tyranny of the Church …
    This is Madrid! It is fighting for Spain, for Humanity, for Justice
    and with the mantle of its blood it shelters all human beings!"

The marching feet and the loud singing of the International Brigades seemed like a miraculous answer to that clarion call.

The first international contingent was made up of three battalions; French and Belgians who named their unit the "Commune de Paris;" the "Edgar Andre" that was composed of German anti-fascists; and a Polish battalion that was called after their legendary hero "Dombrovsky." The whole Brigade, later to be known as the XIth International Brigade, was under the command of Emil Kleber, who had already fought in Russia and China. A big, broadshouldered man wearing a thick grey sweater, this man, originally from Austria, commanded immense authority by reason of his record, military ability and personality.

Altogether there were no more than 2,000 men in the first (XIth) International Brigade that reached Madrid. Amongst them were two squadrons of cavalry, composed of French volunteers; their carriage and discipline alone put new life into the Madrileños.

Four days later the second International Brigade arrived. It was the XIIth Brigade composed of German, French and Italian Anti-Fascists. This Brigade was commanded by the Hungarian writer, Máté Zalka who had adopted the nome-de-guerre of General Lukács. (He was later killed in action in 1937). In the first world war he had served in the Austrian Army, but later joined and fought with the Red Army.*(4)

In this Brigade was the "Thaelman Battalion" of German Anti-Fascists commanded by Ludwig Renn the author of the famous book, "Krieg," a story of World War I. This battalion was divided into "Zugs" of 30 men. In "Zug No. 2" was Bill Scott of Dublin. He had come from Ireland in early September 1936. He was a member of the Communist Party of Ireland, having been formerly a well known member of the Irish Republican Army. Like his father and the rest of his family he was a bricklayer by trade, and like them an active and well known member of the Bricklayers Union of the (Irish) Building Workers' Trade Union.

Bill Scott's father was a Dublin Protestant worker who had been a member of Connolly's Citizen Army during the Irish Rising of 1916. Bill himself had a very good record in the Irish revolutionary movement having served a sentence as a political prisoner in the Military Detention "Glasshouse" in the Curragh Camp only 16 months before he went to Spain. A short while after the Spanish War broke out, he had travelled to Barcelona where he linked up with a group of French, Italian, and English volunteers who formed themselves into a fighting group of approximately 100 men in the "Thaelmann Centuria," which in fact was one of the groups that anteceded the International Brigades.

In the defence of Madrid, Bill Scott fought with the XIth Brigade and later with the "Fifth Regiment" that was commanded by Enrique Lister, a Spanish stonemason who later developed into one of the outstanding military leaders, reaching the rank of General. Scott took part in the battle of Boadilla del Monte, a small town 20 kilometers south west of Madrid alongside the English poet, John Cornford. On the 13th of November he took part in the assault on the positions of the Civil Guard*(5) in University City.

In a letter to Sean Murray (quoted in "The Worker," December 19th, 1936) he recounted his experiences on the Madrid front. Despite the diversions and the strains of the battles he still displayed his awareness of the activities of the reactionary forces at home in Ireland:

"You needn't mind who knows I am in Spain. I won't be ashamed to go back to Dublin when it is over for I am convinced now that we're going to win, and it's the most sacred cause in history to defend Freedom."

The effect of the arrival of the International Brigades in Madrid was that the Fascists to their consternation were flung back, but over one-third of the Brigaders died in battle.

In the early days of the Madrid fighting, Ireland was not alone represented by Bill Scott. In the first days of the defence, two Irishmen fell, Gaelic-speaking Tommy Patton*(6) of Achill, County Mayo, who paradoxically was to be the first English-speaking volunteer to die in Madrid, and William Barry of Dublin who had come from exile in Melbourne, Australia.

The International Brigades, appearing in Madrid at such a crucial moment, were a great demonstration of international democratic solidarity at a time when Fascism was rampant throughout Europe. It was only 17 years after the defeat of the German workers revolt and the crushing of the Hungarian worker's republic. A dictatorship ruled in Greece; Pilsudski was in power in Poland; the reign of fascism was strongly entrenched in Nazi Germany, Mussolini's Italy, Horthy's Hungary and in neighbouring Portugal. The attack on Abyssinia had been both successful and uninterfered with by the western "democracies." In all the fascist countries the trade unions had been destroyed. In Britain, Sir Oswald Mosley was on the march. In France, the "Croix de Feu" was strengthening its ranks. Fascism, supported as it was by powerful conservative circles in the West, seemed all powerful.

In this situation the Spanish people had dared to light a torch of freedom, and to the world's surprise, many hands from many lands came to help keep that flame alight despite the overwhelming odds against them.

In the course of the war, thousands volunteered from 53 different countries until there were six International Brigades: —*(7)

XI Brigade of German and Austrian anti-fascists.
XII Brigade of Italians who were known as the "Garibaldi Brigade."
XIII Brigade of Poles and Hungarians
XIV Brigade of French and Belgians
XV Brigade the English-speaking one that was composed of four battalions; British; the American "Lincoln-Washington;" the Canadian "Mackenzie-Papineau," and a battalion of Spanish speaking volunteers from Latin America. It had also in its early days attached to it the Bulgarian "Dimitrov" and French battalion named the "6th of February." It was in the ranks of the XV Brigade that the Irish volunteers mainly fought.
129 International Brigade of Yugoslav, Bulgarian, Czechoslovak, Rumanian, and Albanian volunteers.

Demarcation was mainly according to nationality and language, but there were Spaniards in every brigade, battalion, company and section.

The International Brigades fought not only at the defence of Madrid, in the Casa de Campo, University City, Las Rosas, Jarama, but also later on many other battle-fronts such as Guadalajara, (where the XII Brigade of Italian anti-fascists routed Mussolini's picked troops), at Pozoblanco, Brunete, Villanueuva de la Cañada, Belchite, Quinto, Teruel, Aragon and the River Ebro.

The entire number of volunteers was approximately 40,000, of whom more than 5,000 died in battle. There were never more than 17,000 at any one time in Spain, and never more than 6,000 in any single campaign.

They came to Spain in small groups, many of them singly, most of them without passports, crossing many frontiers, and overcoming many obstructions. After February 1937, when the London Non-Intervention Committee closed the frontiers of Spain by a blockade on land and sea, the Volunteers had to climb over the Pyrennees Mountains at night, engaging in a muscle-racking experience whilst all the time finding the way of slipping in between the guards on the French side. Many others made their way to the Spanish Republican coast in small boats in a Mediterranean Sea that was patrolled not only by "Non-Intervention" observers but also by marauding Italian fascist submarines.

On the Franco side there were far larger bodies of regular foreign troops; complete units of the Italian and German armies. In all the number of Italian troops may have amounted to 100,000 with their ships transporting them to Spain and their submarines sinking ships that tried to run the blockade to Republican territory with either food or guns.

The Nazi Air force—the Condor Legion—played the main part in Franco's air attacks; as well there were units of artillery and tanks; altogether over 26,000 German regulars served with Franco.*(8)

There were tens of thousands of Moorish troops and cavalry, and two complete divisions of the Portuguese Regular Army.*(9)

Chapter 4 Notes

*(1) Dolores Ibarruri known as "La Pasionaria"—the Passion Flower—because of her fiery oratory and passionate dedication to the cause of the Spanish working people. The eighth of the twelve children born to "Antonio the Gunner" (he worked as such in the Asturian mines), she had a hard life of poverty as a young child. As a young girl she worked as a domestic servant and waitress. At the age of twenty she married a miner, becoming more and more prominent in strikes and demonstrations. She was later elected as a Communist M.P. to the Spanish Cortes. For more information on this legendary figure in the Spanish people's struggles, see her autobiography, "No Pasaran—They Shall Not Pass;" International Publishers, New York, 1966.

*(2) "El Quinto Regimiento" (The Fifth Regiment). Words and music recorded by Folkways Records (Album No. Fh 5436), 701 Seventh Avenue, New York, 1961.

*(3) In an attempt to present the war as one of the Christians of Spain holding "back the atheistic materialism of Moscow" (as by Aodh de Blackam) false reports were published of the presence of Soviet army units on the side of the Republic. What *was true* was that the Soviet Union—then the only Socialist state in the world, exhausted after its own bloody Civil War, military intervention by 14 imperialist states, famine and blockade—helped Republican Spain with arms and other supplies. This solidarity with peoples struggling for their freedom was repeated consistently in the later years as in the case of China, Cuba, Vietnam and the national liberation movement throughout the world. General Ignaco Hildago de Cisneros, head of the Republican Air force, who negotiated the supply of Soviet arms wrote of such help: "I have the right to declare to the entire world that Soviet aid was completely unselfish, not to mention that the Soviet people had to make great sacrifices for this aid." Rendering such aid was a difficult and dangerous task because of the geographical position of the two countries. In running the gauntlet of Italian submarines and planes, Soviet ships were attacked 86 times with three of them being sunk—"Komsomol," "Timiryazev" and the "Blagoyev." During the autumn and winter of 1936–37 as many as 23 ships arrived from Soviet Black Sea ports with military equipment. (see also, Note No. 7 in Chapter 14). The number of Soviet *volunteers* in the army of the Republic never exceeded more than 2,000 during the whole of the war. These included 772 airmen, 351 tankmen, 222 advisers and instructors, 77 naval personnel, 100 artillerymen, 52 other military experts, 130

engineers, 156 radio workers, 204 interpreters and journalists. The quality of the Soviet volunteers was to be demonstrated in the later fight against the Nazis in World War 2. Many of them rose to great prominence in that war. They included, Rodion Malinovsky (known in Spain as 'Malino') who became an Army Marshal and the U.S.S.R. Minister for Defence; N. Voronov who became a Marshal of Soviet Artillery; Pavel Batov, at present an Army General who was awarded, on two occasions, the Medal of Hero of the Soviet Union for his leadership in the battle of Stalingrad; Colonel-General A. Rodimstev, likewise Twice Hero of the Soviet Union, whose celebrated Division played an outstanding part in the same famous battle. Inscribed there today on the Volga Embankment are the words: "Rodimstev's Guards stood here to death. But they held out and conquered death!" (in the same battle Reuben Ibarruri, the son of "La Pasionaria" died in action in the ranks of the Red Army). Other volunteers who later attained distinction were Kiril Merskov who was a Divisional Commander in Spain; and Ivan N. Nesterenko a Divisional Commissar. For more information on Soviet assistance and military participation, see:—"International Solidarity with the Spanish Republic," Progress Publishers, Moscow, 1975, "Pod Znamenem Ispanskoi Respubliki" by Nauka, Moscow, 1965 and "Leningradi V Ispani," Lenisdat Publishers, Leningrad, 1967.

*(4) Ilya Ehrenburg, in his "Eve of War, 1939—41," wrote: "According to biblical tradition, Sodom and Gommorrah might have been saved had ten just men been found. This is true of all cities and epochs. One such just man was Máté Zalka, General Lukács, dear Matey Mikhailovich."

*(5) The Civil Guard noted for their three-cornered hats were organised as an army in the mid-eighties. They were led by a General and were composed of ex-regular army N.C.O.s. A ruthless force against the people, they were never quartered in the part of Spain they came from. They were always lodged in separate barracks and were not allowed to mix, or even converse, with the people in whose areas they were stationed.

*(6) Peadar O'Donnell dedicated his book, "SALUD!"—"TO A BOY FROM ACHILL who died fighting in Spain and his comrades who went the same proud way." In the concluding paragraph of the book, he wrote: "Irish Republicans smarting at the thoughts that Facist Ireland should have sent soldiers to fight the Spanish people, stole quietly away from their homes and made the trek to Barcelona and Madrid. Tomas Patton of Achill fell outside Madrid one cold day when a shower was pelting down on the grey earth, in the winter time too when his townland was full of the laughter of young folk gathered back after the season work in the Scotch tatie fields. I had to send them the word ... His name will live on in Achill when yours and mine are forgotten." The first English-speaking person to be killed fighting with the Republican forces, in Spain as distinct from Madrid, was a London young woman artist, Felicia Browne, who died in action at the Aragon Front on August 25th, 1936. See: "Britons In Spain" by William Rust, Lawrence & Wishart, London, 1939. p. 20.

*(7) For more detailed information on the composition of the Brigades, see: —
— "L'Epopee de l'Espagne" published by the L'Amicale des Anciens Volontaires Francais en Espange Republicaine. Paris, 1956
— "Pasaremos," Deutscher Militärverlag, Berlin, German Democratic Republic, 1966.
— For the Decree that incorporated them into the Spanish Republican Army see Appendices X and XI
— They were not 'Communist Brigades' as the capitalist press described them. The volunteers reflected a wide spectrum of political parties and its ranks included many of no party, but indisputably the vast majority were Communist Party members. The political basis for the type of Popular Front government which they defended had been formulated by the VII World Congress of the Third International (Comintern) in 1935. The Comintern acted as the International organising centre for the transportation of the volunteers, under illegal conditions, to Spain whilst the Communist Party in each country (as in the case of Ireland) were the links in that operation and the national centres for the recruitment of volunteers from its own ranks and other organisations. Though Communists formed the overwhelming majority their policy was for the merging of all different political viewpoints and affiliation into a single united military and political international solidarity movement. Thus each member of the Brigades in his military pass-book described his party affiliation simply as "Antifasciste."

*(8) The precise figures of Italian and German regulars who fought for Franco are uncertain. On one hand, some of the estimates made by the Spanish Republic during the war may be too high; on the other hand historians in West Germany and elsewhere have attempted to play down the figure. On German participation, a military historian of the German Democratic Republic with access to secret Nazi files states: "Reactionary historians have claimed that only about 16,000 Germans, soldiers and civilians, were engaged on the 'national Spanish' side. In fact, after the war, no fewer than 26,116 members of the intervention troops were decorated with the (Nazi) Spain Cross, instituted on 14. 4. 39." (Horst Kühne "Revolutionäre Militärpolitik," Deutscher Militärverlag, Berlin—G.D.R., 1969, p. 109).

*(9) The British consul general in Tangier estimated in June 1938 that 70,000 Moroccans had been sent to fight for Franco by that date (see "The Historian," November 1974).

THE
CONNOLLY
COLUMN

"Músgluighidh, a bhrothuine na cruinne!
a dhioghadh an ocrais, aire dhaoibh!
Tá an tuigsint in—a buabhall buile
Saghdabh an duine chun malrait saoghail.
De shaen—ré na ngeasróg déanam casair,
Al na laincise, músgluighidh
Sinne nach faic muid, gheobhamuid gradam
An sean—reacht leagfar bun os cionn."

Sí'n troid scuir í, a bhráithre,
Eirighimis chun gnímh
An t-INTERNATIONALE
Snaoidhm—comhair an cine daonn,
Sí'n troid scuir í, a bhráithre,
Éirighnimis chun gnímh
An t-INTERNATIONALE
A bhéas mar chine daonn."

The news of the arrival of the International Brigades and the presence of Bill Scott in Madrid quickly raised the question of Irish participation in the military struggle against Franco.

Despite the strong pro-Franco feeling in Ireland, old traditions of progressive international solidarity began to bubble to the surface. There was Wolfe Tone, the first Irish Republican, who had been at one with the French Revolution when the word "Jacobin" conveyed the same feeling of fear and horror as the title "Communist" did in 1936. The Fenians, it was recalled, were linked with Marx and Engels through the International Working Mens' Association. That one of the most famous of them, O'Donovan Rossa, had in his native West Cork organised, in spite of police intimidation, a demonstration in support of the Polish Rising of 1863. It was remembered also that it was not a one-way traffic of solidarity; that Marx and Engels had championed the cause of Irish independence; that Jenny Marx (Marx's daughter) had actively and courageously campaigned for the release of the tortured

53

Fenian prisoners. That working with her had been Gustave Flourens who later died in the defence of the Paris Commune of 1871, an event that had been as badly castigated as the then occurrences in Spain. There was the case of that Fenian leader, James Stephens, who had fought with the workers of Paris in 1851 against Louis Napoleon, and who wrote ...

> "Since '48, since the day I became a Soldier of Liberty I should proudly, nay joyfully, have given up all, even to my life, for my country. Still my motives and feelings would not be at all intensely national. For I would fight, for an abstract principle of right, for defence of any country and were England a Republic, battling for human freedom, on the one hand and Ireland leagued with despots and struggling for despotism on the other I would unhesitatingly take up arms against my native land." *(1)

There was even, ironically enough, the resurrection of a poem that had been written by none other than Aodh de Blacam himself. Composed in 1920 when he was dabbling with socialist ideas it nevertheless did express the growing feeling of international humanism in many in 1936. He had titled it "On Freedom' Eve":

> "When comes the Revolution and the world
> Storms the Bastille that holds its hopes in thrall,
> When States like tumbled walls are overhurled,
> Then loudly Freedom's call
>
> Shall summon men with streaming eyes to pray
> For those who died before the dawn,—the dead
> Who won for us, but never saw the day;
> And it shall then be said:
>
> In all your orisons remember Pearse
> (That dreamed and did), Connolly, Mitchel, Tone,
> Gentle O'Leary, O'Donovan the fierce,
> Emmet, who died alone,—
>
> Liebknecht who fell ere German freedom rose,
> Shelley and pitying Marx and gallant Paine.
> But highest honour shall we yield to those
> For whom we'll rear a fane
>
> Where ceaseless incense to the Crucified
> Shall smoke and ceaseless Offices be prayed—
> For those, the humble and the nameless ones, who died
> Upon the barricade."

The old Irish tradition of progressive struggle, of solidarity with peoples fighting for their freedom elsewhere could be stifled by the propaganda of the Christian Front, but it could not be completely killed. Direct news was coming from Spain in letters from Bill Scott. Writing from the headquarters of General Mangada, (who was both a poet and one of the few regular army officers who remained loyal to the Republic) Scott penned these lines to his friends in Dublin:

"Having witnessed some of the horrifying acts of terrorism committed on the Spanish people, and the wholesale massacre of innocent women and children in Madrid, and being your representative in Spain's fight to preserve World Democracy, I feel I would be failing in my duty if I did not report to you a little of what I have seen, and warn you of what awaits you if Fascism is allowed to grow in Ireland.

"Two weeks ago I returned from the University City sector of the Madrid front. On this front six thousand trained Germans, thousands of Italian Fascists and Moors, supported by German bombing planes, Italian tanks and artillery, with expert operators to use them, are in action against the defenders of the Capital ...

"I was free for a few days and decided to see Madrid. Here is what I saw: On December 4th, thirty low flying Fascist planes loomed over the city as if considering where to release their loads of death. Suddenly a succession of terrific explosions shook the city, and dense volumes of smoke were seen rising about a mile from the centre. I went to the scene of the raid. I saw firemen and militiamen endeavouring to rescue dying men, women and children from the burning pile, which half an hour before had been a block of tenement flats. I saw heaps of bricks and mortar mingled with human flesh and blood. I saw the mutilated bodies of children wedged between heavy beams. In the midst of the street I saw, what on examination proved to be a child's cot containing a mangled body. People in adjoining streets, not fortunate enough to be killed outright, were blinded and shell-shocked by the explosions.

"The 'Irish Independent' describes this carnage as a war to save Christianity'" ... (Quoted in the "Worker," January 9th, 1937).

Above the clamour of the loud hypocritical singing of emotive hymns, the call from beleaguered Madrid was nevertheless heard in Ireland albeit by a relative few—but by a minority who were prepared to match their sentiments with their lives, and who felt with a burning sense of anger that Ireland's good name had been tarnished by the O'Duffy link with International Fascism and by the Christian Front's campaign of support for Franco, the mutinous Generals, and the Landlords of Spain.

In September 1936 a decision was taken by the very small Communist Party of Ireland that an Irish Unit of the International Brigades should be formed. The task of recruitment and organisation was given to Bill Gannon* (2), a member of the party who had considerable experience as a Republican fighter in the war against the British Imperialists and the Free State forces.

By December 1936 the first group was on its way to Spain. It was led by Frank Ryan who prior to the departure made a public press statement:

"The Irish contingent is a demonstration of revolutionary Ireland's's solidarity with the gallant Spanish workers and peasants in their fight for freedom against Fascism. It aims to redeem Irish honour besmirched by the intervention of Irish Fascism on the side of the Spanish Fascist rebels. It is to aid the revolutionary movements in Ireland to defeat the Fascist menace at home, and finally, and not the least, to establish the closest fraternal bonds of kinship between the Republican democracies of Ireland and Spain."*(3)

Thus was declared the credo of all the Irishmen who went to fight in the International Brigades in the years 1936–37–38.

Frank Ryan, the spokesman and commander of the Irish in the Brigades, personified as no one else did the best militant and revolutionary characteristics of the Irish people. He was born at Elton, Knocklong in County Limerick on September 11th, 1902. Both his parents were national teachers; his father exercising a very formative patriotic influence on him as a youth. Educated at the local national school he made contact with the Irish Volunteers, being accepted at the age of 16 years into the East Limerick Brigade by Seamus Malone. In 1920 he secured a scholarship to St. Colman's College Fermoy, County Cork. There his national feelings were further cultivated by frequent historical and political talks that one of the lecturers used to give to the students. His military training was also further developed when he and some other students used to climb the college walls at night in order to take part in the secret "drilling" parades of the local I.R.A. unit.

From there he went to University College Dublin to study for a degree in Celtic Studies and Master of Arts. It was not until 1925 that he was able to secure his degree because of his participation in the Irish War for independence. When the Civil War broke out he was on a visit to his family home. He straightaway left to participate in the fighting with the Anti-Treaty forces in Kilmallock. He was later arrested by the Treatyite Government and lodged in the Internment Camp at Harepark, County Kildare in the period of 1922–23, being one of the last of the prisoners to be released.

On his release he returned to his studies at U.C.D. and there continued his Republican activities. He had a burning enthusiasm for every organisation that strove for the political, cultural and social liberation of Ireland. He was one of the founders of the U.C.D. Republican Club and became Auditor of the Cumann Literardha Na Gaelige (Gaelic Language Literary Society) in the College. In later years he became an active figure in the Gaelic League being a member of Craob Moibhi and Craob na Cuig Cuighi, writing many articles under the pseudonym of "Seachranaidhe." He was also the Chairman of the "Sean Cole" Gaelic Football Club*(4).

In the Irish Republican Army he blossomed out to become one of its leading personlities. He was the Editor of "An Phoblacht" (The Republic) which he made into an eagerly read weekly radical national journal. He was also one of the founders of the Dublin Branch of the National Union of Journalists. For his activities he was arrested many times. In 1928–29 he was arraigned on the charge of possessing seditious documents. There were three trials—on each occasion the jury disagreed and he was therefore freed of the charge. It was this failure of the Government to secure conviction by juries that led them to abolish trial by jury and to set up a Military Tribunal.

On December 8th, 1931 he was imprisoned with other Republicans in

Arbour Hill Military Prison. The fact and the conditions of their imprisonment became one of the issues in the 1932 March General Election. On the day of the defeat of the Cosgrave Government the new Ministers-elect of the de Valera Government went immediately to the prison to see the prisoners. There they saw Ryan and the others lying naked in their cells. The next day they were released and were greeted by a mass meeting of welcome at College Green. After his release Frank Ryan returned to his work at the editorial desk of "An Phoblacht" and to his position as a leader of the Irish Republican Army. In 1933 he was Director of Organisation of Fianna Eireann, the Republican Boy Scout Movement.

To his forthright opposition to British Imperialism, and to native capitalism in Ireland, he had coupled a deep detestation of Fascism. When the Republican Congress was formed he was its Joint Secretary along with George Gilmore. He was a respected figure even outside the Republican and Anti-Fascist movements because of his integrity and fighting personality, and for his active interests in all matters relating to Ireland.

He was also a versatile organiser. Armistice Day in Ireland of the thirties was always an occasion for a display of British jingoism, and for native subservience to imperialist ideas. Irish ex-service man and their families were always mobilised for such an occasion, with the inevitable reaction by Republicans of the seizing of Union Jacks and the Poppy Wreaths. In November 1934 Frank Ryan organised a counter demonstration of another kind. To the annual anti-poppy day meeting, there marched to an audience of 10,000 in Abbey Street in Dublin a procession of Irish veterans of World War I wearing their medals and carrying slogans of opposition to War and Fascism—and British Imperialism. Speakers like Bob Smith (Royal Tank Corps), and Tom Ellis (Royal Garrison Artillery), shared the same platform as Roddy Connolly (son of James Connolly), Peadar O'Donnell and Frank Ryan himself. The ex-service men for that unique occasion were mobilised by two first world war veterans—who were close friends of Frank Ryan—Sam Nolan and Danny McGregor.

To Spain in that month of December along with Frank Ryan went other outstanding figures in the Irish Republican and Communist movements. Amongst them was "Kit" Conway, originally from Tipperary who was a legendary figure of the "Black and Tan" and Irish Civil Wars. In the early days of the Irish Civil War, when considerable confusion existed not only about attitudes to the Treaty, but to ones specific military units, Conway masqueraded as a Captain in the Pro-Treaty forces, based at the Curragh Military Barracks. When a keen provost-marshal discovered his presence there, he led a detachment of military police to arrest him—but the bird, having been warned, just flew in time bringing with him two Lewis Machine-Guns and a considerable supply of ammunition pans to an anti-treaty flying column that was operating in his native Tipperary. After the end of the Irish Civil War he was forced to flee to the U.S.A. A fighter who believed in "keeping his hand in" he joined the U.S. National Guard. He returned to Ireland after the election defeat of the Cosgrave Government in 1932, when he became National Training Officer of the I.R.A. Afterwards he joined the Communist Party of Ireland. He died in the Battle of Jarama, February 1937.

Also in the first Irish group was Jack Nalty, also of the Communist Party, who had been a well known member of the I.R.A. and the Republican Congress. He was a well known athlete, also, specialising in crosscountry running. He had been a fellow prisoner of Bill Scott's in the Curragh Camp's "Glasshouse" in May 1935. Previous to this he had been jailed in Mountjoy Prison for incidents arising from a campaign against the non-recognition of trade unionism in the Dublin "Bacon Shops" chain.*(5) Imprisoned with him, on that occasion, were Charlie Donnelly and Dinny Coady—all three were later to fall in battle in Spain.

With Ryan, Conway and Nalty went the latter's close friends, Paddy Duff and Donal O'Reilly.*(6) Other members of the group included Frank Edwards of Waterford who had been dismissed from his position as a teacher by the local Bishop, Dr. Kinane, because he was a member of the Republican Congress*(7) and Jim Prendergast, activist of the Communist Party of Ireland.

The first Irish detachment went to the International Brigade base in Madrigueras to be shaped into a military unit. This did not take long, as most of them, including the youngest, had at some time or other been members of the I.R.A. in which they received military training.

They choose the title of the "James Connolly Unit" to designate the Irish Section of the Brigades. This choice was inspired not only as a tribute to the memory of a great Irish Marxist and revolutionary soldier, but also as expressing in the conditions of 1936, the national and working class principles of Connolly who said that the Irish struggle for national freedom should be expressed "as part of the creed of the democracy of the world."

The ranks of the Irish at Madrigueras were continually augmented by new arrivals from Ireland as well as by Irishmen who had come from Britain and the U.S. They had been driven into exile by the economic pressure of unemployment. Many of them had, also, been forced for political reasons to leave the island after the victory of the pro-treatyites in the Irish Civil War.

The national-revolutionary background of the Irish, their fighting traditions, political conduct, and the keen desire to master military techniques, attracted to their ranks many English speaking volunteers who could by no stretch of imagination claim any relationship with Ireland. Among such was Samuel Lee, a young Jewish volunteer from London (later to die with many of his Irish comrades in the battle of Jarama, February 1937). Attached to the Irish Section were also a group of Dutch comrades.

Amongst the Irish there were two sets of brothers; John, Willie, and Paddy Power from Waterford; and the three O'Flahertys—Frank, Eddie and Charlie—from Boston, the "little Ireland" of the U.S.A.

On Christmas Eve, 1936 the Irish Unit went to the front for the first time. It marched with the 12th French Battalion of the XIV Brigade, and the No. 1 Company of the British Battalion, 145 strong. Their task was to take part in a Republican offensive in the South with the express duty of capturing the village of Lopera from the Fascists.

Into action at Christmas! Writing about it ten months later, in the "Irish Democrat," (Dublin) October 2nd, 1937, Donal O'Reilly recalled that "Christmas time refreshed memories. Childhood days of well kept promises that brought days of happiness. The memories of co-operative efforts that lightened the corridors of Mountjoy and other evil spots.

"A war in Spain. The old enemies of our National struggle taking the side of bloody Fascism. Stampeding the Irish people with the prostitution of ·ideals, they send a challenge to many resolute heads.

"Grim faced men from Ireland answer the challenge. Sharp differences of years makes talk a danger. Then the swift journey to take our place and prove our mettle in the great test.

"Spain. A few days of restless training, checking the impatience of those 'old soldiers' who had worn the by-roads of Ireland forming fours and taking cover" . . .

In preparation for the coming battle, O'Reilly noticed that, Conroy, Fox, and May can't be stopped taking down and cleaning their 'Betsy' (machine-gun). "A comradeship of heroes," he remarks.

Before the 50-strong "Connolly Column" moves off, there was a wait for food that was delayed in coming.

O'Reilly and Nalty saw a herd of goats nearby, and proceeded to milk them, procuring almost a quart of that delicious liquid, making the best use of the Spanish words they had, they succeeded in getting it heated, but never succeeded in drinking it, as the draft then moved off and they had to go "on the double" to join it.

At first, the Irish went into a reserve position. Their forced march to the front lines was broken half-way with the arrival of lorries. Then there was the sound of planes overhead, and the transport halted, and the occupants scattered for cover. The planes kept going on overhead, and the Irish clambered aboard the "camions" once again. An order was transmitted to them: "When the lorries stop you are under fire, jump out and take up positions!" The lorries did stop, at an olive grove, and out they jumped to take up positions among the trees. There they lay for half-an-hour, with the war seeming very far away. Then came the planes back again, sweeping over them, and spraying them with machine-gun fire. A Jewish volunteer is seen to be in an extraordinary position. Somebody shakes him and he falls back dead—with four bullet wounds across his back.

They advanced up a sand road and the enemy machine-guns opened fire on them; they continued through an olive grove and swung left to begin climbing a bare ridge. "The Company forms," related Donal O'Reilly, "and moves to the attack. A V shaped movement with the Irish advancing on the left flank. Kit Conway is fair bursting to get to grips, but first we must lend two of our best gunners—May and Conroy—to the main French Battalion. We move through the olive grove with the zing-zung of the bullets playing a tune. Occasionally the snick as a bullet clips off a cluster of leaves. Out from the friendly trees, down a short valley crossing a stream then up, up, among the hills. It's tough work with our tremendous load." The Irish carried trench-helmets, 250 rounds of ammunition, grenades, gas masks, machine-guns, spare pans of ammunition. But the old-style Austrian rifles had to be fired single shot because there were no ammunition clips available, and the even older machine guns, Chauchots, continually jammed.

"We halt for a break. Kit calls for a volunteer scout. Refusing to wait until we get our wind, away goes Kit."

Up and up they went, continuing to advance over the ridge in short rushes. "We move to the crest. The fire is terrific. The language is terrific. Joe Monks is hit. Prendergast's and Dinny Coady's guns are shot to pieces. Bits of the guns fly and we think we're all hit."

They are only 350 yards from the village of Villa del Rio. They stood up and went vigorously on the offensive. The Franco forces broke and retired, using all the time Verey lights and tracer bullets in an attempt to draw the fire on to worthless targets.

The "Connolly Column" waited for support before making the final assault. In preparation for this blow they moved in a sweeping right movement in order to find a better position. After they moved, the Fascists raked, with machine-gun fire, the position they had left. "That right swing served us well," wrote O'Reilly. Back on the crest of the hill, they discovered that they had advanced too well! In the darkness they dug in, and then lay down in groups to rest, huddled together against the cold of the night.

When the dawn came, they went on their way again. This time towards a road on their right. Republican big guns came into play, but their fire was largely ineffective, two out of every five shells failing to explode. Singing, the Irish advanced but on an angle on the road they came under heavy fire. "Kit is a trojan, darting up and down our Indian files. It's clear the enemy have stiffened their resistance and cheering will not dislodge them." They cross open ground, with clouds of dust being thrown up by the enemy's bullets. A large-scale machine-gun barrage signalled the beginning of a heavy Fascist counter attack. The Irish fired away at the Franco forces who wore clearly identified Nazi uniforms. The weapons of the Anti-Fascists were completely inadequate, but they continued to take up a position on a sloping piece of ground. "Kit spreads us out. Duff, Nalty and myself are on the edge of the road." They are told that Mick May and Frank Conroy were the only two left out of their machine gun crew, and that they were coming back to them. "We realise we are now fighting a rearguard action. Cummins and Gough are wounded and move back. Jack Nalty is hit. I won't look. Paddy Duff attends him. I glance and see both sides of his chest are hit. I must cry or act the pig, so I go back to the gun for relief. It's clear Jack is badly hit. I think he is finished ... We advise Jack to start making his own way back. We'll cover the ground later, perhaps. Jack crawls away."*(8)

The Franco planes came over against them, and without any aviation support or adequate artillery help the Anti-Fascists had to withdraw. In combat formation they fell back, group by group. The Thaelmann Battalion of German Anti-Fascist Germans came up and helped to turn the Fascist's left flank. The Irish moved back to the shelter of the olive groves.

Cordova was the fount in which the "Connolly Column" received its baptism of fire. It was an introductory session to warfare, that was to take the toll of eight Irish lives:—John Meehan*(9) of Galway; a group of Dublin workers, that included that "comradeship of heroes" Frank Conroy, Tony Fox and Mick May, as well as Henry Bonar, Jim Foley, Leo Green and seventeen-year-old Tommy Woods.*(10)

The Irish spent nearly a month on the Cordova front, yet they had barely time to mourn their dead, because they were soon transferred to another front. The news had come through that thousands of German and Italian

troops were being mass(
it. New forces of the Int(
again in the repulsion of
darkness they evacuated
a·journey that took two
offensive was to be fores1
tive also of recovering sor
in this operation were al:
Battalions.

The lorries drove in the
evening, they stopped and t
to be reserve ones. There the
into action the next morning
They were awakened early
fire. The Fascist drive had b
troops. The "Connolly Col
positon. Paddy Smith of Du
our Brigade, Irish, English a
formation across a flat plain. 1
the Fascist observers must h
a heavy artillery barrage. A
comrades fall. It was getting v
safely to our allotted position:
exchanges of rifle and machin
ourselves in. We were instructe

Coady*(13) from Dublin's Corporation St
killed. A few days after his death Frank
his friends:

"We were lying in po
with another Irish
between Coady
my side. M
envelope
he wa
our

Chapter 5

on the alert for the Fascists
were expected to attack. However, as their planes were no use for night
attack, they did not come over. They seldom attacked without their planes." *(11)

Next morning however the attack took place, on the right flank of the
Irish, on a position that was being held by the Italian Garibaldian Anti-
Fascists ... "but they might as well have been attacking a stone wall with
their bare fists as attacking these men who knew what Fascism was and who
had suffered so terribly under Mussolini in their native Italy. The cheering
and singing of the Garibaldis as they went into action against the oncoming
Fascists gave new courage and inspiration to the other battalions along the
line." The Fascists, meeting such resistance, retreated in disorder. Instructions were issued that the Internationals were to get ready to "go over the
top"; there was going to be a counter-attack along the whole Republican
front. "The receipt of this news was greeted with the singing of the 'Internationale'. The inspired singing of this great song coming from thousands
of throats in many different languages, gave the Fascists warning that something was amiss, for they sprayed our lines with machine-gun fire and trench
mortars exploded all around us. This surprise burst of fire took a terrible toll
of life among us and the stretchers were hastily loaded with wounded men."
... "Since then in other battles many Irish have fallen in defence of the
Spanish Republic. We shall never forget them. Their spirit will guide us in
the fight at home and the four winds of Ireland will re-echo these works which
gave courage to the people of Spain: 'They Shall Not Pass'!" *(12)

At Majadhonda the Irish took part in its capture; At Las Rozas, Dinny

...eet, son of the 1913 Striker was
... Edwards wrote the news home to

...sition on a ridge. Dinny Coady lay near me
...man, Pat Murphy, between us. A shell landed
... and Murphy. I immediately felt a sharp pain in
...urphy screamed. I glanced towards him. He was
... in a cloud of smoke and dust. But I cold see his face ...
... ghastly pale. I got up and walked down to a ravine where
...Company Headquarters section was posted, and told them
to send up a stretcher at once. I thought Murphy had been badly
hit. Then I got a Red Cross man to rip my clothes off. I had a
very deep wound under my left armpit, and a slight scratch on
my leg.

"While I was being dressed the stretcher-bearers came back with
a body. Someone pulled back the blanket, and I saw his face. It
was Dinny Coady. I got a hell of a shock ..., perhaps I had known
him longer than of the other lads." *(14)

In the fighting on this front, Kit Conway won unstinted praise from the
other International fighters for his outstanding leadership in the repulse of
an attempted counter attack by the Moors at nightfall on the Majadahonda
position.

For the first time there then reached Ireland an account of the combat
activities of the "Connolly Column." Writing from Madrid in a letter dated
January 21st, Frank Ryan reported:

"The military training of our lads has been turned into good account. Our section is one of the mainstays of the Company. They
were rushed off to the Cordova front on Xmas Eve. They were
in action from December 26th, till about January 8th. On the
Madrid sector of the front they captured a village, with a battery
of artillery, the Fascists retreating. In this action they took and
sent to G.H.Q. prisoners and also some machine-guns. Here on
the Madrid front there was really brilliant fighting. Our fellows
were in support when they came under heavy and accurate
shelling. It was here Frank Edwards got wounded. Others wounded are:

Donal O'Reilly, J. Hillen, J.J. O'Beirne, J. Monks, T. Woods
Jerry Doran, Sean Goff, Seaumas Cummins, P. Smith and Pat
Murphy. All are slightly wounded are progressing favourably.

The same shell that wounded Edwards killed Denis Coady.
We buried him in Torredodones, and his comrades, under Kit
Ryan*(15) fired three volleys over his grave. A true man and a
fine soldier. J. Meehan of Galway and W. Beattie*(16) were killed
in the fighting on the Cordova front.

Jack Nalty*(17) was wounded on the Cordova front by a burst
of machine gun fire in the chest; and walked three miles to the
dressing station. He is in hospital in Albacete, doing well. His

absence is a great loss to the crowd. Mick May did great work one black day in Andalusia covering off his comrades as they went back under shell and machine gun fire. Frank Conroy fought like a hero the same day.

The morale of the lads is very high now. Their repulse in Andalusia is forgotten in their victories near Madrid.

To all my friends on the anti-Fascist home front I send greetings."

Along with their dead of Cordova and Las Rozas the Irish also mourned the death of 33 year-old Ralph Fox who had endeared himself to the Irish fighters because of his authorship of the volume "Marx, Engels and Lenin on Ireland." Many of them had read it before they came to join the International Brigades, and it had strengthened their convictions on the necessary relationship between the issue of the national liberation of their own country and the cause of international solidarity.

The harsh reality of lives lost and of grievous wounds suffered made necessary a re-statement of why such should be so. This came from Frank Ryan who no doubt felt a keen sense of personal responsibility for those who followed his leadership in going to Spain; writing from Madrid he had this to say:

"... *Our 50,000 who died in the Great War* were sacrificed uselessly; *no life here is given in vain*... I read in the 'Irish Press' that 'the Wild Geese have flown again'; I read in the 'Irish Echo,' New York, of the 'tragedy' of men like me coming out here. The type of canned nationalism that inspires such talk is THE tragedy I deplore. They ignore the changes in world politics, they would have us ignore the Great Danger until it is on our shores. 'We serve Ireland only,' they cry, but they would have us wait until it would be too late to make effective use of our services. Catalonia recognises that it must not wait until Franco reaches its borders. Is Ireland to commit the error Catalonia avoids?

Is the 'Irish Press' comparing the Wild Geese*(18) to O'Duffy's hirelings? The Wild Geese were honest-minded men who went out to fight against their country's enemy. (Incidentally, their fate should have forever *killed the slogan: 'England's enemy is Ireland's friend.'*) To compare O'Duffy's dupes with them is an insult to national tradition. Does O'Duffy go to fight even 'England's enemy'?

What mistakes—yes, tragedies—are caused by failing to face facts. Not ten per cent of O'Duffy's forces in Spain are Fascists; the rest of them are just dupes who go to 'fight for the Faith.' The 'Irish Press' refused to say that, for it fears to tackle the pro-Fascist Irish Hierarchy, yet to avoid alienating Republican opinion, it has to shadowbox with O'Duffy. And there is no paper to champion truth and justice unequivocally. How can we let the world know that the lives of Conroy and Coady, Meehan and Boyle, have not been wasted, that their deaths are no 'Tragedies'

63

that need not have happened? Honour to those who died for the freedom of the Irish people; honour even greater to those who die here for the freedom of All Humanity. No 'Wild Geese' were these lads. You remember how I warned them before they left home, what their life here—as long as it would last—would be like. You remember how I discouraged every suspicion of adventurism. You know how they could have stayed at home and be regarded by their friends as 'soldiers of Ireland.' They chose to *come here asking neither for pay or preferment, coming because they believed it was their duty to come to participate in this decisive fight against Fascism.* And, for my part, while it would be wrong to accuse me of bringing them here, I would never regret having done so. Our 50,000 who died in the Great War who died in vain were sacrificed uselessly; *no life here is given in vain.*

And look at it from the purely selfish viewpoint. Which is better; That some of us should die here, or that thousands should die at home? For if Fascism triumphs here, Ireland's trial will soon be at hand." *(19)

Chapter 5 Notes

*(1) "Chief of the Comeraghs," p. 100, by James Maher, Kickham Street, Mullinahone, County Tipperary.
*(2) Bill Gannon (1902–1965) was the son of a 1913 striker and a Fenian mother. He was a member of Fianna Eireann (Republican Boy Scouts), later joining the Irish Republican Army, being one of the first to be chosen for the Active Service Unit of the Dublin Brigade taking part in all the engagements of that specially picked body of fighters against the "Black and Tans". During the Civil War he was of the Republican Garrison of the Four Courts along with his close colleague, Donal O'Reilly, (later of the Connolly Column of the I.B.) With the fall of the Four Courts, he was imprisoned in Mountjoy Jail. After his release he resumed activity with the I.R.A. and was associated with that body's formation of Saor Eire, a radical political organisation based on workers and small farmers. On the occasion of his funeral on September 15th, 1965, his coffin, as he wished, was covered by both the National and Red Flags. At the graveside an honour guard from the 2nd Battalion the Irish Army, Cathal Brugha Barracks, rendered military honours.
*(3) The Worker, December 19th, 1936.
*(4) So named after Sean Cole, a leader of Na Fianna Eireann (Republican Boy Scouts), who with another young comrade, Alf Colley, was murdered by Free State troops at Yellow Lane, Santry, Dublin on August 26th, 1922.
*(5) Also jailed during this agitation were Roddy Connolly (son of James Connolly), Eugene Downing (who later fought in Spain), Nelly Plover, and a god-daughter of Eamon de Valera's — Cora Hughes.
*(6) Donal O'Reilly (1903–1968) was the son of J.K. O'Reilly, composer of the well known Irish song, "Wrap the Green Flag Around Me Boys." His father and Donal's three brothers took part in the Irish 1916 Rising. Donal, then 13, was left at home but he found his way to the centre of the fighting, at Dublin General Post Office, on the second day of the fighting. He was sent home. However, he later served with the 5th Battalion of the I.R.A. in the "Black and Tan" War, and was with Bill Gannon in the Four Courts Garrison in the Irish Civil War, later, they were together in Mountjoy Prison. There he became particularly friendly with Liam Mellowes who, prior to his execution, gave him a chessman as a keepsake. O'Reilly was held later in Newbridge,Internment Camp where he participated in the hunger strike of 1923. In Spain he was wounded in the Battle of Cordova, December 1936. After Spain, he returned to trade union activities in Ireland. He was an Executive Committee member of the Plasterers Union, delegate to the Dublin Trades Council and the Irish Congress of Trade Unions until his sudden death on May 7th, 1968. As a recipent of the Irish Government's "War of Independence Medal" he was, like Bill Gannon, accorded military honours by the Irish Army at his funeral..
For his political apologia see Appendix III, and this writer's obituary tribute in the "Irish Socialist", May 1968.
*(7) "In 1937, Bishop Kinane of Waterford pointed to the recent strikes in his city as illustrating the need for corporate organisation" Church and State in Modern Ireland by J.H. Whyte, Gill & Macmillan, Dublin, 1971, p. 74.

The Irish Citizen Army at Liberty Hall, Dublin, 1914

Revolutionary Warfare

1/6

By JAMES CONNOLLY

James Connolly's
articles on revolutionary military struggle,
first published in the "Workers' Republic,"
May–July 1915
(See Appendix 2)

In the early weeks of Franco's rising, Junkers planes
supplied by Nazi Germany, flown by Luftwaffe pilots,
ferried thousands of Moorish troops from Spanish Morocco
to Spain proper. They played a decisive part in
consolidating fascist rule in the western part of Spain

Civilians slaughtered by Franco troops in Badajoz,
August 1936

"The Crusade." Catholic dignitaries give the fascist salute, 1936

*(above) The Spanish people, bombed from their homes by German Nazi
and Italian Fascist pilots flying for Franco*

(left) The People's Militia sprang to arms to defend the Spanish Republic

*In November 1936 Spanish Republican troops halt the Franco advance
in the outskirts of Madrid.
In the same month the first of the International Brigades
—volunteers from over 50 countries—come to the aid of the Spanish Republic*

(above) Sean Murray, General Secretary of the Communist Party of Ireland,
speaking at Abbey Street Dublin at an anti-Franco meeting,
September 1936

(below left) Cover of a pro-Franco pamphlet by Aodh de Blacam,
published in Dublin in October 1936.
The pamphlet received the "Imprimi Potest"
of the Primate of Ireland

(below right) Father Michael O'Flanagan,
who championed the Spanish Republican cause

*Some of the first Irish volunteers
killed in action with
the Spanish Republican Army.*

*(top left) Frank Conroy (Kildare),
Cordoba front, December 1936*

*(top right) Michael Nolan (Dublin),
Cordoba front December 1936*

*(bottom left) Denis Cody (Dublin),
Las Rosas, January 1937*

Bringing in a wounded soldier of the International Brigades,
Jarama front 1937

Irish volunteers killed in action with the XV International Brigade, Jarama front, February 1937

(top left) Charles Donnelly (Tyrone)

(top right) Captain "Kit" Conway (Tipperary)

(below) Liam Tumilson (Belfast)

Taken on February 2nd, 1937,
four days before the fascist
offensive at Jarama
(left to right, seated):
W. Garland (U.S.A.),
John Hunt (Waterford)
(standing) Peter O'Connor (Waterford),
P. McEvoy (Dublin),
Johnnie Power (Waterford)

*Spanish volunteers in the ranks
of the XV (English-speaking) International Brigade, 1937*

Machine-gun post of the XV International Brigade,
Jarama front.
The gun is a Soviet Maxim.
On the left,
Lieutenant Oliver Law,
later commander of the American Lincoln Battalion

Olive-tree memorial at the Jarama front
for the dead of the VX International Brigade.
The inscription reads:
"To our fallen comrades.
Our victory is your vengeance.
June 1937"

*(8) Nalty though hit by a burst of machine-gun fire in the chest, walked the three miles, by himself, to the first aid station.

*(9) The news of the death of Meehan inspired a fellow-country man, "Tribesman" to write a poem of salutation which linked two Galway men; the one who had sailed with Columbus, and the one who had gone to fight with the International Brigades:

> *To James Meehan of Galway*
> "When the world was small. Levant a far voyage to Cadiz,
> Cathay people with firedrakes and Africa a legend.
> When merchant-men along the shores of Europe
> Coasted the western fringes cautiously;
> Then when a few left the known shores behind them,
> Advanced upon the unfrequented sea
> And having passed through doubt and thirst and tempest
> Saw on the hot horizon the rim of the New World lifting;
> Then there was one man from our western city
> That looks upon the Atlantic, there was one
> Who sailed with them: one of us went undaunted
> On with the vanguard into the unknown.
> And in later days
> When certain men, gathered from all over the world,
> Guarded Madrid, machine-gunned, battered and shelled.
> Forging the fellowship that moves the earth,
> Building for our children a New World with their blood;
> Then in those winter days of terrible glory
> We had our share of honour, too, for one
> Redeemed it and is dead. A man of ours,
> A man of Galway, was there too."

*(Irish Democrat", Dublin,
June 19th, 1937)

*(10) Tommy Woods, Buckingham Place, Dublin, had been a member of Na Fianna Eireann (the Republican Boy Scouts). His uncle, Patrick Doyle, was hanged by the British in Mountjoy Jail, March 14th, 1921. Another uncle, Sean Doyle was killed in the I.R.A. attack on Dublin's Custom House – the record centre of the British administration – May 25th, 1921. Before leaving for Spain, Tommy left a letter for his mother ..." I am going to Spain to fight with the International Column. I left a message to be delivered on Sunday. We are going out to fight for the working class. It is not a religious war, that is all propaganda. God Bless you."

*(11) "Irish Democrat," Dublin, October 9th, 1937.

*(12) Ibid.

*(13) Again a tribute by a friend was expressed in poetry. It was by Tom O'Brien, who himself later was to join the International Brigade:

> DINNY COADY
> *"One whom I knew."*
>
> "We who live to remember—
> We who have to die eventually,
> in deaths like this,
> It is not simple;
> it is something that was sunk deep,
> torturously down the centuries –
> this emotion we feel
> at the death of men we knew,
> Killed in such action.
>
> Emotion heavy with centuries of suffering
> and struggle and sacrifice
> of oppressed peoples everywhere.
>
> We know that he must have died,
> We know that he should not have died,
> These comforts the mangled mind of man,
> the simple mind of man,
> Knowing what is good and noble,
> faced with a thing called Fascism –
> killing men who would have lived
> ordinary happy lives;
> men like Dinny Coady."

*(14) The "Worker", January 30th, 1937.

*(15) "Ryan" was a "nom de guerre" used by Kit Conway in Ireland.

*(16) William Beattie of Belfast was incorrectly in this case reported as dead. He was later killed, July 1937, at the battle of Brunete.

*(17) Jack Nalty survived this and all subsequent battles only to fall in the last day of the last battle of the XV Brigade on the Ebro front, September 23rd, 1938.

*(18) The Wild Geese: Following the defeat in Ireland in 1691 of the cause of James the Second of England, the native Irish soldiers and officers who supported him went into exile in the service of the King of France. Their departure was known as "The Flight of the Wild Geese." Their leader Patrick Sarsfield fell in battle in Landen on July 29th, 1963. Lifting his hands that were covered with his life's blood he whispered: "Would that this were shed for Ireland."

*(19) Quoted in the "Worker", February 27th, 1937.

THE BATTLE
OF JARAMA

The Tolerance of Crows
"Death comes in quantity from solved
Problems on maps, well ordered dispositions,
Angles of elevation and direction;

Comes innocent from tools children might
Love, retaining under pillows,
Innocently impales on any flesh.

And with flesh falls apart the mind
That trails thought from mind that cuts
Thought clearly for a waiting purpose.

Progress of poison in the nerves and
Discipline's collapse is halted.
Body awaits the tolerance of crows."

    The high rate of casualities among the small Irish group affected its ability to continue as a single unit. When the first U.S. contingent, later to be expanded to form the "Abraham Lincoln Battalion" *(1) which had set out from New York on Christmas Eve, 1936 with an illegal vanguard of 96 men, arrived, the Irish were divided between it and the British Battalion.

    Frank Ryan in the Albacete base sent a letter on January 1st, 1937 to all the Irish volunteers:—

> A Chairde,
>   As most of you will have read in the newspapers before leaving home, an Irish Unit of the International Brigades is being formed. It may be necessary to make clear to some why *all* Irish comrades are not just now together. The fact is that the military situation does not allow the war to be held up so that all Irishmen can be collected and formed into a unit. At the earliest possible opportunity that will be done. The unit now at the front, the unit now in training and the other comrades now on their way to us will be united in one unit.
>   This unit will be part of the English-speaking Battalion which

is to be formed. Irish, English, Scots and Welsh comrades will fight, side by side, against the common enemy—Fascism.

It must also be made clear that in the International Brigades in which we serve—there are no national differences. We are all comrades.

We have come out here as soldiers of liberty to demonstrate Republican Ireland's solidarity with the gallant Spanish workers and peasants in their fight against Fascism.

If we stress the fact that we are Irish it is mainly to show the world that the majority of the Irish people repudiate Fascist O'Duffy and his mercenaries who are helping Franco and his Moors.

Finally, we insist that the closest bonds of comradeship must unite us with all fighters against Fascism from other countries. Rival national war-cries will never be raised by us.

It should be unnecessary, too, to point out that as we came out voluntarily, men of different parties, and men of no party, so may we go back when this fight is over.

There is no compulsion on any of us to form any new party, or belong to any party. But — one bond will always unite us—the bond of comradeship in a common cause here and at home.

As soon as possible I will visit every Irish group in this country and at the first available opportunity I will in co-operation with the Officers of the English-speaking Battalion—re-unite all groups in a distinctive Irish Unit. Until then, I ask every man to play his part as a disciplined and eager soldier—just as if we were all together in one Unit.

For the sake of the people of Spain and for the success of the fight against Fascism and in the name of the folks at home whom we must never disgrace I ask for complete unity and the fullest co-operation in this the decisive fight for the liberty of the human race."

—Frank Ryan,
Commander, Irish Unit,
Albacete,
New Years Day, 1937*(2)

The arrival of more English-speaking volunteers and a reorganisation of those already there made possible the formation of another Brigade, the XV. In February it was to go into battle for the first time. In its ranks were 600 of the British Battalion, 500 of the American "Lincolns", 800 from a number of Balkan countries and 800 French and Belgian volunteers. Along with the XI (German anti-fascists) Brigade it took part in one of the bitterest battles of the whole Spanish War — the Battle of Jarama.

This battle was occasioned by the Franco failure to capture Madrid, as they thought they would, by November 1936. To overcome this situation a new Fascist offensive was opened south-east of the city. Its objective was to cut off the road linking the capital with the major city of Valencia.

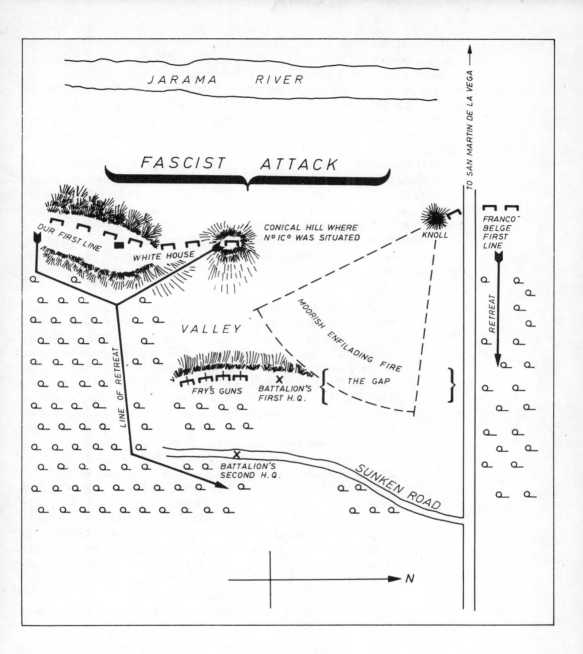

Jarama front, February 1937 (contemporary sketchmap)

The offensive that lasted a month began on February 6th, 1937. With 5 mobile brigades, 6 batteries of 155 mm calibre, a Nazi Condor Legion unit of 88 mm guns as well as squadrons of Moorish cavalry the Fascists advanced. The power of the offensive overwhelmed the Republican forces. Despite the fact that two Republican battalions fought to the last man, the Franco forces kept advancing. By February 12th they had captured Pingarron Hill after crossing the Jarama River with 10,000 troops supported by tanks and artillery.

On the same day (12th) the 15th Brigade with its Irish complement went into action. With few armaments, no trench-spades the Republican forces had little firepower and less cover. To add to the misfortune; there was no ammunition for their old-type machine guns, the munition lorry on the way to the front had crashed and overturned.

Eventually in the raging battle, the Republican lines broke before the weight of steel poured on them. A disorganised retreat began, and as Frank Ryan described it:

"On the road from Chinchon to Madrid, the road along which we had marched to the attack three days before were scattered now all who survived—a few hundred Britons, Irish and Spaniards. Dispirited by heavy casualities, by defeat, by lack of food, worn out by three days of gruelling fighting, our men appeared to have reached the end of their resistance. Some were still straggling down the slopes from which had been, up to an hour ago, the front line. And now there was no line, nothing between the Madrid road and the Fascists but disorganised groups of weary, warwrecked men. After three days of terrific struggle, the superior numbers, the superior armaments of the Fascists had routed them. All, as they came back, had similar stories to tell; of comrades dead of conditions that were more than flesh and blood could stand, of weariness they found hard to resist. I recognised the young Commissar of the Spanish Company. His hand bloody, where a bullet had grazed the palm, he was fumbling nervelessly with his automatic, in turn threatening and pleading with his men. I got Manuel to calm him, and to tell him we would rally everybody in a moment. As I walked along the road to see how many men we had, I found myself deciding that we should go back up the line of the road to San Martin de la Vega, and take the Moors on their left flank."

"Groups were lying about on the roadside, hungrily eating oranges that had been thrown to them from a passing lorry. This was no time to sort them into units. I noted with satisfaction that some had brought down spare rifles. I found my eyes straying always to the hills we had vacated. I hitched a rifle on my shoulder. They stumbled to their feet. No time for barrack-square drill. One line of four. 'Fall in behind us!' A few were still on the grass bank beside the road, adjusting helmets and rifles. 'Hurry up!' came the cry from the ranks. Up the road towards the cookhouse I saw

Jock Cunningham assembling another crowd. We hurried up, joined forces. Together, we two marched at the head. Whatever popular writers may say, neither your Briton nor your Irishman is an exuberant type. Demonstrativeness is not his dominating trait. The crowd behind was marching silently. The thoughts in their minds could not be inspiring ones. I remembered a trick of the old days when we were holding banned demonstrations. I jerked my head back: 'Sing up, ye sons of guns.'

"Quaveringly at first, then more lustily, then in one resounding chant the song rose from the ranks. Bent backs straightened; tired legs thumped sturdily; what had been a routed rabble marched to battle again as proudly as they had done three days before. And the valley resounded to their singing:

> Then comrades, come rally,
> And the last fight let us face;
> The Internationale
> Unites the human races.

"On we marched, back up the road, nearer and nearer to the front. Stragglers still in retreat down the slopes stopped in amazement, changed direction and ran to join us; men lying exhausted on the roadside jumped up, cheered and joined the ranks. I looked back. Beneath the forest of upraised fists, what a strange band; unshaven, unkempt, blood-stained, grimy. But full of fight again, AND MARCHING ON THE ROAD BACK. Beside the road stood our Brigade Commander, General Gal*(3). We had quitted; he had stood his ground. Was it that, or fear of his reprimands, that made us give three cheers for him? Briefly, tersely, he spoke to us. We had one-and-a-half hours of daylight in which to recapture our lost positions. 'That gap on our right?' A Spanish Battalion was coming up with us to occupy it. Again the 'Internationale' arose. It was being sung in French too. Our column had swelled in size during the halt; a group of Franco-Belge had joined us. We passed the Spanish Battalion. They had caught the infectio: they were singing too as they deployed to the right.

"Jack Cunningham seemed to be the only man who was not singing. Hands thrust into his great-coat pockets, he trudged along at the head of his men ... we were singing; he was planning.

"As the olive groves loom in sight, we deploy to the left. At last we are on the ridge, the ridge which we must never again desert. For while we hold that ridge, the Madrid—Valencia Road is free. Bullets whistle through the air, or smack into the ground, or find a human target. Cries, shouts. But always the louder interminable singing. Flat on the ground, we fire into the groves. There are no sections, no companies even. But the individuals jump ahead, and set an example that is readily followed—too readily, because sometimes they block our fire. In the thick of the battle we organise ourselves with a certain amount of success into sections. The Spanish problem is quickly solved. 'Manuel! What's the Spanish for 'Forward?' 'Adelante!' yells Manuel, and waves the Spanish lads on. 'Abajo!' and down they flop to give covering fire. A burly French lieutenant runs over to ask me for grenades. We have none. Waving a ridiculously tiny automatic he advances shouting 'En Avant!' Ahead of us are little cones of blue–red flame. Now we know where the Moorish and German machine-gunners are. Oh for grenades! As we hug the earth we call to one another to direct group fire on those cones. Flat on our bellies we push forward. Inch by inch. Darkness falls like a blanket. Advancing! All the time advancing. As I crawl forward I suddenly realise, with savage joy, that it is we who are advancing and they who are being pushed back. And then in actual disappointment: 'The bastards won't wait for our bayonets!'

"We are in the olive groves. Firing ceases. We are on our feet, feeling for one another, in the inky blackness. I stumble against a soft bundle. I bend down. His spiked bayonet scrapes my hand. He is one of ours. His face is cold. He has been dead for hours ... So we are back where we were at midday.

"Manuel, Andre and I dig in. Our rifle-pit completed, Manuel reaches back for the blanket he had so carefully laid down it is missing. Manuel rattles his bayonet and shouts lurid threats to the "'bloody bastard' who stole my blanket!" From the trees, all around he is answered with roars of laughter."

"And thus the men who had been broken and routed a few hours ago settled down for the night on the ground they had reconquered. They had dashed Fascist hopes, smashed plans. Thenceforward, for more than four months, they were to fight, and many of them to die, in these olive groves. But never again were the Fascists to rout them. They were to hold that line, and save Madrid; fighting in the dauntless spirit of the great rally of that afternoon, fighting too, in the spirit of those reckless roars of laughter that night in the Wood of Death."*(4)

The mighty enemy offensive had been hurled back, but the International Brigade paid a high price in lives. Some of the best and bravest of the Irish fell in the Jarama battle, men like the Reverend Robert M. Hilliard, a Church of Ireland clergyman. He was a graduate of Trinity College Dublin where he had won the Read Sizarship. Along with a number of other nationally minded students he had formed the "Thomas Davis Society". Whilst in college he had taken part in the last stages of the Irish Civil War on the I.R.A. side. In the University he also became editor of "T.C.D." the college magazine. He was a keen amateur boxer, winning the College Featherweight Championship*(5) and was picked to represent Ireland in the Olympic Games. Because of this interest in he was known Spain as the "Boxing Parson." Born in Moyeightragh, Killarney he functioned as a clergyman in Dernaghy, Co. Antrim and the Cathedral Mission in Belfast. He was one of a party of four who had fought, on February 14th, against the advancing tanks with neither an anti-tank gun or even grenades.

With the Protestant minister, there fell Eamon McGrotty of Derry who had been a member of the Catholic teaching order, the Irish Christian Brothers, and previously a member of Na Fianna Eireann, I.R.A., and Gaelic League (the Irish Language Revival Movement).

With the Protestant Minister and the Catholic Monk from Ireland, died William Fox; Bill Henry who had been acting commander of the No. I Company of the Lincoln Battalion; Dick O'Neil*(6), Danny Boyle, and Bill (Liam) Tumilson*(7) (who had taken over command of the "Tom Mooney" Machine-Gun Company)—those five from Belfast, Catholics and Protestant workers had as companions in death—Hugh Bonar of Donegal, who was a Section-Commander; T.T. O'Brien of Liverpool, Maurice Quinlan of Waterford, Paddy McDaid whose battles before consisted of the defence of the Dublin Four Courts in the Irish Civil War; and Mick (Blaser) Browne who was burned to death by incendiary bullets being fired at him as he crawled wounded across "no man's land".

Nineteen Irish anti-fascists fell at Jarama. They included Charlie Donnelly*(8) the young Irish Poet. When the news of his death reached Dublin, his close friend and college contemporary, the Irish poet, Donagh McDonagh, wrote the following lines in mourning:

> *HE IS DEAD AND GONE, LADY ...*(9)*
> (for Charles Donnelly R.I.P.)

> "Of what a quality is courage made.
> That he who gently walked our city streets
> Talking of poetry or philosophy,
> Spinoza, Keats.
> Should lie like any martyred soldier
> His brave and fertile brain dried quite away
> And the limbs that carried him from cradle to deaths outpost
> Growing down into a foreign clay."

> "Gone from amongst us and his life not half begun
> Who had followed Jack-o-Lantern truth and liberty
> Where it led wavering from park-bed to prison cell
> Into a strange land, dry misery,
> And then into Spain's slaughter, snipers aim
> And his last shocked embrace of earth's lineaments.
> Can I picture truly that swift end
> Who see him dead with eye that still repents.
> What end, what quietus, can I see for him
> Who had the quality of life in every vein?
> Life with its passion and poetry and its proud
> Ignorance of eventual loss or gain.
> This first fruits of our harvest, willing sacrifice
> Upon the altar of his integrity
> Lost to us; somewhere his death is charted —
> Something has been gained by this mad missionary."

However, the greatest loss of all was sustained in the death of Captain "Kit" Conway. More than sixteen years before he had earned for himself the reputation of a tough guerrilla commander both against the British and pro-treaty "Free State" forces in Ireland. An indomitable opponent of Fascism, he joined the Communist Party of Ireland, and was well known in many parts of the country for his fighting opposition to the Blueshirts. Because of the near pogrom atmosphere in Ireland against anyone who sympathised with Republican Spain, most of those who volunteered for the International Brigades had to leave the country quietly. Not so Conway. An active member of the Building Workers' Section of the Irish Transport & General Workers' Union, he, on the day of his departure for Spain, mounted an oil barrel on the site where he worked and addressing his fellow workers he explained what was happening in Spain and told his mates that, "Sooner than Franco should win there, I would leave my body in Spain to manure the fields."

In the battle of Jarama he played an outstanding part as a Company Commander. Recalling that battle and the incredible bravery of the Republican troops, the Spanish history book records ...

> ... "Los combatientes internacionales, que rivalizaron en heroismo con los espanoles, pagaron tambien un gran tributo de sangre: mueieron, entre otros, el commandante del 'Batallon Dimitrov', Grebenarov, el pastor protestante, *Reverendo Hilliard*, el escritor comunista ... Christobal Caudwell, *el irlandes Conway*, el frances Brugere, los garibaldinos Tamango, el mas antigue de todos ellos, Valentino, Negroni, Bassi, Carloni, Borrini, Cerruti, Fogaci, Garofanos y otros" ...*(10)

James Prendergast, who was beside Conway when he was killed, described the circumstances in the following words ...

> "February 12th. Noon We had just swung through the bottleneck of a valley and were beginning to deploy. I had been told to look out for a bridge, our objective. Just then we came under direct fire. Men were hurriedly seeking good cover among the scrub but once we lay down we saw that we had no view ahead. For a while we fired from standing positions. Suddenly Peter Daly shouted that they were advancing on our left. I looked across. We concentrated fire on them at 500 yards range.

> "But the Fascist fire, front and flank was now pretty heavy. Men were being hit all around. Somebody was hit beside me. A yell for stretcher bearers. Goff tumbled over, his hand to his head, his face white. It was a narrow shave; his helmet was dinged. 'Kit' was everywhere at once, directing fire, encouraged us all.

> "The fire on us had grown so heavy now that nobody could tell what would happen, and fear was not felt any more, because it was no use feeling afraid. A Spaniard who had got mixed up with us somehow moved over to my side. The bush he left had been

denuded by a stream of bullets. He looked at me, laughed. We moved to the right, to higher ground to get a better field of fire.

"We took up new positions. I saw Paddy Duff moving back, hit in the leg. Shells were exploding on the left. Holy God! If they fall on this bare ground we are finished! Low-flying planes scream towards us. Now we are for it in earnest. They pass over and soon they are back again with our chasers at their tails. A faint cheer from us.

"Now if we quit these positions, the Fascists will break in on the road. So here we must stay, even though the Fascist fire is literally eating the top of the hill away. Men from three Companies are now here on the hill. Things are a bit mixed up. 'Kit' takes command of all.

"As I move up the hill, Jack Taylor, a big Cockney, with whom I had one unforgettable night at Figueras, is dressing a wounded comrade. 'Hit bad?' 'Unconscious, thumbs up, I guess.' There is blood on the seat of Jack's pants. Only a flesh wound he says, and he won't go back."

"I settle into a new firing position. My rifle is soon burning hot. 'Kit' comes over. I notice his face with lanes of sweat running through the dust. He hands me a note. It is from Brigade H.Q. telling us that we must hold out at all costs. He tells me to transmit these instructions to the section on our left flank. I look through my binoculars before I move off. The Moors are sneaking up there on the left. Oh, where are our Machine-guns?

"I speed away to the left to deliver the message. What's left of others are around the White House, I am told. I get to the house, and on my way, it seems as if a thousand bees are buzzing past my face. So, it does take a man's weight in lead to kill him.

"I get to the yard and shout. No reply. No noise from within. I clear the low wall and go in. Yes, they are there all right, all dead. I shiver as I move back.

"I am more reckless. No fear now. Why? I do not know. Somebody calls my name. It is Pat Smith. Blood streams from his head and arm. Tom Jones of Wexford is there. Good man, Tom. Always dresses a man where he falls. A hero. He tells me Goff and Daly are hit. I reach the hill-crest where 'Kit' is directing fire. He is using a rifle himself and pausing every while to give instructions. Suddenly, he shouts, his rifle spins out of his hand, and he falls back.

"He is placed in a blanket. No stretchers left now. His voice is broken with agony. 'Do your best boys, hold on!' Tears glisten in our eyes. Many are from other Companies. But all remember 'Kit' at Cordova and Madrid. His gallant leadership then and today won them all.

" 'Kit' is taken away. I see Ken Stalker. He is the only experienced man left. I run to him and he takes Command. I see Fascist tanks rolling up the road to the right. The Moors are sweeping us front and flanks. We'll never hold out now. I move to a firing position. Suddenly, I am lifted off my feet. Something terrific has hit me in the side. I cannot breathe. They are dressing me now . . .

"In the ambulance I meet 'Kit'. He is in terrible agony, and can talk little. 'How are the rest?' is his constant question . . .

"Next morning they told me our great leader was dead."*(11)

Chapter 6 Notes

*(1) Altogether, in the course of the war, 3,300 came from the U.S.A. More than 1,600 were killed in action.

*(2) Copy of letter preserved by Peter O'Connor of Waterford.

*(3) A Hungarian International Brigade General whose real name was Janos Galicz.

*(4) "The Great Rally" by Frank Ryan, "The Book of the XV Brigade" (pp. 58—61) edited by Ryan and published in Madrid, February 1938 by the Commissariat of War, XV Brigade. This book (306 pages) was written and printed 'under fire.' Amply illustrated it contains many well written articles dealing not only with the three main constitutents of the XV Brigade—English, American, Canadian—but also the "Franco-Belge" and Dimitrov Battalions. The battles of Jarama, Brunete, Aragon, Quinto Belchite and Fuentes de Ebro, are dealt with in detail.

*(5) For details of his college championship bout, vid: "Irish Independent", May 29th, 1931.

*(6) O'Neil from the Falls Road area of Belfast was one of the few Catholics, at that time, having the trade of a Compositor. He joined the Communist Party of Ireland just before he went to Spain.

*(7) Tumilson came from a typical Protestant working class family which had long connections with the Orange Order. He first crossed the "divide" when he frequented the Falls Road area. He changed his name to the Gaelic form of "Liam". During the Unemployed Riots described in footnote 2 on page 122, he was an invaluable liason between the Protestant and Catholic unemployed. On February 20th, 1932 he wrote in a friend's autograph book: "I would rather die as James Connolly died than to die peacefully without having fought in the cause of working class freedom." On another occasion he met up with an ex-Black and Tan who boasted of his activities in County Cork. The next evening, Tumilson and his friend, Jimmy Straney from the Falls Road (who was killed in Spain in 1938) accosted the British mercenary. They threw him over the Lagan Bridge in Belfast into the river. Another friend Paddy Roe McLaughlin (also of the International Brigade) recounting this story says: "With his rare dry wit, and without event a smile, he finished with, 'We never asked him if he could swim, but it seems he could as he was seen again—but not in Belfast!' "

*(8) Charles Donnelly (July 10th, 1914—February 26th, 1937) was a young poet of great promise. Born in Dungannon, County Tyrone, he moved with his family to Dublin. He attended the O'Connell's Christian Brothers School, and later University College Dublin. He came into conflict with the right-wing university authorities because of his membership of the Communist Party of Ireland and had to leave the College. In 1935 he was imprisoned in Mountjoy Jail and, there, wrote the poem, "The Mystery of the Flowering Bars." After his release he found employment in London as an unskilled worker. There he helped to organise the London Branch of the Irish Republican Congress. He wrote a memorandum on military strategy, and left his work on a biography of James Connolly to go to Spain. In the battle of Jarama he was killed by an explosive bullet, his body lay for four days on the battlefield before it could be recovered. A description of his death appeared in "Hello Canada," a pamphlet published by the "Friends of the Mackenzie-Papineau (Canadian) Battalion 1937: "We run for cover. Charlie Donnelly, Commander of the Irish Company, is crouched behind an olive tree. He has picked up a bunch of olives from the ground and is squeezing them. I hear him say quietly between a lull of machine-gun fire, 'Even the olivers are bleeding'! A bullet got him square in the temple a few minutes later. He is buried there now beneath the olives."

(For articles and poems by and about Charlie Donnelly see: "Ireland To-day" (Dublin); "Left Review" (London) Vol. II, No. I. October 1935, Vol. II April 1936 and Vol. III, 1937—38; the "Irish Times" (Dublin), December 1970, and Hibernia (Dublin), April 2 1971.

*(9) Published in "Ireland To-Day", Vol. 2. No. 7. July 1937.

*(10) "Guerra y Revolucion en Espana, 1936—39." Tome II, Editorial Progreso, Moscu, 1966, p. 247. Here is a translation:

". . . The international fighters, who rivalled the Spaniards in heroism, also paid a great tribute in blood: amongst those who fell were Grebenavov, commander of the Dimitrov Battalion; *Reverend Hilliard*, the Protestant clergyman; . . . Christopher Caudwell, the Communist writer; the *Irishman Conway*; the Frenchman Brugere; the Garibaldinos Tamango—the oldest of them all—Valentino, Negroni, Bassi, Carloni, Borrini, Cerruti, Fogaci, Garofanos and others . . ."

*(11) "The Book of the XV Brigade", pp. 64—66.

FROM VINEGAR HILL TO CHIMORA

... "For Connolly was there,
    Connolly was there,
    Great, brave, undaunted,
    James Connolly was there" ...

In the battle of Jarama, 25,000 of the Spanish Republican forces died in combat. The casualities of the International Brigades were relatively higher, —but the road between Madrid and Valancia was held open!

After the bloody thrust back of the fascist offensive there began an extraordinary long period of continual trench duty in which the Irish—those not dead or wounded—remained with the rest of the XV Brigade for a nerve-wracking period of seventy-three days, from February 12th, until June 17th, when they were finally relieved.

It was a terrible strain after the holocaust of the earlier battle with the continual anticipation of another mighty fascist offensive. The time was utilised in digging in, trench building and the erection of barbed wire fortifications.

For the Irish however there was a short break in early May when they were accorded absence from trench duty by the "Estado Mayor" (headquarters) of the XV Brigade for an important commemorative function.

On May 12th, 1937, the 21st anniversary of the execution of James Connolly, the Irish sponsored a unique ceremony in his honour. It was held on the very battle field of Jarama, under the protecting cover of a hill just behind the front line. The background noises were the daily strafing of artillery and machine-guns. Every unit in the XV Brigade was represented at a meeting in which the speakers dealt with the national and international aspects of Connolly's life and teachings. The gathering of international anti-fascist fighters endorsed a resolution which read:*(1)

"We of the James Connolly Unit of the International Brigade, alongside the democratic forces in Spain fighting against International fascism send revolutionary greetings to our comrades in Ireland who are commemorating the 21st anniversary of the

77

death of James Connolly, murdered on May 12, 1916 by the forces of British Imperialism.

"We together with comrades from all over the world, pledge ourselves to the International struggle against the International enemy—Fascism. We fight the enemy here in Spain to-day, knowing that by defeating it here, Ireland will be spared the horrors which Fascism inflicts on the peoples it dominates.

We salute our comrades at home, who are carrying on the struggle against Imperialism, native and British, and we call for a closing of the ranks against the common enemy.

We stand in silence here for two minutes in salute to the memory of Connolly, and to all our comrades who gave their lives in Ireland's fight against oppression, and to the workers of the entire world who have died for freedom."

Signed on behalf of the Organising Committee of the Irish Section, Lincoln Battalion:

Sean de Paor, Peadar O'Concobhair, P. de Stainligh, Kevin Blake, Joseph F. Rehill, P.C. Haydock, T. Hayes, Michael O'Ceallaigh, James O'Regan, J. Hunt, P. Power, D. Holden, A. MacLarnan, Paul A. Burns.

Signed by:

Martin Hourihan, Commandant*(2) 17th (Lincoln) Battalion; Frederick Lutz, Political Commissar, do; Fred Copeman, Commandant, 16th Battalion; R.S. Elliot and B. Williams do; Aratchovis, Commandant, Dimitrov Battalion; Dobrett, Political Commissar, do; Lantz, Commandant, Franco-Belge Battalion; Jose Cavalle, Captain Estado Mayor (on behalf of Spanish Comrades) Capt. Allan Johnson, Operations Officer, 15th Brigade; Harry Haywood, Political Commissar, 15th Brigade.

Signed also by:

J. A. Demetriar (Greece), R. Kerr (Canada), Juan Santiago (Cuba), A. J. Thornstanje (Holland), Alfons Bircht (Germany), Bernardo Cappadona (Italy), Artemio Luna (Philipines), J. Shiva (Japan), Edward C. Flaherty (American-Irish), Ralph Bates (Editor, Brigade Journal).

After the "Connolly Commemoration" they returned to the trenches. Life there was described by Paddy Roe McLaughlin of Donegal: "The day dawned cloudily which was rather a disappointment to those of us who had intentions of giving ourselves a fine coat of tan. It was chilly, so we put on our sweaters and other warm clothes. Today the men were not running around as usual in their trunks, with bare feet and bare backs, baking under the hot sun. The trunks of the olive trees were cold and their leaves sweaty.

As the day passed with light exchange of rifle fire, a few dark clouds blanketed their huge shadows over us. On a few occasions when it attempted to rain, comrades who were extra cautious threw towels or pieces of rags around the rifle bolts to keep them dry.

"The Fascists across the way were particularly quiet, a fact that created

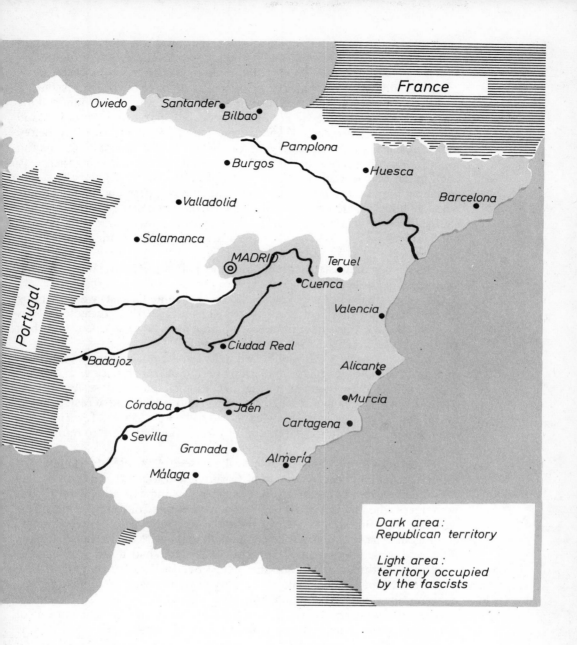

France

Oviedo • Santander •
Bilbao •
Pamplona •
Burgos • Huesca •
Barcelona •
Valladolid •
Salamanca •
MADRID ◎
Teruel •
Cuenca •
Valencia •
Portugal
Ciudad Real •
Badajoz •
Alicante •
Murcia •
Córdoba • Jaén •
Cartagena •
Sevilla •
Granada •
Almería •
Málaga •

Dark area:
Republican territory

Light area:
territory occupied
by the fascists

Spain, the front line, summer 1937

in many of us an increased feeling of the gathering storm. But we felt certain that we could meet the enemy under any conditions and defeat him.

"Eat, sleep, watch! When is it all going to end? Why don't the bastards come out and fight? We felt as if we were being cheated out of our just due.

"Some of us returned to our dugouts and waited, others sat around talking and joking. All of us failed to notice the formation of a particularly dark cloud almost directly overhead. A sudden peal of thunder, followed by heavy rain-drops sent everyone scurrying for shelter. It was almost malicious fun to sit in our rain-proof dugouts and watch the food detail making their way back in the midst of such bedlam. With food cans in their hands, they ran splashing themselves with water and mud, slipping here and there, cursing when a bullet whizzed by their ears, and finally upon arrival at the dugouts, sliding down the watery earthen stairways. One comrade made a perfect two point landing on his back, and held the precious food high in the air to prevent it spilling.

"As we began to eat, the familiar sound of fast increasing musketry and machine-gun fire came to our ears. Sure enough it was an attack.

"From our trenches we were able to see that some Fascists were charging but because we met them with a terrific barrage, they retreated. They foundered back into their trenches; some Fascists were killed, and their wounded were left to die in 'No Man's Land'."*(3)

On June 17th the XV Brigade eventually left Jarama where they had been in a month-long bitter battle and a long period of trench duty with its daily routine of alternating tension and almost "idyllic" quiet as described above. Their seventy-three days at the front line had only one period of rest; in billets at Alcala de Henares, when they expected to be able to relax for a long and deserved period—only to find that after three days they were to return once again to Jarama!

Three months previously going to the base at Albacete; the numbers of the Irish who had been wounded at Cordova and the early days at Jarama had already arrived at this Brigade base. They, along with a number of fresh volunteers who had just arrived in Spain, were formed into another unit. This was the 20th Battalion which in its make up was a truly "international" contingent. The Battalion's four component units were the French, German, Slav, and Anglo-American Companies. The latter had three sections; the American, Latin American and the "No. I Section" of Irish and British.

Two Irishmen—Peter Daly and Paddy O'Daire—were tenientes (Lieutenants) in the Anglo-American Company.

Peter Daly, was a native of Vinegar Hill, Wexford—the scene of one of the most historic battles in the United Irishmen's Rising of 1798. He came from a place and a family steeped in Irish revolutionary traditions. His father had been one of the founders of the Tom Clarke Society in Liverpool (named after the famous Fenian who had survived 15 years of savage imprisonment by the British, to fight as a leader in the Easter Revolt of 1916, and who died before the firing squads that executed James Connolly and the other leaders of the Rising).

Peter Daly himself joined Fianna Eireann, and as a youth took part in the fight against the Free State Army. In this struggle he was wounded and taken prisoner. After 17 months in jail he finally secured his release by an

18-day hunger strike. Having to leave Ireland after the victory of the Cosgrave forces, he went to Britain where he worked for a while before joining the British Army for a period of four years, reaching the rank of Sergeant. However he had "to leave in a hurry" when it was discovered that he was smuggling arms to the I.R.A. and he returned to Ireland in the thirties, to take up the position of Training Officer of the Wexford Brigade of the I.R.A. In 1934 he joined the Republican Congress, but after long spells of unemployment he chanced it to return to England again. There he worked as a navvy for Wempeys of Hammersmith, London.

One of the first to volunteer for the International Brigades, he was a group leader in the Irish Section at Jarama, being wounded in the hip on the fourth day of the battle there.

His close companion and fellow officer in the 20th Battalion, Paddy O'Daire was a native of Glenties, County Donegal. Although but a youth at the time (as was Daly) he also played his part in the last stages of the Irish War of Independence. He also had to emigrate after the Irish Civil War, in his case to Canada. There he became active in the Canadian worker's movement, serving a sentence of 15 months hard labour for his activities. On his release he was deported. In December 1936 he was with the Irish on the Cordova front where he was wounded. (In the course of the Spanish war he developed into an outstanding military leader, being in 1938 "Director of Operations" of the XV Brigade. In World War II he joined the British Army in the fight against Hitler as a private and held the rank of Major on demobilisation.)

The 20th Battalion, its Anglo-American Company with its "No. I Section" of Irish and British were sent out on March 20th, 1937 to help out at Pozoblanco which was under very heavy enemy pressure. On arrival they found that the Republican forces had by then in fact routed the Fascist attackers and that the later were retreating so quickly that the Republicans had to take over a train. On this they mounted machine-guns, in an effort to make contact with the enemy. When they did, the men of the 20th Battalion then found that they were pinned down by a heavy Fascist artillery barrage. A few days later, however, the Battalion succeeded in taking one of the most important hills in the area. After this feat, the Anglo-American Company was sent to Chimora to assist a Spanish Battalion engaged in battle there. Placed on the left flank of the Spanish comrades, the Company took a hill by surprise from the Fascists; an operation that was necessary to secure the flanks of the Spanish Republican unit. Fierce attacks and counterattacks continued for the possession of the hill; the capture of which in the first place had in fact, exposed the Company's own left flank to the dominating fire of the enemy, who only a few thousand yards away held the superior force of Moors with a superiority of six-to-one whose attack was preceded by a continuous artillery bombardment of two hours. This forced the defenders to retire from the hill.

Throughout this action Peter Daly, played a leading part. Writing of his conduct, his fellow International Brigader, Alec Donaldson, said that "He was courage incarnate ..." On one occasion, with two others he manned a machine-gun and covered the withdrawel of the Company (of which he had been appointed Commander during the battle) keeping off the hordes of

Moors who had advanced under the cover of a heavy barrage of shells. "He was the type of leader for whom men would have gone through Hell and his qualities were such that he merited this high regard of his comrades" ...*(4)

Wounded again in the hip he was forced to go back to hospital. At the conclusion of the action his Anglo-American Company was paraded before the rest of the 20th Battalion as an example of a brave and efficient combat unit—as well it might, because the hill was retaken by them. Paddy O'Daire arranged a night attack, since without artillery it was impossible to attack in daylight. It was imperative that the hill should be re-taken, since it gave the enemy the opportunity to throw grenades right down on the Company's new position. It was retaken.

After four months on the Southern Front, the 20th Battalion was withdrawn to Albacete for the purpose of integrating all the English-speaking volunteers into a re-organised XV Brigade.

New battles were on the agenda.

Chapter 7 Notes

*(1)   "Irish Democrat (Dublin) June 12th, 1937 and mentioned in "Notre Combat" p. 123 "Book of the XV Brigade".
*(2)   Martin Hourihan was an Irish-American, born 1906. He served at sea for a while, and was in the U.S. Army for six and a half years. Later he became a teacher and organiser of sharecroppers. He was jailed by the Philadelphia police during a seamans strike.
*(3)   Page 108, "Book of the XV Brigade".
*(4)   "These Men Have Died," published by the Commissariat of War, International Brigades. Madrid, 1937, p. 17.

THE BRUNETE
OFFENSIVE

... "Viva la Quince Brigada
     Rumbala, rumbala, rum-ba-la" ...

The Irish, those who had been relieved at Jarama on June 17th, 1937 and those who were withdrawn from Chimora, met in Albacete. It was a joyful reunion marred only by the sense of loss of the dead and the absence of the wounded. For those who came back from Jarama, after their 73 days in the front line, it was to be only a short rest, for on July 6th, there was to begin a Spanish Republican offensive at Brunete.

In the intervening period since Jarama and Chimora, the Franco forces had concentrated on subjugating the North of Spain. On April 26th, Guernica, the ancient and sacred city of the Basques was subjected to a terrific bombing by the Nazi Condor Legion air force. By June, the Italian regular army had taken Bilbao with the overwhelming support of 150 planes, 150 big guns and 100 tanks.

In view of those Fascist victories, the Government decided to launch an offensive at Brunete which lay west of Madrid. The offensive had a dual purpose — to relieve the pressure on the North; and to strengthen the position at Madrid with the aim of pushing the besieging forces back to a position where they could no longer shell the capital.

This development was new. Heretofore the Republican forces had been on the defensive at Madrid and Jarama, and Brunete was to be the first real offensive of the Republican command. The forces at its disposal were the V Army Corps under the leadership of Juan Modesto, the Communist woodcutter who became a General; the XVIII Corps led by another Spaniard, General Jurado, and the 35th Division with the Polish General Walter at its head.*(1)

Under the slogans of "Relieve the pressure on the Northern Front!" and "Raise the Beleaguerment of Madrid!" the attack was opened up on a stretch of approximately 20 kilometres. In the first few days advances were made into the enemy-held territory, and some 150 square kilometres taken. The aim of relieving the pressure on the Northern front was successful — too successful in fact, as Franco brought down from the North a mass of troops, aircraft and artillery to stop this Republican advance.

The advance continued with the morale of the Republicans at its highest. On the eve of the offensive they had been addressed by "La Pasionaria" whose words still rung in their ears. In the course of their advance, Brunete was captured in a dawn attack; and then Villanueva de la Cañada, and on the following day Quijorna was taken. On the third day they were set to attack Mosquito Crest, after crossing the Guadarrama River. The weather was of intense heat, and there was no water or food for the 15th Brigade. This had the severe effect of exhaustion.

From July 9th, to July 18th, there was a fierce contest for Mosquito Crest, with more and more Fascist reinforcements arriving there until their aircraft and artillery outnumbered the Republican forces by three to one. But still the anti-fascist attack continued. On July 18th, however, the Fascists counter-attacked, and after six days succeeded in retaking Brunete, only to have it taken from then again by a counter-charge!

In the taking of Brunete the XV Brigade played a prominent part. Along with the "Dimitrovs"*(2) it was the force that finally stormed it.

The fighting on this front was a severe test of courage, military training and physical staminia—and with a very high rate of casualties: the British Battalion was reduced from 630 to 180 men; the Polish "Dombrovskys" losing 121 killed and 320 wounded.

On July 18th, a Fascist counter offensive opened with a overwhelming superiority of planes and artillery which succeeded in pushing back the Republican lines which, however, by disciplined withdrawals, kept the front intact.

By July 26th, the fierceness of the Fascist offensive was exhausted; and a fortified line developed between the opposing armies.

As at Jarama, the cost of this battle against Fascism was 25,000 Republicans dead. In this number were seven Irishmen, William Beattie and William Laughran of Belfast, (both of these comrades had come from different religious backgrounds in Belfast, Beattie a Protestant, and Laughran a Catholic; their deaths in Spain together superceded the age-long sectarian animosity between the workers of both religions in that northern·Irish city); with them died Michael Kelly, William Davis (Dublin), Joe Kelly from Roscommon and Paddy Stuart O'Neil who had come to Spain from Vancouver.*(3) Another Irishman to be killed was George Browne.*(4)

George Brown was born, 1906, in Thomastown, Killkenny, but as a young lad was taken by his parents, in emigration, to Manchester—there he became a popular figure; he was a member of the Hugh Oldham Lads Club. He was an all-round sportsman, being a winner of the Metro-Vicks Works Sports in running and walking,—he was also a good boxer. In his work at Metro-Vicks and the Manchester Corporation Highways Department he was an active trade unionist, all the time maintaining his connection with the Irish Clubs in Manchester. He became a member of the Manchester and Salford Trades Council. He was a leading figure in the unemployed struggles of 1931, and later became a leader in the Communist Party in Manchester. Wounded in the battle of Brunete he was shot by the Fascists as he lay disabled on the road side.

How did the Irish behave in the Brunete Battle? Again, Frank Ryan recorded it*(5): "Our boys were all in the big push on the Centre Front. Their first objective was Villanueva de la Cañada, a town nearly as big as Bray, Co. Wicklow. To get there they had to drive in outposts, capture a line of trenches strongly fortified with barbed wire, break through a line of pill-boxes, and finally storm the trenches at the entrance to the town."

Paddy Duff commanded a machine-gun section. He got as far as the block-houses. While dashing between two of them he got a bullet in the ankle, in the same leg he was wounded in at Jarama. He rolled into a shell hole, would let nobody near him, yelled them onward and waited for the First Aid men. "Great, cute, old soldier" commented Ryan.

The final storming of the town was a desperate affair just carried at nightfall; the attack that had begun at dawn was ending at dusk. The Americans of the Lincoln Battalion along with the Irish tried fo find cover in ground a few hundred yards from the houses. The Republican aircraft had bombed the place well, but the church, the most prominent and dominating building in the town still stood, with its tower manned byy Fascist machine-gunners.

Just at dusk there occurred an amazing piece of deceit by the Fascists. From the town there came a procession of women, children and old men. From their ranks came the cry, "Camaradas." Pat Murphy who was lying behind a heap of earth, came out to greet what appeared to be a group of refugees. Just as he approached them, there was a sharp burst of fire from rifles, sub-machine guns, and the explosion of hand-grenades. Behind the lines of civilians were the Fascists using them as a screen. Murphy engaged with the leader of the enemy, they fell into a ditch, and Murphy shot him. Beside them fell a little girl of about ten years, who had been placed at the head of the group. "Lie quiet girlie," said Pat, and the girl looked at him as if she understood. Using the dead body of the Fascist leader as a shield, Murphy continued firing until he was seriously wounded in the groin by an hand-grenade. With the assistance of other Republican soldiers, the battle with the Fascists continued—and in ten or less terrible minutes it was all over. All of the Fascists were killed, but so were many of the civilians they had used as cover.

A few minutes later the town was stormed from two opposite points. By then it was dark, and the only light was provided by the bursting grenades. The grenade work was done so well that the two storming parties were within an ace of bombing each other. The job of mopping-up took all the night. "There were weird sights", wrote Ryan, "In one house you went to talk to three men lolling on chairs. Not a scratch on them. They had all been killed by the concussion of aerial torpedos. And every Fascist prisoner, if you could believe him, was either a Communist or a Socialist. It was the most People's Front town in all Spain."

Michael Kelly of Ballinasloe was killed that day. He was a Battalion runner, and was out with the Observation Officer. He was killed instantaneously by a bullet in the head. He was always a good type, full of energy, and always linked up the struggle in Spain with the fight at home in Ireland. He had been the chief organiser of the Connolly Commemoration which had been held in the Jarama trenches the previous May. He was a man who never shirked work, and according to Ryan, "he was actually an embarrassment by his habit of volunteering for dangerous work for which he was not capable. His loss is universally regretted here. Unfortunately the papers he was carrying with (he was a walking library) were lost"...*(6) Mick Kelly was very well-known in Irish Republican circles in London where he

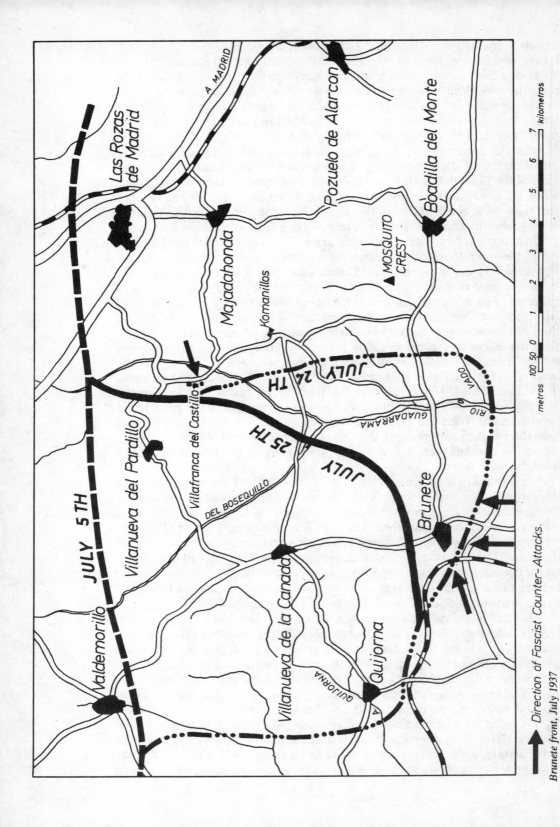

A MADRID

Las Rozas
de Madrid

Pozuelo de Alarcon

Boadilla del Monte

Majadahonda

Komanillos

MOSQUITO
CREST

JULY 24 TH

GUADARRAMA

RIO

RIO VADO

JULY 25 TH

Villafranca del Castillo

JULY
25 TH

Villanueva del Pardillo

DEL BOSEQUILLO

JULY
25 TH

Brunete

JULY 5TH

Villanueva de la Canada

Valdemorillo

QUIJORNA

Quijorna

▲ Direction of Fascist Counter-Attacks.

Brunete front, July 1937

metros 100 50 0

kilometros 0 1 2 3 4 5 6 7

played an active and leading part in the work of the Republican Congress Groups, being editorial adviser to its paper, "Irish Front" before he went to Spain.

He was killed as he and the Observation Officer went ahead as part of an advance patrol which pursued the retreating Fascists following the capture of Villanueva de la Cañada. He had come unscathed through the heavy fighting of the previous day, only to fall in an encounter with the retreating Fascists.

· He died in action on July 7th, 1937 at the age of 38 years.

Bill Davis of Dublin was killed when a burst of machine-gun fire from the church tower caught him as he was charging forward; his friend, Tom Murphy of Belfast, was beside him as he fell, "He curled up," said Tom, "his fist shot out clenched, 'Salud, Camaradas', he smiled, and died."

Frank Ryan in his letter home endeavoured to give a complete account of the battle. "I wish I could give you certain pictures of the fighting certain pictures of the fighting—and there's some I try to forget myself. At times I saw it all like a panorama in front of me; then there were hours when my nose stuck further and further to earth. Ludwig Renn says it was like the Somme only a bit worse.

"One sure thing you never get inured to bombardment; used to it certainly. But every time the torpedos start to fall, you feel your guts contract, and the blood gets sucked up out of your body. Of all the reading matter, what should I have in my hand one such day but the story of Guernica. Then I really realised what it must have for the women and children." ...

"War's hell. There is little glamour in it when you're there, especially when you see what's left—after shell and heat—of fellows that were joking with you a few hours before. But this one has got to be done and won, so that makers of war can never again cause Guernicas and Almerias and Bilbaos."

On July 23rd, William Beattie was killed and his fellow Belfastman, James Hillen was wounded. Eight days later, the fascist attacks petered out to a standstill, and the front lines were drawn.

One Irish participant, Peter O'Connor, kept in his diary an account of these days. Under the relevant dates he recorded the happenings:

"June 30th: (1937). At 9 p.m. received the order to 'stand to.'

July 1st: 'Standing to!' Paddy Power left for home at 12.30 p.m. this morning. I feel very lonely after Paddy as we had been in several battles together. (I would like to state here, that this is the eve of the Great Republican Offensive of the Brunete Front. There were three brothers, Johnnie, Paddy and Willie Power in the Irish section. Frank Ryan decided and it was agreed by us that at least one of the brothers should be sent home. It was decided to send Paddy who left under protest.)

July 4th: Left for the front. Went for swim in river with Frank Ryan.

July 5th: Encamped in a beautiful forest on the side of the mountains. We are about to enter a battle which will prove decisive in the war against fascism.

July 6th: Attack started at 5 a.m. Fascists in rout at 9 a.m.

July 7th: Mick Kelly killed. Advancing steadily, took the village of Villanueva de la Cañada.

July 8th: Made a great advance today, had very narrow escapes all day.

July 9th: Fascists counter-attack today. Got as far as our lines but driven back with heavy losses on both sides. Johnnie Power and Paul Burns wounded, both in the legs. Our Batt. Commander Law killed. Our great Spanish comrade Humanes was also killed besides many other comrades. Just heard of the death of George Brown our great comrade of the British Communist Party.

July 11th: Fortifying our positions, holding our lines in spite of repéated enemy counter-attacks.

July 12th: Here I must pay tribute to Comrade Nelson, our Batt. Political Commissar who took command of our Batt. On the death of Comrade Law. It was up to his resourcefulness and coolness in desperate situations that our positions which we took from the enemy, were held with a minimum number of men. I feel very lonely now as I am the only Irishman left in the line. The rest being either wounded or killed.

July 14th: Went to the rear for re-organisation.

July 16th: Leaving for the front lines 9 p.m. Marching all night until 9 a.m. In the second line of reserve outside the village of Villanueva del Pardillo. Moved to the front line 8 p.m.

July 17th: Got the heaviest aerial and artillery bombardment yet received during the war. One piece of Artillery shrapnel missed my head by inches and buried itself in the ground at my feet. Left this line for another part of the front 12 kilometres away.

July 18th: Marching all night through soft sand at the end my feet are raw, no socks. Went into battle immediately. Nearly collapsing with heat and exhaustion. We are still holding out. Both feet had to be bandaged by First Aid men.

July 19th: The scorching heat is terrific. We are holding our advanced positions against heavy counterattacks from the enemy using immense aerial artillery, anti-tank and anti-aircraft bombardments. .

July 20th: The Fascists made a fierce attack this morning on our right flank using 40 or 50 bombers, machine guns and tanks. Our flank gave way. We are retreating slowly. The heat is terrific. We are parched with thirst, we are now 12 hrs. without a drink. Some of our Spanish comrades have collapsed with the heat. The bombardment and machine-gunning from the air by Hitler's Junkers is terrible. It is the most demoralising of all, but still our troops are holding heroically under the strain.

July 26th: Our Brigade is withdrawn for a rest behind the lines. Major Nathan one of the greatest soldiers taking part in the fight against Fascism was killed today in an aerial bombardment. His last words were "Do a good job boys." Frank Ryan arrived from Albacete on the 27th and told me I must leave the Battalion as he has some other work for me to do. I protest on leaving my comrades and I have made a lot of friends since I came here. But, he says, I must obey orders. I feel like a deserter.

July 30th: On the way to Albacete I visit the American Hospital at Villa Paz where I see Paul Burns, my company commander who was wounded in both legs, also Captain Hourihan one time our Batt-Commander, now on Brigade Staff. He was wounded leading us on the attack on Villanueva de la Cañada. I was nearest to him when he fell and bandaged his wound. He hopes to visit Ireland some day."

Chapter 8 Notes

(1)   General Walter, whose real name was Karol Swierczewski, was at that time 39 years old. He was a veteran of the Russian Revolution and of the subsequent Civil War against the Whites. He had been Commander of the XIV International Brigade in which some Irish fought during the early days of Madrid. In World War II he was the Commander of the Polish Army (part of the Red Army) which liberated Warsaw. Later he became Minister for Defence in the Polish Peoples Republic. In 1947 he was shot down by right-wing Ukrainian assasins. See—"W Bojach o Wolnóść Hispanii"*, published by Wojskowy Institut Historyczny, Warsaw, 1966.

*(2)   The "Dimitrov" Battalion was composed of German, Bulgarian, Rumanian, Hungarian, Austrian, and Yugoslav anti-fascists. At Jarama, it was commanded by the Bulgarian, Grebenarov (who was mentioned in "Guerra y Revolucion" along with Kit Conway and R. M. Hilliard.)

*(3)   Paddy O'Neil commanded a section of Canadians attached to the American "Washington Battalion."

*(4)   "George Brown" by Mick Jenkins, published by the North West Communist Party History Group, 28, Hathersage Rd., Manchester 13, 1973.

*(5)   "Irish Democrat" (Dublin), August 28th, 1937.

*(6)   Ibid.

ON THE ARAGON FRONT

... "No tenemos ni aviones
Ni tanques, ni cañones, ay Manuela!" ...

After the Brunete battle the XV Brigade was withdrawn for a few weeks' rest in a group of villages north-east of Madrid. The period was utilised, also, as an opportunity for the reorganisation of the Brigade. Discharged wounded returned to its ranks and new volunteers, who had climbed over the Pyrenees, enlisted.

Peter Daly, who could never stay in hospital, rejoined the Brigade and was given the position of Commander of the British Battalion. He had spent the major portion of his rehabilitation at an Officers' School, both learning and teaching.

After its short rest the XV Brigade was on the march again. On August 24th, 1937 it set out for the Aragon Front.

The first objective in the Aragon offensive—the fourth one that summer of the Republican Army—was the town of Quinto. In Brunete the International Brigades comprised one-fifth of the Spanish Peoples' Army, forces, but now they were not even a twentieth part. The Government, by the respite given to it by the International Brigades, had now built a new regular Republican Army.

The purpose of this new offensive on the Aragon Front was to apply pressure on the enemy-held city of Saragossa. The terrain did not lend itself easily to an offensive. There were great ranges of hills with deep wide valleys, and the Fascist front-line consisted of strong points. This front had been manned by the Anarchists*(1) (who behaved more as "caretakers than combatants") and had enabled German Nazi experts plenty of time to build extraordinary fortifications which they considered impregnable.

Porburell Hill, on the outskirts of the XV Brigade's objective—the town of Quinto—was a veritable fortress. It was fortified on all sides with barbed wire, tank traps, artillery and machine-gun emplacements, magazines and dug-outs that were reckoned to be bomb proof. Its garrison was equipped with the latest type German and Italian guns and a plentiful supply of anti-tank guns and Krupp anti-aircraft guns.

The Republican offensive which started from Azaila, crashed through towards Saragossa, north along the railway line. Quinto fell through the perfect coordination of Republican planes, tanks, artillery and infantry. The taking involved three days of street fighting including the storming of a church with its dominating tower which had been converted into a fortress. Its seven-foot thick walls were heavily fortified with machine guns. Though the town had fallen, the objective had not been fully realised because from the super-fortified Purburell Hill fire was being poured on the town and its captors. The Hill had to be taken.

There was no way of knowing how many of the enemy garrisoned it; because of its position and armoured defences, it could in fact be held by a small group. On the afternoon of August 23rd, the Battalion under the command of Peter Daly took up position for attack. Under heavy cross fire, it advanced across a gully to secure a foothold on the Hill itself; as they did so the Fascist trenches near the top of the Hill became alive with continuous machine-gun fire. There could be no further advance in face of such murderous fire. Peter Daly, who again displayed great qualities of leadership, was caught in that fire and was wounded in the stomach. He was brought back under the same fire by his comrades. This was his third—and last time—to be wounded; it had already happened at Cordova and Jarama. In few days he was dead in Benicasim Hospital. A great Irishman and a great Commander.

His place as Battalion Commander was appropriately taken by his friend and colleague, Paddy O'Daire.

There was no doubt about it now; the Hill was manned by a strong force. It was considered suicidal to keep on trying to take it then. At nightfall, the Battalion withdrew from its position. The night was not spent in rest, but in preparation for another attack at dawn.

For eight hours under a broiling sun the attack went on. Republican artillery gave perfect protecting fire as the assaulting party fought up the Hill. Fascist planes went over the heads of the advancing party, and bombed the Hill! They had mistakenly believed that the Hill had already been taken by the Anti-Fascists. Under the impact of the air bombing, the Fascists on the Hill hoisted the white flag of surrender, then realised that the planes were not Republican, and hauled it down again. They opened up a murderous fire on those who dashed up to take the surrender. With the blazing battle continuing, they ran up the white flag on two other occasions, but the attackers refused to expose themselves again to such false moves.

"I remember," said one of the storming party, "seeing barbed wire ahead, and the brown earth of parapets. I remember Paddy O'Daire's yell: 'Charge the trench!' As we ran up the last few yards, the trench became alive." *(2)

After they had taken the trenches, shots rang out, it was several of the Fascist officers—including a German Nazi and a "White" Russian committing suicide.

Purburell was taken. To everybody's surprise, as the enemy dead and captured were counted, it was discovered that their total of over 500 vastly outnumbered the size of the attacking force.

A fortress had been taken by an attacking force that was less in number than the defenders.

The main force of the Fascists on this front had fallen back on the town of Belchite. The XV Brigade's next task was the capture of this stronghold. On the way there they passed through the small town of Codo from which the Franco forces had already retreated. One International volunteer on his way in saw that the dead had already been moved and

> "Around the barricades were scattered sheaves of religious pictu-
> res. I pick one up. A composite photo of Franco, Christ and Mola
> — in that order. Ugh! What would Christ say to this prostitution
> of his teachings? ... I pick up a Fascist newspaper. Photos of
> Mussolini and Hitler. Big splashes about the value of Fascism to
> Italy, Germany and Spain. War news: the Reds are defeated
> everywhere; thousands of prisoners! The lies so blatantly told
> that I'd nearly believe them myself if I were not twenty miles into
> Fascist territory these last two days ... Here is news of Marqui-
> ses and Dukes. No Marquises or Dukes on our side; no Trade
> Unions on theirs. This is no Civil War; ... This is a war between
> the grandees and the people. ... The Shrine of Codo. A command-
> ing knoll, its flat summit encircled by fourteen pillars, with a
> little Chapel in the centre. The Chapel overlooked the line of the
> Republican advance, so the Fascists loopholed and sandbagged
> it, and built other machine-gun posts beside two of the pillars,
> just as they also fortify their Churches. This is the modern way
> of fighting for Christianity—turn the Churches into fortresses, and
> then blame us 'Reds' for smashing them up in order to get the
> garrison out! There's a Cathedral and a few Churches over there
> in Belchite. The Fascists will use them as strongholds too. Villa-
> nueva. Brunete, Quijorna, Quinto—every time it is the same story;
> the Church is the Fascist key-fortress ... A whistle blows. We
> run back to the Square. The battalion is falling in. The advance
> is resumed." *(3)

Belchite had been surrounded by Spanish Republican units before the XV Brigade had come to it. The encircling force had built trenches about 400 yards from the town—the Lincoln-Washington Battalion, in which some of the Irish were, took over these positions; the rest of the Irish in the British Battalion were taken out, with the main body, and they marched north towards Mediana, with the task of fighting off any Fascist attempt to relieve Belchite.

The Fascists were attempting to break through the line that had been established. It ran for a distance of 17 miles, north of Belchite, running over the hills, from Fuentes de Ebro to Mediana and in a westernly direction it curved back to Puebla de Alborton.

The trenches that had been dug outside Belchite were very shallow ones. Once one lay down, there was nothing else one could do but wait; but in vain for either food or water, because of the exposed position. The Franco forces in Belchite had them well covered with machine-gun fire, and one could not move. Only at night was it possible to bring up the much-needed supplies of food and water. This was the position for a number of days until the order came through for the direct attack on the town.

Led by Carl Bradley, an American docker, one party charged up-hill under enemy machine gun fire. The party consisted of 29 men, including Charlie Regan of Dublin. In the first phase of the charge there were lost three

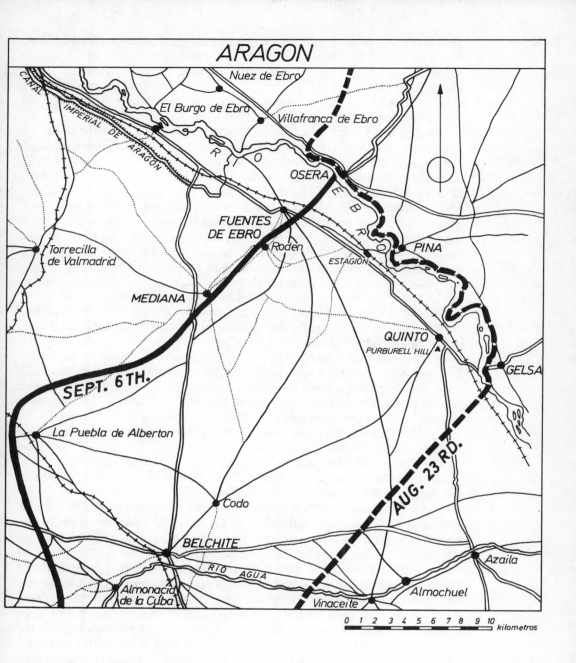

ARAGON

Nuez de Ebro

El Burgo de Ebro

Villafranca de Ebro

CANAL IMPERIAL DE ARAGON

RIO

OSERA

EBRO

FUENTES DE EBRO

Torrecilla de Valmadrid

Roden

ESTACIÓN

PINA

MEDIANA

QUINTO

PURBURELL HILL

GELSA

SEPT. 6 TH.

La Puebla de Alberton

AUG. 23 RD.

Codo

BELCHITE

Azaila

RIO AGUA

Almochuel

Almonacid de la Cuba

Vinaceite

0 1 2 3 4 5 6 7 8 9 10 kilometros

Belchite front, August–September 1937

93

dead and seven wounded. The advance continued, and they took an outlying street where Charlie Regan was killed. "We named the place where he was killed" ... this "fighting Irishman with a burning hatred for Fascism" Dead Man's Point. We built a barricade here of bags of grain taken from the cellars of abandoned houses and fought the Fascists from there with rifles and hand-grenades" wrote Carl Bradley in his report.*(4)

After a while Bradley's section decided to move forward the barricade a few feet at the time. Two volunteers were needed, and two stepped forward. One of them was a miner from Colorado, with Indian blood in his veins. With his back to the side of the building, he took sack by sack from the barricade. Holding them in front of him in direct fire of the enemy, he piled them into position until the whole barricade was moved forward. Later on the section advanced through the buildings by breaking through the house walls, until they reached a position where they commanded a field of fire over the Fascists. They fought their way into the town all that night and day. The Franco forces were able to retreat through a maze of underground tunnels and passages until they massed their forces in a big stone house in the Plaza of the town, which gave them control of the entire end of the town.

Efforts to take this position were not successful. The International fighters crawled along a gully that lay close to the Fascist position, and began throwing grenades, endeavouring to bounce them down on the fascist positions. This did not succeed either. The Fascists were in a higher position and they unleashed plenty of grenade fire on the attackers. Another method was tried. Sandbags were filled with dirt and flung into the gully to build some sort of protective barricade. Again the Fascists were able to keep up their grenade attacks, destroying any possibility of building the barricade. Eventually, Belchite was taken, but many paid the supreme price. "Another fine fighter all that day was Jim Woulff from Limerick, Ireland. He was killed by a grenade in the last hour of the final day's fighting."*(5)

On September 6th, 1937, the fortified town of Belchite surrendered to the forces of the Spanish Republican Army.

Before that, the British Battalion under the command of Paddy O'Daire had been dispatched to Mediana. The Fascists had attacked there for the express purpose of trying to raise the siege of Belchite, and had in fact succeeded in taking two hills that dominated the latter town. The Battalion had to move up during the night. The camions on which they were mounted ran into long-range fire. On the way they actually came face to face with a column of Fascists, who retreated, and after a short struggle the two hills were recaptured. Then began a very heavy fascist counter-attack. For three continuous days and nights an artillery and aviation series of attacks pounded them; but because they had dug-in well the number of casualties was comparatively light. There were two direct night attacks on them, but these they defeated. Bright light was provided by a series of electric storms that lit up the whole area.

Despite the aerial and artillery bombardment the line held. After the fall of Belchite, the XV Brigade was moved into reserve positions in the mountains north of Saragossa. It was then the end of September and the winter had set in—and the Brigade rested.

However, on October 12th, fresh orders came; the XV Brigade had to return to the Aragon front. The strong Fascist fortifications had halted the Republican Army advance that was planned to take place after the fall of Belchite. The Brigade was moved into a position facing Fuentes de Ebro. The Brigade was now strengthened by the appearance of the Canadian Mackenzie-Papineau Battalion fighting for the first time as a single unit. It was to play the major part in the Brigade's attack on the fortifications near the town. The Canadians had arrived behind time, as the transport was held up on the roads that were jammed with military traffic. In the attack the Spanish Republican troops of the 24th Battalion rode into battle on the tops of Republican tanks, clinging on to the turrets of the armoured vehicles as they drove at 40 miles per hour. The Canadians, the Americans and the British followed behind the tanks, to be met with a massive fire of hundreds of machine guns, trenchmortars and artillery. In a brief period their ranks were raked by fire and reduced to half. The gap between the Republican tanks—one of which was driven by the Canadian, Bill Kardash who lost a leg—and the infantry widened; and then the tanks were cut off, and the Fascists opened fire on them and destroyed most. The attack failed.

The XV Brigade remained in the trenches for a period of duty until they were relieved by fresh Spanish troops and were moved back to the village of Mondejar for a badly needed rest an for reorganisation.

Chapter 9 Notes

*(1) Associated with the Anarchists were members of POUM (Partido Obrero de Unificación Marxista), a Trotskyist organisation. Both were "bitterly anti-Socialist, anti-Communist, and anti-Government, they accepted into their ranks any who voiced these same tenets ... were infiltrated by outright Fascist and other undesirable elements, who sought only a place to hide, or a base from which to effect the greatest harm to the Republican war effort" ("The Abraham Lincoln Brigade", Arthur H. Landis, Citadel Press, New York, pp. 252–254)

*(2) "Storming Purburell Hill" by H.M.A., "Book of the XV Brigade," p. 253.

*(3) "The Shrine of Codo," by R.F., "Book of the XV Brigade," p. 257

*(4) "Street-Fighting in Belchite," "Book of the XV Brigade," p. 269

*(5) "Street-Fighting in Belchite," "Book of the XV Brigade," p. 272

THE HOME FRONT

... "There can only be one side for the Irish people!
And it is on the side that has been shamefully traduced.
As yesterday, so it is to-day.
The lordlings and generals, with wealth
and the mighty ones of the earth behind them,
have made the world ring with new 'Scullabogues'
and 'Wexford Bridges';
the men in frieze-coats and dungarees,
the poor teachers and scholars, cannot be heard,
though every fact attests the justice of their cause" ...

The deaths up to now of the Irish anti-Fascists had produced little re-action in their own country. Amongst friends and comrades they had how-ever the effect of strengthening the resolve to counter the seemingly allpow-erful campaign of the pro-Franco forces.

In March 1937, in face of great difficulties, a group of Irish progressives launched the weekly "Irish Democrat." It sought to explain the political issues in Spain as well as in Ireland and of a Europe where Fascism was going from strength to strength. It was the only journal which chronicled the doings of the Irish in the International Brigades and which called for support for them.*(1)

The committee of "The Irish Friends of Republican Spain" had to do its work in the most difficult of circumstances. Its appeals for help only reached a limited circle because of the press suppression of its activities. Neverthe-less it went on organising support.*(2)

The campaign of the Christian Front continued with success. In early 1937 it developed its attack on the de Valera Government's policy of neutrality to the war in Spain. On Monday February 23th, Paddy Belton in the Parlia-ment *demanded* the recognition of France. He waxed furiously against the Fianna Fail government's introduction of a "Non-Intervention" Bill which enabled it to support the policies of the British and French Governments who under the alibi of the same "non-intervention" were denying the vital right of the Spanish Republican Government to get supplies to defend itself against an international Fascist attack.*(3)

Advocating intervention in support of Franco, Belton thundered: "We got 100,000 to declare for Franco in College Green, and we will get 200,000 to tear up this Bill."

How the neutrality of the Irish Government was viewed in Spain itself

"Catalonia, who when Ireland was fighting to conquer her liberty and sought for the warm aid of Nationalists throughout the world, put herself at the front of the defenders of your legitimate rights and many of her sons, for this act, were persecuted and maltreated by the monarchist police.

"Catalonia, in spite of being enslaved by an oppressor state, put herself courageously at the side of your country the noble Ireland to whom the Catalan Nationalists gave with veneration the title of sister country, because her misfortunes were ours and her sufferings were felt in our own flesh.

"Catalonia, in this tragic hour when hundreds of thousands of her sons are giving their blood at the front and are offering their lives in the defence of the Republic and of liberty, attacked with premeditation and treachery by the professional militarists and by international Fascism, has suffered the greatest disappointment possible and has received the most cruel lesson she could expect; the conduct of the President of the Irish Free State, of that sister country, in the Assembly of the League of Nations, has not been worthy of a country that has known slavery.

"Eamon de Valera, you have not been liberal nor generous. You are therefore not a good nationalist." *(4)

In the tumult of the Christian Front's offensive, the Irish Labour Party and top Trade Union leaders remained silent. Their condemnation in the Joint Manifesto on Fascism in 1934 was well and truly buried. Tracing the period since the publication of that document one can almost see them retreating before the reactionary propaganda which had become more and more effective.

In the 1935 Annual Conference of the Irish Trade Union Congress there was only a passing reference to Fascism. In fairness this could be taken as a reflection of the fact that the "Blueshirt-Fascist" threat in Ireland itself had been defeated on the streets, and on the credit side, there was the passing of a resolution opposing the idea of the Corporative State.

However, at the Trade Union Congress at Tralee on August 5–7th, 1936 after the outbreak of the revolt in Spain, there was a deliberate skirting of the issues. Whilst Bob Smith (Plumbers, Glaziers and Domestic Engineers Union) made a positive reference to Spain in the context of a debate on unemployment, Ted Harte (Amalgamated Transport and General Workers' Union) contented himself (and obviously many of the other trade union leaders) with this kind of statement: "It was only by using intelligence and commonsense that they could make progress and prevent happenings such as these in other countries. If they wanted to prevent happenings such as these in Spain they would have to get their own house in order and get the rank and file into the movement and prevent their disintegration." *(5)

This gem was only outshone by the Presidential Address of M. Drumgoole

97

(Irish Union of Distributive Workers and Clerks) who devoted his speech to the social theories of Popes Leo XII and Pius XI.

In 1937 when the Christian Front was exercising its highest degree of intimidation, clear feelings of fear were reflected by the most pious of attitudes. Dealing with the 6th Annual Conference of the Irish Labour Party, the fraternal delegate of the T.U.C. in his report back to the Congress in Dundalk on August 4—5th, said: "Arising out of the resolution dealing with 'Fascism' and on an amendment to include 'Communism', Deputy Norton (the leader of the Labour Party) made a stirring declaration on the Labour Party's attitude towards both these menaces, which were described as the 'negation of democracy and the cemeteries of any true conception of liberty.' So enthusiastically was Deputy Norton's speech received and endorsed that it was ordered to be printed in pamphlet form."*(6) The Norton speech was an unashamed retreat from the 1934 Labour Party attitude.*(7)

The same phamphlet never saw the light of day, but its draft contents succeeded in forcing the withdrawal of the one resolution calling for a struggle against Fascism despite the spirited protests of a small number of delegates including Michael Price, Roddy Connolly, and Seamus O'Brien.

So concerned was Norton with any possibility of the Labour Party being regarded as "red", that he paid an official visit of loyalty to the Papal Nuncio, Monsignor Robinson, and wrote an entirely unnecessary letter, to the same effect, to the Vatican.

Such displays of cowardice only stimulated reactionary elements to demand more. The "Irish Catholic" (of 1913 and 1916 ill fame) opened up an attack on the Trade Union Congress because it had passed a resolution favouring affiliation—not to the Red International of Trade Unions based in Moscow—but to the eminently reformist International Federation of Trade Unions with its headquarters in Amsterdam!*(8)

The Lenten Missions, the annual period of highly charged religious sincerity and emotion, were in 1937 used to endorse the Lenten Pastorals of the Irish Bishops.*(9)

Singled out as a target by one of the Missioners was the Teachers' Club in Dublin's Parnell Square where the "Irish Friends of the Spanish Republic" had a meeting some time before. Preaching at the Pro-Cathedral, Rev. B. O'Sullivan, O.P. delivered a tirade against the teachers in whose club, he said "A 'Communistic' meeting had been held."

With a little bit more courage than that displayed by the Norton leadership of the Labour Party, Mr. J.J. Sharkey, Honorary Secretary of the Teachers' Club hit back with the statement:—

"The only charitable conclusion that can he placed on the reverend preacher's words is that he was unacquainted with the facts. The menace of Communism can surely be met without the setting up of imaginary Communists and using the Pro-Cathedral pulpit to threaten that 'appropriate action must and will be taken' against them. It cannot be unknown to Father O'Sullivan that attacks have been made on Communists and on known Communist premises. Is it not then a grave responsibility to use a solemn occasion to make serious insinuations against teachers?"

The degree of courage can be measured in the light of the fact that the religious orders controlled education and the manager of every lay national school, the employer of teachers, was the local Parish Priest.

The campaign of the Christian Front, itself, had some revealing moments. In December 1936 it held one of its rallies in the town of Drogheda. Involved as one of the speakers was the Labour Party Councillor Blood who found himself subjected to two pressures, that of the Front and its clerical champions, and on the other side from a group of local workers who refused to let themselves be intimidated.

Councillor Blood tried to cancel out the pressure in his speech by denouncing Fascism as well as Communism. For his pains he was rebuked by another speaker, Reverend Father O'Connell who said: "Italy and Germany today would be Communist but for Mussolini and Hitler. *Hitler persecuted the Church to a certain extent, but that was no reason for running him down.*"*(10)

Inevitably, with its phoney character, there began to appear strains in the Front. Its first Annual Conference was scheduled for February 1936 and the first indication of internal disquiet was the decision of the Drogheda Branch to oppose Paddy Belton for the position of Chairman. The Drogheda members of the Front indicated their preference for either Lord ffrench or Dr. Brennan, because as one of them, Mr. T.P. Clarke, said: "Some Executive members are putting politics before Catholicism and are doing more harm to the Movement than many Communists. It is very hard to convince many people that the Movement is not political when some heads of the Movement are politicians."

However, at the Annual Conference, Paddy Belton triumphantly overcame what opposition there was to him.

It was apparent, nevertheless, that disillusionment with the leader of the Christian Front was growing. Even as early as December 1936 there were some—though not supporters of Republican Spain—who saw through Belton's antics. Thus at a meeting of the Dublin County Council when Councillor McCabe was eulogising Belton for "crushing Communism", Councillor Clare interjected with the derogatory remark:— "This is only blowing more froth off a creamy pint."*(11)

Even a month previously when Belton went off on a visit to Franco-held territory, another leading member of the Front, Dr. Brennan (then Coroner for South County Dublin, and later a member of Parliament for the Clann na Poblachta party), made the cryptic statement:

> "I do not agree with any one going to Spain from the Christian Front. Some weeks ago I would have welcomed such a step as an investigation of actual happenings there, but I cannot agree with it now."*(12)

However, the greatest blow suffered by the Christian Front was the return of O'Duffy's Brigade on June 19th, 1937. It was back less than six months after it set out on its crusade.

The "exploits" of O'Duffy and his Brigade were well and colourfully chronicled by a Special Correspondent of the "Irish Independent", Miss Gertrude Gaffney, and also by that 'charming young woman' of the "Pro-

Deo" Society, Aileen O'Brien, who turned up in Spain and got herself attached to Franco's Press Department.

The truth was the the "Crusaders" had taken part in only one action when they clashed with a Moorish unit of Franco's army! The Moors killed four, and three others were to die later during a short period of trench duty. On the one occasion when they were ordered into attack O'Duffy refused to obey because it would possibly cause a "huge loss of life." Demoralised they demanded to be sent home. In the course of their short service their only vigourous activities consisted of numerous mass parades and a mutiny against O'Duffy himself.*(13)

Nevertheless, the men who had gone to Spain with O'Duffy to the accompaniment of blessings returned to be greeted with a similar ritual. On their arrival in Dublin they marched to the Mansion House, to be welcomed back by the Lord Mayor, Alfred Byrne, Monsignor Waters, Paddy Belton and the General himself. They were applauded for their service, and there was a touching moment when a salutory address to "His Excellency, General O'Duffy" was read out. The ceremony concluded with Monsignor Waters calling on the returned to continue the fight in Ireland by joining the Catholic Young Mens' Society.

It was clear, however, despite the carefully 'Heroes welcome home' reception that all was not well within the Brigade. A large section refused to march to the Mansion House. One of them, the one-time Brigadier-General of the Free State army, Horan of Tralee, County Kerry said: "Instead of returning with honour and renown we return humiliated and disgraced. The responsibility rests with General O'Duffy. We were not long in Spain until we were convinced that it was a political campaign." Likewise, ex-Colonel Thomas Carew of Tipperary said: "We are home because the Irish Brigade was badly led."*(14)

An impending scandal was hushed up by the private appeals of a number of clergymen. By appeals to loyalty in face of the "Cummunistic threat," and a number of glorification functions, the dissident elements were influenced not to talk publically about what really happened in O'Duffy's "Bandera of the Tercio Extranjero" (the Foreign Legion).*(15)

When the Kilkenny Corporation conferred the Freedom of the City on the returned O'Duffy, the Kilkenny Workers Council demanded an explanation from two of its members Messrs. Lennon and Connell who had attended the ceremony. They were subjected to straight-forward criticism from Mr. Leahy (Postal Workers' Union) and Patrick Farrell, delegate of the Woolen Mills workers, who asked if O'Duffy and his like got their way what would become of trade unions in the country? "Organised workers", he said, "met O'Duffy and the Blueshirt menace and beat them. If any leader, or so-called leader, rose up and tried to smash organised labour they would harken to the standard of Jim Connolly, and their cry would be 'no surrender'. There would not be a dogs life for them in the country if O'Duffy got his way."

A statement that was fully consistent with the 1934 Trade Union Congress policy of opposition to Fascism, but an articulation of which was a rare feature by workers' leaders in the later period of 1937.

The fortunes of the Christian Front were not helped either by the scandal concerning a Councillor of the Dublin Corporation who had been elected as an "Anti-Communist" candidate. He had to face charges in the Dublin Police Courts of allegedly "trying to bribe Gilbert Lynch, G. Doyle" and other members of the Grangegorman Mental Hospital Committee in connection with the purchase of a site for a new mental home. Messrs. Lynch, Doyle and the others alleged that they had been offered as a bribe the sum of £ 25 and a trip to Paris each.

On July 1st, 1937 a General Election took place. In the Dublin South City Constituency Frank Ryan was nominated as an "Anti-Fascist Republican." It was not an easy election campaign. Though the Christian Front had been somewhat discredited the seeds of their propaganda was still bearing poisoned fruit.

On Tuesday June 30th, the supporters of Frank Ryan held an election meeting at Christchurch Place. An earlier meeting in York Street had been broken up by a hostile mob which had as its nucleus members of the Christian Front, the Catholic Young Mens' Society and remnants of the Blueshirts. They followed to Christchurch Place to repeat the operation, and when Peadar O'Donnell began to speak he was met with a volley of stones and bottles from a crowd singing the hymn, "Faith of Our Fathers." The platform was wrecked beneath him, but he sought another vantage point to address the meeting. He climbed up a gas-light standard and from there continued to speak, ducking, now and again, to avoid the shower of missiles that were hurtled at him. The situation seemed hopeless.

Suddenly, some one remembered that the I.R.A. (who were boycotting the election) were having a meeting in O'Connell Street, and an urgent message was sent to them. Although the I.R.A. believing in armed force only did not look kindly on Ryan's policy of social action (which led to the split in 1934 with the formation of the Republican Congress) once the name of Frank Ryan was mentioned, they abandoned their own meeting, and several hundred of them marched in formation to Christchurch Place and made quick work of the mob.

In that General Election, the de Valera-led Fianna Fail Party received 599,636 votes as against 689,043 in the previous election of 1933. The Blue-shirt-Fine Gael Party also dropped from 549,214 to 461,176, whilst the Labour Party increased its votes from 79,224 to 138,656.

The votes cast for Frank Ryan amounted to 875. This was of course a reflection of the atmosphere, but could have been higher only for the rigid I.R.A. Republican boycott of the polls.

One of the pleasant surprises of the election however was the defeat of Paddy Belton and others prominent in the Christian Front. One of them, its National Treasurer, Corr, had been confident of victory, but instead he got such a low vote that he lost his deposit.

Paddy Belton reacted to his defeat with the statement that "The people of the Free State had endorsed the policy of recognising and helping the Government of Anti-Christian Spain!" This was his simple equation: any-body who did not vote for Belton was a "RED." ·

From that day he retired from both politics and the onerous task of defending Christianity. Not that his labours in that field had affected him materially. Unlike the early Christians who were really poor from defending the teachings of Christ—Belton contracted out of that arduous struggle an affluent man. He retired, the owner of a big farm and a pub, a succesful building contractor, a merchant with a number of shops that included a profitable pharmacy, and a housing estate in North-East Dublin that bears his name to this very day.*(16)

After his election defeat, he again lashed out, but this time his fire was not directed against the "Reds," but at his former colleague, O'Duffy.

The General started him off by stating that whilst he was in Spain he never received any financial help, despite the £ 44,000 collection that had been raised at the Masses by Belton's Christian Front.

Belton's reply was to ask irrelevantly if O'Duffy's Brigade had fought for Franco why were they not treated as part of the Army. (This was in reference to the fact that O'Duffy's "Bandera" had been regarded as a unit of the Spanish Foreign Legion, which vied with its French counterpart in having the largest number of European and African cut-throats in its ranks).

O'Duffy replied to this a rather hurt manner:—

> "I regret that Mr. Belton in reply to my mild statement of facts should display such an uneven temper, *and am inclined to think that he is annoyed about something* (this author's italics). I would be very happy to give favourable consideration to any advice from Mr. Belton, if I knew exactly what he wanted to say ... If outsiders cannot be helpful perhaps they would refrain from being harmful."

He then listed some complaints that he had to make against Mr. Belton's Christian Front:

> "Our troops could not march properly to Spanish music and band and I was requested to get an Irish Pipe Band out"*(17)

To this Belton retorted:—

> "The sending out of a band 'to enable our troops to march properly' could only be conceived by O'Duffy."

In his reply to further O'Duffy letters, Belton was to exclaim:

> "The statement published by O'Duffy on Saturday last is a national shame and humiliation."

> "The Irish Christian Front wants nothing to do with the splits in the Brigade."

> "The Irish Brigade of our day should not have gone to battle unless it was prepared to uphold the tradition of Irish valor."

The inimitable "Somhairle Mac Alstair" dealt with this new and last stage in the life of the Chairman of the Christian Front with a two verse satirical poem: *"DOLEFUL DITTIES OF DONNYCARNEY"*(18) (On 'Beltona' Two-Faced Record: Nr. 1916)

Set to the obvious melody of the well known song, "Oft in the Stilly Night" by the Irish poet Thomas Moore it ran as follows:

"Oft', in the recent past,
'Ere Bolshie billows drown me.
I stood basking in the light
With all the Mugs around me:
And in me ears
I hear their cheers,
By all my praises spoken.
Bright hopes that shone
Are dimmed and gone,
My heart is nearly broken,
Thus now I stand aghast
With shattered dreams around me.
Nemesis has come at last
And in her death-clasp bound me.

When I remember all
The Gang that flocked together
Now scattered (with the Bishops Fund)
Like leaves in wintry weather.
I feel like one
Who treads alone
Some battle-field deserted,
By Duce's troops
And Duffy's Moors-Beshirted.
Thus blows the wintry blast
Of parted fame around me.
Lay me down when Death comes at last
Where the 'Independent' found me."*(19)

The antics of Belton and O'Duffy provided ample material for light-hearted cynicism, but unfortunately contributed little to an understanding of the struggle in Spain.

In view of this a number of the Irish who had come home on leave, because of wounds received with the International Brigade, issued a Manifesto. This recapitulated what had happened in Spain, why they had gone there, and what Ireland should do in the bloody and grim situation in which the Spanish people were not only fighting Francoism but the combined might of International Fascism.

The Manifesto was issued to all the newspapers, but it only saw the light of publication in the "Irish Democrat:"*(20)

We the undersigned wounded members of the Irish Unit serving under Frank Ryan with the Spanish Republican Army feel that it is now necessary to raise our voices in a direct appeal to the Irish nation. In the name of our fifty comrades whose graves dot the Spanish battlefields, in the name of our comrades still in action, we speak on behalf on their cause.

When the conflict in Spain opened in July 1936 we saw Ireland deluged by a propaganda such as had not been seen since 1914. An attempt was made to sweep the country in a wave of hysteria.

We were told that the Government elected by an alliance of Trade Unionists, workers parties, liberal Republicans, tenant farmers, and separatists of Catalonia and the Basque country, were really no Government, but a mob of assassins, priest-murderers, and church burners.

We saw Franco and the rebel generals described as the "Patriot Forces" and as defenders of Christianity. It was represented that every Irishman and woman could be only on one side in this dreadful struggle—on the side of the rebels.

We saw the powerful nations of Europe uniting—possibly for the first time in history—to deny a properly elected Government its right, long established under international law, to purchase arms and other supplies abroad. We saw Franco bringing back the Moors to Europe, to crush his own people. We saw later a regular Italian Army landed in Spain. Yet the Spanish people, whom we were told was against their Government, fought on, almost without arms against both the military forces that had risen against them and the new foreign invaders.

Then we saw Franco's acts in the territory conquered by him. While claiming to be a Republican, he abolished the Republican flag and restored the monarchist standard. Though we were told he was a man of the people, he executed Trade Union leaders, made the Fascist salute compulsory, outlined a 'corporative' system, and sent as his representatives abroad the marquises, counts, and grandees of the old regime.

Above all, we noted those who supported Franco in this and other countries. We saw the "Irish Independent" spreading atrocity propaganda as it did about "Catholic Belgium" in 1914. We saw that its allies in Britain were the "Daily Mail", the "Morning Post" and diehard Tories, well known to us for their attitude to Ireland and any other people striving towards liberty. We saw General O'Duffy, Mr. Patrick Belton and others, who but three years ago were in the forefront of a blatant effort to uproot democratic government in this country, organising financial and even military support for the war to overthrow the Spanish Republican Government.

It was now clear to us that the same sinister forces that had stampeded the Irish people into the Great War in 1914 were again at work, for as false a cause, with as cynical a propaganda.

Madrid was ringed round with enemies, foreign artillery and aircraft raining death upon its people, destroying its treasures of art and architecture, while even its women and children were digging trenches to hold back the invaders. At that moment the call went out to the democracy of the world to rally where their rulers had failed.

Their response was the most moving episode of latter-day history. By sea and illegally across frontiers, 30,000 men of all nations answered the call. Men of all parties and none, of all creeds and colours and tongues, staking their lives as proof of their unity with the outraged Spanish people. The International Brigade marched into beleaguered Madrid, to give new heart to its ill-armed defenders.

Ireland, with its matchless record of resistance to oppression, would have been found wanting before the eyes of the world, had it stood apart. But we did not stand apart. We assembled under Frank Ryan in Spain.

We were less than 200 in number, and have been in action since last December. We will leave it to the Spanish historian of the near future to tell whether we worthily acquitted ourselves, whether we upheld the honour of Ireland. We will say only that we fought on five fronts, that our small band has lost nearly 50 dead and at least another 50 wounded, and that our Irish Unit still holds their line.

In Andalusia, on Christmas Day, we lost our first seven heroes. In January we were transferred to Guadarrama and lost more. At Jarama, in storming the heights of Pingarron, our captain, Kit Conway, fell and our commandant and leader, Frank Ryan, always with his men in action, was twice wounded. Here, too we lost the Rev. R.M. Hilliard, a Church of Ireland clergyman, who had taken his place in the ranks. At Brunete, in July, four of our Unit were killed and a number wounded.

Our experience in Spain has convinced us that we were right in taking the step we did. We saw for ourselves that the propaganda still being circulated here was a grotesque misrepresentation. We say to the Irish people that there is no "Red Mob" in Republican Spain; that all parties have united to defend the Republic, so that the Spanish people may freely determine their own destinies in the future; that in the Spanish Republic there will be unqualified liberty of conscience and freedom to practice religion, with an end to attempts—such as that made by the "Christian" Front here to make the Church of the majority of us an adjunct of political parties; and that all the Spanish people want are the independence of their historic country, the right to work and live in peace on the land they till, and the means to educate their children out of the illiteracy they have been condemned to themselves.

And we ask these questions of the Irish people:
Is a nation that has striven for centuries to rid itself of an alien yoke now to support those who would deprive Catalans and Basques of their national liberties, customs and language and who will make the whole Iberian peninsula a Fascist colony?

Are Irish farmers, whose fathers fought under Davitt, to support a merciless and rackrenting landlord class in its efforts to crush tenant farmers?

Are Irish Trade Unionists to support those who have outlawed all Unions and executed thousands whose only offence was that they carried a union card?

Are Irish teachers and others engaged in cultural work to take sides with those who aped Hitler barbarism by burning the works of Spain's greatest thinkers, who dragged Spain's greatest poet, Frederico Garcia Lorca, through the streets of Granada before killing him, who hurtled bombs upon the Prado?

There can be only one side for the Irish people! And it is the side that has been shamefully traduced. As yesterday, so it is to-day. The lordlings and generals, with wealth and the mighty ones of the earth behind them, have made the world ring with new 'Scullabogues' and 'Wexford Bridges'; the men in frieze-coats and dungarees, the poor teachers and scholars, cannot be heard, though every fact attests the justice of their cause.

We call on the Irish people, then to rise up against the Press Lords and unscrupulous politicans who are misleading us now as they misled us before. We call on the Government of the Irish Free State to end its subservience to this powerful and noisy group, and to grant the Spanish Republic the full recognition it had before the conflict.

We demand this in the name of our comrades who have died to redeem this nation's honour, in the name of our comrades who are ready yet to die, and in the name of the traditions handed down by our National Fathers.*(20)

Signed:

William Scott. Terence Flanagan. James Prendergast. Joseph Monks. Patrick Smith. Sean Goff. Patrick Duff. Frank Edwards. John Power. Peter O'Connor. James O'Beirne. Donal O'Reilly. Jack Nalty.

Chapter 10 Notes

*(1)   There existed also the monthly journal, "Ireland Today" which had its first issue in June 1936. It adopted an objective stand on the Spanish struggle. In its fourth issue (September) it published a symposium on the war and its issues. It also published some of Charlie Donnelly's poems and articles by Peadar O'Donnell and Mairin Mitchel. Its objective neutrality did not save it from being a victim of the Christian Front's opposition. Its final issue was in March 1938.

*(2)   One feature of its work was the organising of sympathisers to write to the men in Spain with a flat paper packet of five Woodbine cigarettes enclosed in the envelope. These were invaluable gifts as tobacco in Republican Spain became an absolute luxury. Men were reduced to smoking dried vine-leaves rolled up in newspaper to supplement the meagre and infrequent ration of the "tabac de guerre" cigarettes which because of their rank strength were nicknamed "Anti-Tanks."

*(3)   The Roosevelt Government also subscribed to "non-intervention" but at same time supplied 12,000 trucks and more than 1,886,000 metric tons of fuel were delivered to Franco by U.S. companies.

*(4)   Irish Democrat, Dublin, October 23rd, 1937.

*(5)   Report of the 42nd Annual Conference of the Irish Trade Union Congress, published by the National Executive of the Irish T.U.C. 32, Nassau Street, Dublin, C 2. p. 100.

*(6)   1937 Irish T.U.C. Report. p. 97.

*(7)   Vid. Appendix VIII.

*(8)   At the 1938 T.U.C. Congress in which the Presidential Address of Jerry Hurley (Irish National Teachers Organisation) consisted of large extracts from a speech of the Director of the International Labour Office on "social justice," there was a motion "viewing with alarm the growth of Fascism throughout the world" ... Its mover, Hugh Todd (Belfast Trades Council) said: "They saw their comrades in Spain and China fighting behind the barricades for liberty. He appealed to them as Irishmen, and lovers of liberty, to protect the freedom they had got." "Big" Jim Larkin (Dublin Trades Council) seconded, but made no mention of Spain or Franco, saying: "The present Government of Ireland were trying to take away from the workers, the right to associate together and formulate and remedy grievances through negotiation. It was high time that someone in the Labour movement and Trade Union movement had the courage to get the workers together." (pp. 152–53) The motion was passed without discussion.

N.B. This report also mentions that Professor Alfred O'Rahilly (of the Christian Front) was one of the lecturers at a T.U.C. Summer School!

*(9)   For an account of the Bishops' Pastorals, see Appendix IX.

*(10)   The Worker, December 12th, 1936.

*(11)   The Worker, December 5th, 1936.

*(12)   Ibid. November 14th, 1936.

*(13)   In the Church of San Domingo in Caceres there is a special plaque commemorating the number of Masses attended by them. For further details of the fiasco of their service in Spain, see:

i) "I Was A Franco Soldier" by Seamus McKee, London, 1937

ii) "New York Times," April 4th, 1937 and the "Irish Democrat," Dublin, March 27th, and April 24th, 1937.

iii) "Crusade in Spain" by Eoin O'Duffy, Browne & Nolan, Dublin, 1938.

iv) The Republican history of the War, "Guerra y Revolucion en Espana," in its description of the Fascist forces concentrated for the Jarama offensive refers to them" ... que en el Jarama empezo y termino su historia en Espana." (Which opened and closed its history in Spain at Jarama.)

v) Documentary Documentary Broadcast by Radio Eireann (Dublin), May 26th, 1974.

v) Duffy (1892–1944) "had suggested to the German Embassy (in Dublin) in the summer of 1943 that he would like to organise an Irish Volunteer Legion for the Russian front in order to save Europe from Bolshevism. He therefore requested that an aircraft might be sent from Germany so that he could conduct necessary negotiations in Berlin. This offer was not taken seriously." (From "Spies in Ireland" by Enno Stephan, p. 212).

*(14)   "Irish Democrat," Dublin, June 26th, 1937.

*(15)   When Brendan Behan, the Irish playwright and charakter, was told by the author of the story of O'Duffy's Brigade in Spain, he quipped: "They certainly made history. They seemed to be the only army that went out to war, ever, and came back with more men than they set out with!" This was in fact true as in Spain they collected a few Irish stragglers in the Spanish Foreign Legion who subsequently returned with them.

*(16)   Belton had been a member of the anti-Treaty Fianna Fail party up to 1927, then became an "Independent" Deputy, later joining the Centre Party, then a Deputy for the pro-Treaty Fine Gael Party, which he left with O'Duffy in 1934 with whom he launched the stillborn National Corporate Party. He was an "Independent" candidate when he failed to re-elected in 1937, but rejoined Fine Gael again to become once more a Deputy for that party in 1938. In 1943 his political career came to an end when he failed to retain his seat having changed his political ticket to that of an "Independent" once again (!)

*(17)   O'Duffy did get his band. The "Saint Mary's Anti-Communist Pipe Band" answered the call with swirling kilts and flying ribbons. The band was based on the Waterford Street area of Dublin (the centre of the "Animal Gang" activities). After its return from Spain it had frequent public collections about which there was great suspicion. In August 1937, two months after the return of O'Duffy's troops, it was unable to fulfill any engagements because its uniform and instruments were in pawn.

*(18)   Donnycarney is a district in north-east Dublin where Belton's residence and his emporiums were located.

*(19)   "Irish Democrat," Dublin, September 4th, 1937.

*(20)   "Irish Democrat," October 23rd, 1937.

THE BATTLE OF TERUEL

"Here they come, here they come,*(1)
In marching step without bugle or drum.
Weidmann whom I liked so well
And never saw since Teruel.*(2)
Here's Peter, Jack, Doc Robins—brothers!
How is Ralph Fox and how are the others
Whom we left where they laid,
Rearguards and scouts of the Brigade?
O how they toss and how they strain
To live again and try again!
Go, comrades, back to Carabanchel
Beneath the mounds. There you must wait
Until you hear flamencos tell
Of better guns and better hate" ...

The fight of the XV International Brigade in Spain went on. It only ceased as far as they were concerned, for a brief period when in late October, the Brigade was moved from the Fuente de Ebro trenches to the rest village of Mondejar, until the first days of January 1938 when it went into battle again at Teruel. In this campaign that lasted three continuous months there were to be other loses including three more Irishmen, David Walshe of Ballina, P. Glacken of Westmeath, and Francis O'Brien of Dundalk, who joined the Brigade from London.

The rest period that began in October was utilised for training and political organisation. In the same month the XV Brigade bade farewell to one of its most outstanding units, the Dimitrov Battalion, which in the process of re-organisation was transferred to the XIII Brigade. It was a moving occasion as the British, American and Irish volunteers said farewell to a fighting Battalion that had fought beside them in the grim battle of Jarama, in February 1936 and in which it had borne a great brunt of the fighting; in the first five days its strength being reduced from 620 to 200 men. It had also been at their side in Villanueva de la Cañada; at Quinto it had carried through the major portion of the street-fighting.

The majority of the Battalion were Czecho-Slovaks and Yugoslavs. Its No. I Company was exceptional in so far as it was composed completely of students. The Battalion was first led by Grebenarov, the Bulgarian comrade killed at Jarama, who was singled out for mention with "Kit" Conway and R.M. Hilliard in the history, "Guerra y Revolucion en Espana." Later it was led by Mihály Szalvai, the 38 year-old Hungarian, who was known by the "nom-de-guerre" of Chapaiev. At the age of 20 he had fought in his native Hungary, and after the overthrow of the Hungarian Soviet Republic he was sentenced to 15 years imprisonment, from which he escaped after 10 months.

Mondejar.was not only the venue for a farewell. It was also the centre for vigourous military and political preparation for the battles yet to be fought.

The Spanish People's Army had come a long way from the early militia units that had first challenged the General's revolt; so likewise had the International Brigades from the groups that had formed the Centurias and from the units that had come to the aid of Madrid on November 9th, 1936. A regular Republican Army had been built up, but always there was continuing effort to make it still more efficient; it had to be, to be able to take on the regular Army that revolted under Franco, and the highly-geared Italian Fascist and Nazi German armies. It was necessary now in the Spanish Republican Army that a regular structure with its complementary code of military procedure be further built up. Regular army discipline was used to further develop that spontaneous moral and voluntary discipline of the Republican forces. Saluting officers which up to now had been a casual and voluntary exercise was now to become a specific military responsibility. This was not an easy duty to enforce; since all officers and men were on the closest possible terms, many of them knowing one another before they went to Spain, in the civilian life of political and trade union organisational "egalitarianism." The mimeographed "Nuestro Combate" (the journal of the Brigades which appeared in an English language edition under the title of "Our Fight") had to make the case why saluting was necessary:—

> "1. A salute is the military way of saying 'hello'. For either to omit it when a soldier meets an officer is as insulting as for two men who know each other to pass without greetings in civilian life.
> "2. A salute is the quickest, easiest way for a soldier to say to an officer: 'What are your orders? I am ready to carry them out'.
> "3. A salute is not undemocratic. Two officers of equal rank, when meeting on military business, salute each other.
> "4. A salute is a sign that a comrade who has been an egocentric individualist in private life, has adjusted himself to the collective way of getting things done.
> "5. A salute is a proof that our Brigade is on its way from being a collection of well meaning amateurs to a steel precision instrument for eliminating fascists."

Such and many other tasks for the instilling of regular army discipline came not as edicts but were the work of the Political Commissars. Those officers, Political Commissars, or "Comisarios de Guerra" (Commissars of War) were an integrated feature of all the units of the Republican Army—including the International Brigades—being set up, four months after the war began, in October 15th, 1936. The prototypes of such a rank had been the

"Commissars of the French Revolution" and of the Soviet Red Army. Their function was to guide the army at all levels, build up morale, produce army journals that ranged from company wall-newspapers to Divisional publications. They had the responsibility of continually raising the discipline level, and widening the understanding of the war amongst the ranks.

The Political Commissars were no armchair political advisers. They went to all the fronts and all the battles alongside the commanders and the rank-and-file. One of the earliest of them, Commissar Belmonte, who died fighting in the early days at Madrid had laid down for them a slogan which they were always expected to live up to; "El primero en avanzar, el ultimo en retro-ceder"! (The first to advance and the last to retreat.)

The Commissar was not only expected to be a good morale builder and clear exponent of all the political questions that arose in the course of the war; he was also a valuable part of the military structure. He had to act as an advisory commander, being involved in all military discussions and decisions, to which he brought his knowledge of the men who had to carry out such plans. Each order was signed by both the Military Commander and the Political Commissar.*(3)

From October to December the XV Brigade was settled in the villages around Mondejar. Before Christmas it was on the move again to Aragon, where it halted at Alcañiz and then at Mas de las Matas in which it was to celebrate Christmas Day. For many of the Irish it was to invoke the memory of the previous year when they had spent the same festival at Cordova, the scene of their baptism of fire. The occasion was made cheerful by the good news from the Teruel front where they were to act as reserves.

Franco had planned an offensive at Guadaljara with the objective of an all-out assault on Madrid. Such plans were upset by the surprise Republican attack on Teruel, in mid-east Spain, on December 15th. The Republican forces led by Generals Lister and Modesto had attacked the town in a snow storm. It was a silent and sudden assault without any aerial or artillery support. They succeeded in encircling and penetrating the town. On December 29th, Franco stopped his Guadalajara offensive to switch to a large-scale counter-offensive to lift the siege of Teruel. His forces consisted of a big mechanised section supported by the German Nazi Condor Air Force. This succeeded in pushing back the Republican lines, which however withdrew from positions in good co-ordinated order.

Fighting continued in bitterly cold weather; temperatures were as low as 18 degrees below zero; there were many cases of severe frost bite to such an extent that many amputations had to be carried out. The Republicans were ill-clad, many wearing only ropesoled sandals. The battle was bogged down for four days because of a heavy blizzard, but eventually Teruel was taken despite the Republican self-imposed disadvantage that no heavy guns should be used in order that the civilian population of the town could be saved.

The capture of Teruel was a brilliant feat by the Republican Generals. They were able to carry out the secret concentration of their attacking forces, and to attack in such a way that the Republican casualities did not exceed 200 men, a very low casuality rate bearing in mind the ferocity of the battle and the consistent superiority of the Fascists.

On January 17th, in the Teruel area the Fascists launched a counter attack under the heavy protection of Italian artillery and Fiat planes. The Republican lines, deprived of sufficient aerial assistance, were pushed back. The XV Brigade which had been in reserve up to now under the command of General Walter was called upon to help to throw the Fascists back.

On January 19th, the latter succeeded in advancing through a valley that led straight to Teruel; an advance that was heralded by the greatest artillery bombardment yet. They captured two important hills which in turn were counter attacked by International Brigade riflemen who failed, and suffered severe losses. The Franco forces pressed on and took control of a number of valleys just north of Teruel. The XV Brigade continued to resist them.

On February 16th, the XV and XI (German Anti-Fascist) Brigades was switched to Segura de los Baños, a hundred miles north of Teruel, in order to strike at the Franco communication lines that linked them with Teruel. Edwin Rolfe, the American poet-volunteer described the plan:—

> "The Thirty Fifth Division composed of the XV and XI Brigades was to strike from Seguar de los Baños at the heart of the Fascist communications over which poured the troops and materials for their Teruel counter-drive. The two Brigades were to assault the rebel fortifications at Atalaya and Sierra Pedigrossa which overlooked the town of Segura and from there to battle southward, sweeping over the enemy forts, and taking possession of the apex formed by the three main roads converging. The task of the assault was given to the XV Brigade which was in far better condition than the XIth. The latter had been practically cut to pieces in the defence of Teruel and El Muleton, and was assigned the job of acting as a rear-guard against any surprise flank attack that might develop after the movements of the XVth Brigade got under way." *(4)

Frank O'Brien from Dundalk, with the rank of sergeant, was one of those who occupied a long ridge that tapered off towards a road that led into a village in Fascist hands. In an early morning action the enemy, beginning with an artillery and aviation attack, tried to dislodge them but they were driven back by excellently co-ordinated machine-gun fire. The same machine-guns with their cross fire later in the day repulsed a strong flanking movement by the enemy. Later the Fascists were chased back down into the village, which could have been taken from them, but for the fact that the Republican forces were not of sufficient numbers to hold it. It was in the counter-attack that Frank O'Brien fell.

Later the Brigade was withdrawn to a reserve position, where its ranks were augmented by others who had come to Spain.

The organisation and transit of volunteers of so many nationalities to Spain was in itself a major operation. After February 20th, 1937 it was a highly illegal activity because of the enactment of the London Non-Intervention Agreement. The Irish who went after that date used to report to an address in Litchfield Street, London and after establishing their bona-fides, they set out for Paris by way of the Newhaven-Dieppe steamer on weekend tickets and with a travel document on which they inscribed British names and addresses. In Paris they made their way to a small hotel on the "left bank"

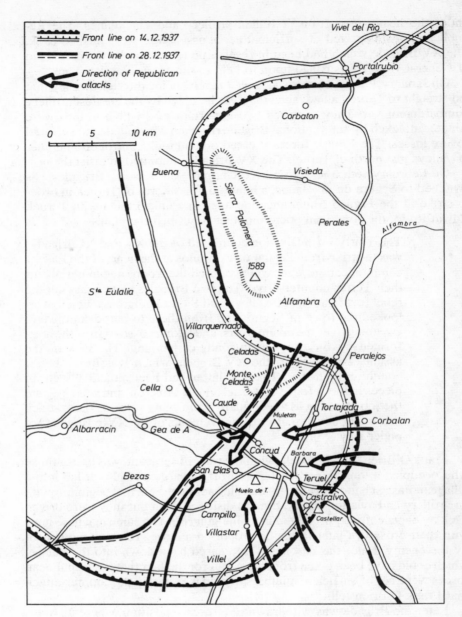

〰〰〰	Front line on 14.12.1937
– – –	Front line on 28.12.1937
⬅	Direction of Republican attacks

0   5   10 km

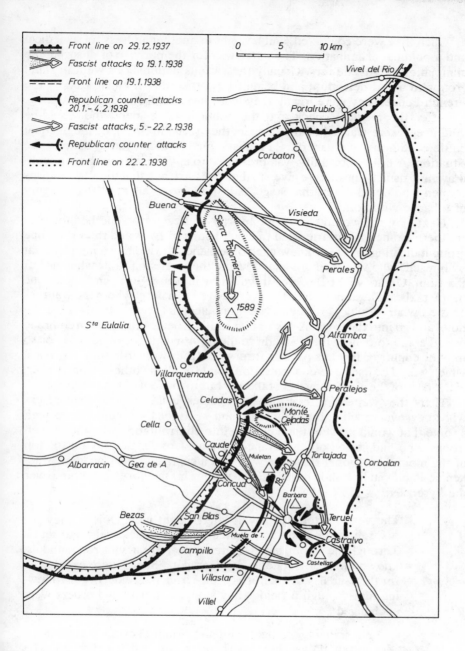

Front line on 29.12.1937
Fascist attacks to 19.1.1938
Front line on 19.1.1938
Republican counter-attacks 20.1.-4.2.1938
Fascist attacks, 5.-22.2.1938
Republican counter attacks
Front line on 22.2.1938

0   5   10 km

Vivel del Rio
Portalrubio
Corbaton
Buena
Sierra Palomera
Visieda
Perales
1589
Alfambra
Sᵗᵃ Eulalia
Villarquemado
Peralejos
Celadas
Cella
Monte Celadas
Caude
Muletan
Tortajada
Corbalan
Albarracin
Gea de A
Concud
Barbara
Teruel
Bezas
San Blas
Muela de T.
Castralvo
Campillo
Castellar
Villastar
Villel

Teruel front, January–February 1938

at which they were contacted, and brought to another address for a medical and a political examination. The latter was for the purpose of ensuring the elimination of adventurers. Usually the various nationalities went in small groups to avoid detection; and being forewarned that if challenged by the French Police, they were to say they were just "weekending" in Paris.

After the medical check and the political assessment, the would-be volunteers were warned of the dangers they faced in Spain, of the unequal battle conditions, and generally a realistic picture conveyed to them of the situation. A last opportunity was presented to anyone who wished to withdraw, and usually the picture given to them was so frank that there were cases of men who opted out at that stage. A last advice to all was "Bring plenty of tobacco with you!"

Next day the volunteers went by rail to Beziers or another town in southern France. They travelled in small goups of twos and threes, no one group indicating that they knew each other, and all watching a man who sat by himself, who was their guide and whom they were to follow when he left the train. On arrival at Bezieres it would be indicated to them to take one of the taxis at the station, and they were driven to a hotel where the waitress or the owner would warn them that on no account were they to leave the hotel and go into the town. A day or two waiting, before the French comrade would come to collect them and drive them for a distance of 15 miles or so into the countryside into a peasant farm where they were ushered into a barn, which would be used as a concentration point for all the other groups. Later, in the dark of the night, they were taken by bus to the foot of the Pyrennees.

There they waited for their mountain guides, usually friendly smugglers who knew every inch of the mountains, and who took the volunteers through a route that would prevent them coming into confrontation with the French troops who had sealed off the Franco-Spanish frontier that lay on the top of the mountain: Lionel Edwards who was a captain in the Canadian Mackenzie-Papineau Battalion committed to writing his memory of climbing over the Pyrenees:

> "The vehicle stopped: it was late twilight now. Quietly they got off, ran to the ditch and waited until the black night had set in. Through the gloom, small figures appeared carrying rope sandals, known all over Catalonia as alparagats. Shoes were exchanged for the sandals and then at a gesture from the guide, began following him through a field. They stopped shortly and orders were exchanged.

> 'No smoking, no lights and no talking! They are watching for us but if we obey instructions, we will get through. The border is at the top of the mountain. It will take all night to get there. It will be tough but we can make it.'

> "The night march began and for those still living, it will never be forgotten. Over rocks, boulders, dry creeks and gullies, the steep path led ever upward. In the harrowing ordeal, three of the oldest did not make it; they were veterans of the First World War. For the others, arms, legs and presently whole bodies were beginning

to ache. Any faltering however, brought the gnome-like guides to the end of the line. 'Allez, allez!' they were whispering to the straggling parade. Joe dislodged a pebble with his foot and then wondered as to where it disappeared, 'My God, we're on a precipice,' he realised. 'Stay on the path or you will be killed,' warned the guide.

"After a few hours, despite his aches, Bill felt a little elated. Possibly the rarified air helped. He looked far along the visible coast and saw a fairy lacework of tiny lights, linking French villages to their Spanish opposites. When a rest was permitted, men would fall with exhaustion and then wait for the stragglers to catch up. With light in the sky heralding dawn, the guides were making their last exhortation, 'Only a little further,' they said, but the volunteers did not believe them. Suddenly a crest was reached.

'Voila, la frontière d'Espagne!' were the shouts from the van.

"It was true as Bill realised when he topped the slope and saw a small white building outside of which a rifleman stood raising his right hand in the salute of the Frente Popular.

"'Salud, Companeros—Mira! Espana, es la Casa Blanca.' He pointed to the white building. They tottered forward and fell with relief at the gate.

"The scholar and historian may tell of Xerxes' Greeks, Caesar's legions and the Old Guard of Bonaparte, but these young men from far-off Canada were to be fighters of a different breed. Their lineage was to be traced back to the Ironsides, the tattered band at Valley Forge, Jemappes, the Commune and the barricades of old Petrograd. They were not soldiers yet but they would learn the trade and apply it well. Most of them sleep forever in the Spanish earth but the memory of those who were heroes will live on in the recollection of man as long as people breathe freely and artists sing.

"The great orb of the sun was rising and together as one, tired limbs stood up and aching eyes viewed the purpling Bay of Roses to the left and then gazed straight and downward to the sweet land of Iberia unfolding before them. Gone were the bitter memories of the past, the cold, the misery and all the ills of the socially disinherited. Cynicism vanished also in this morning sun; it was good indeed to be alive but to be also young, was bliss beyond the dreams of man. They had arrived." *(5)

Chapter 11 Notes

*(1) From the poem, "The Burning River" by David Martin, Fore Publications Ltd. 28/29 Southampton Street, London, March 1944.

*(2) Doctor Robbins, a young American from Hollywood, California, who was attached to the International

Brigade Medical Service. During the fighting before Mosquito Crest (see p. 84 of this book), he had been trying to organise clean drinking water for the men fighting in the lines. "He found the water, apparently, in the only place it existed—in the remaining crevices and potholes of the Guadarrama River. He worked diligently to make the brackish-tasting stuff palatable and free of mud and germs. Then he had it loaded in drums onto a truck and personally escorted it to the lines. A flight of low-flying Heinkels caught him on the open road. The truck with its precious water was destroyed, and Dr. Robbins and his assistant killed. He was the first American doctor to die in Spain." ("The Abraham Lincoln Brigade" by Arthur H. Landis, pp. 213–214).

*(3)   See Appendix XII for details on the role of the political Commissar.

*(4)   "The Lincoln Battalion" by Edwin Rolfe, New York, 1939. Rolfe was editor of the XV Brigade Journal "Volunteer for liberty."

*(5)   "In Retrospect: The Going" by Lionel Edwards, the Marxist Quarterly, Progress Books, 44, Stafford St., Toronto 3, Ontario, Canada, Summer 1966.

THE CAPTURE
OF FRANK RYAN

... "A Felon's Cap the noblest Crown
An Irish head can wear ...

The battle of Teruel demonstrated the newly developed ability of the Republican forces, but the recapture of the town also showed the determining effect of the massive Italo-German aid to Franco. On March 8th, 1938 the Fascist forces launched their biggest offensive yet on the Aragon front. This was preceded by a telegram from Eberhard von Stohrer, the Nazi Ambassador to Franco, who informed Hitler that if Franco was to win he would need even more war material as well as more technical experts and officers with a high standard of general staff experience.

On March 13th, international Fascism gained a big victory when Hitler entered Vienna. A short time later the Mediterranean Pact was signed by Chamberlain and Mussolini, where by the intervention of Italian Government troops in Spain was "legalised." Fascist intervention and the British Tories were tightening the noose around the neck of the Spanish Republic.

The March Fascist offensive on the Aragon opened up with what was again to be the greatest aerial and artillery bombardment of the Republican line. The main thrust on a fifty-mile front was at Belchite, Alcañiz and Caspe. The fascist forces were augmented by a Nazi air force that comprised two Messerschmitt groups of four squadrons, two Heinkel 51 groups of two squadrons, a reconnaissance group of Dorniers 17 and of three squadrons of Heinkel; four bomber groups of three squadrons of Heinkel 111 and Junkers 52. General Ritter Wilhelm von Thoma, the Nazi, commanded a Tank Corps that consisted of four battalions, each of three companies with 15 light tanks in each company, plus 30 anti-tank companies with six 37 millimetre guns each. There also participated the 'Black Arrows' Division under the command of the Italian General Berti.

The Republican troops that faced them were weary and illequipped after the exhausting battles on the Teruel front. On the Aragon the front, that was weakly fortified and undermanned, they only had 60 planes against the Fascists' 800. They had to endeavour to fight back against 10 divisions of the enemy that included tens of thousands of Italian regulars, 30,000 Moors and many thousand Nazi specialists. The lines broke completely.

At the same time there began a series of murderous air raids on Barcelona. Beginning on St. Patricks Eve, (March 16th) they continued until late afternoon of March 18th; over 1,300 civilians were killed and 2,000 badly wound-ed*(1).

The lines crumbled. Here and there groups of men began to make a fighting and orderly retreat, but the overwhelming might of the enemy turned it into a rout.

The British and Canadian Battalions had moved into position near Cala-ceite and the American "Lincolns" were beyond Batea. The three Battalions found themselves encircled as the flanks broke, and they had to fight their way out in small groups.

Chaos reigned everywhere as the Fascist war machine overan the Re-publican positions. It seemed hopeless, and it was hopeless—but groups of men still fought on, and died. One of them was Ben Murray, a member of the Communist Party of Ireland. Murray had received his baptism of fire in his own native Belfast in 1932 when he played a prominent part in the United Catholic-Protestant unemployed movement.*(2)

At Aragon also fell Johnny Riordan who was London-Irish and Tom Donavan, of Skibbereen, County Cork, who before emigrating to Britain from where he went to Spain had worked as a printer in "The Southern Star" weekly paper in his home town.

Hundreds of the best commanders and political commissars were either killed or left to die of their wounds in that terrible retreat, as the combined Fascists drove headlong into the Republican territory. Their planes machine-gunned both the fleeing refugees and retreating soldiers who streamed along the roads before the enemy's war machine. The Fascist artillery played an important part in their advance, their fire being co-ordinated by radio direc-tion from their airmen. But the decisive factor was their overwhelming aerial superiority. There was nothing with which the Republicans could hit back against these armadas of the sky.

The XV Brigade moving back, like the rest of the others, took up new positionons, after the fall of Caspe, near the town of Gandesa. For over ten days the retreat had been in progress. The Fascists, for the first time, used smoke screens to cover their massive offensive.

On March 26th, 1938 the Brigade passed through Calaceite, near Gandesa, and came face-to-face with a column of enemy tanks on the roadway. A bitter fight ensued. The Brigade was scattered in the unequal battle. They sub-sequently reformed—being now without food for many days—and with rifles, a few machine-guns and some hand grenades began to organise a withdrawal in some order. Two hundred of them held a mountain pass, against a two-kilometre long Fascist column, in order to cover the withdrawal of other units. They were attacked by tanks, artillery, planes and by cavalry. The tank forces was firing special incendiary explosive bullets.

"The price for this was high" wrote Landis. "By the end of the day the British had lost more than a hundred and fifty men killed and wounded, in addition to upwards of a hundred captured. Among them was the famed Irish commander, Frank Ryan, who had fought with the first centuria at Mad-rid."*(3)

The pass was held long enough to allow the other units to get away and reform the front—somewhere. Acting under orders, the pass-defenders withdrew from their position—and then had the task of finding their own way in the now enemy-occupied territory to the River Ebro where the main Republican lines were now being established. In small, scattered and combat-weary groups they had to march some 28 kilometres to the river in a defeatist atmosphere that seemed to signal the end of the war and the bloody triumph of the Fascists. They eventually reached the river and began to cross, some in the few boats there were, others scrambled on logs, and the remainder swam across, and some were drowned.

It was a terrible ordeal, but they succeeded in reaching the other bank with the Fascists at their heels. There a new line of defence was established (from which, on July 25th, they were to recross the Ebro in a final attempt, to thwart a Fascist victory).

25 years later, one of the American International Brigaders recounted the circumstances in which he and others were taken prisoners on the Fascist bank of the Ebro:

"We were to the west of Gandesa. Finally, and at about 11.30 p.m., we were stopped by a roadblock and instantly surrounded by men with machine guns. We were ordered out of the truck. Someone asked me in Spanish from the darkness: 'What battalion?' I answered 'American.' I didn't recognise them as Fascists and thought we just might be being hijacked. A Spaniard with their group began yelling hysterically: 'Shoot them! Shoot them!' ... then they took me to the side of a hill and forced me to sit down. From there I watched them line up our Spaniards from the truck, question them, *and shoot three of them on the spot.* They took me to a hut then with my hands tied behind my back.

At 6.00 a.m., dawn or thereabouts, they took me outside again and shoved me to my knees, my hands still tied. The other prisoners (Spanish) were forced to watch. They (the Fascists) were cursing and yelling. I think they wanted me to beg but I wouldn't demean myself. This went on for about ten minutes. Then they stood me up and told me I was lucky and took me back to the hut.

Right after that they brought up Frank Ryan and about thirty British prisoners. (Taken in the tank battle a Calaceite) ...

A Fascist officer demanded to know who their (the British) commanding officer was. Captain Ryan immediately stood up. The English prisoners—all of them were in pretty bad shape, but fearing for Ryan's life they all shouted, 'No, Frank! No! Sit down.' But Ryan said simply: 'I am.'

We marched for some distance. Around 12.00 noon we were put in an area off the main road. Captain Ryan—he was deaf himself—then demanded loudly to know when we would be fed and given water. I acted as his interpreter, speaking Spanish to an Italian officer who approached us. Frank repeated his demands for food and water.

The Italian officer told us that Gandesa had fallen. Ryan didn't believe him and told him so. At that point another officer joined us. He was German—Gestapo. He told us who he was. He got into a discussion in English with Captain Ryan—about why he was in Spain, etc. Frank told him—spelled it out for him; then asked the ·Gestapo officer *what he was doing in Spain.* The officer said simply: 'You're a brave man,' Then he turned around and left us.

A couple of our planes came over then, and despite the fact that their anti-aircraft guns immediately blackened the skies they all ran like a bunch of scared rabbits. It did our hearts good to watch them.

At the next command post we got the word that Captain Frank Ryan had been sentenced to death. He was taken away. That was the last we saw of him ..."*(4)

Among the prisoners taken were two other Irishmen, John Lemon of Waterford and Bob Doyle of Dublin.

As Ryan was being taken away, he was lined up on the road in front of another group of prisoners. With bayonet-prods they tried to make him give the Fascist salute. He refused. Under the threat of an immediate execution they persisted in their efforts. They placed him in front of a firing squad and proceeded to enact the motions of a mock execution, but he still refused.

In fact all of the Internationals expected to be executed when captured as this was the usual practice of the Fascists, but in that period, just before their capture, a new order had been issued from the Fascist Headquarters (at Italian and German insistence) that International Brigaders should now be kept alive for the purpose of exchange for the Italians and Germans who had been captured by the Republican forces. Ryan with his rank was a good prize and the Italian officers of "The Black Arrows" accordingly did not shoot him.*(5) At no time, however, were he and the other International prisoners aware of this new ordinance.

He was taken to a concentration camp which had been set up at Miranda de Ebro. After a while there he was transfered to another detention centre at San Pedro de Cardenas. The conditions in this prison were described thus by Brigader Joe Norman:

> "It looks like a cemetery inside and feels like one, too. We were very badly treated there. Our clothes were taken and we were knocked about with sticks ..."*(6)

Clive Branson, who survived this prison to die later in action in Burma against the Japanese third party of the Rome—Berlin—Tokio Axis, said that the prisoners had to work in labour gangs which were run by a Fascist Sergeant-Major who simply used a stick on the prisoners as if they were cattle:

> "There were no sort of regulations at all, and no time tables. If the guard didn't feel like letting the prisoners out, he didn't. The sanitary conditions were simply terrible. There were two broken down lavatories for six hundred and fifty prisoners and the water supply came through the same pipes as used for the lavatories. There were no medical supplies."*(7)

Ryan was in the forefront in the struggles against the jailers. He was considered as being a dangerous influence and he was transferred to the Central Prison at Burgos and there arraigned before a Courtmartial. There he was charged with taking up arms against the Franco government and, secondly, "that he had outstanding responsibility in Irish politics." Ryan took strong exception to the latter charge, but he was told by the Presiding Officer that "we can decide on your future by studying your past." A letter from an Irish woman was read to the court. It said, "Frank Ryan is not a good Catholic and he was responsible for the murder of Admiral Sommerville."* (8)

Also listed as evidence against him was information from the right-wing Irish Catholic weekly, "The Standard."

The Courtmartial sentenced him to death.

However, ever since the first news came to Ireland that he was being held in a Franco prison, there was, because of his personal prestige and well known integrity, a campaign waged for his release. A "Frank Ryan Release Committee" was formed. In a headed notepaper (May 15th, 1940) there was listed its composition:

> CHAIRMAN: Aodghan O'Rehilly; HON SECRETARY: Sean Nolan; HON TREASURER: Michael Cremin; *Committee*: Senator Miss M. Pearse; Michael Price; Cu Uladh; Senator David L. Robinson; R.M. Fox; Mrs. L. Kearns-McWhinney; Con Lehane; Mrs. Mollie Hall; Simon Donnelly; Madame MacBride; George Irvine; Miss R. Jacob; Mrs. Austin Stack; Miss McCarthy; P.T. Daly; Mrs. Aileen Walsh Edwards; P. O'Keefe, Maire Comerford; Tom Barry; Eamonn de Barra; R.J. Connolly.*(9)

The work of this Committee in its initial stage secured a great victory. As a result of the pressures it generated many pleas were made that Ryan should not be executed but released. Among the interventions was one from the Irish President, Eamon de Valera.

The death sentence was commuted to 30 years imprisonment. Burgos Prison, in which he spent most of his incarceration, was built to contain 500 prisoners but Ryan had to share it with 5,143 others. It was very cold in winter and very damp and warm in summer. The only newspaper the prisoners were allowed to receive was the weekly prison journal "Redemption" which was issued by the Jesuits. The prison chaplain was Father Marcelino Balinaga, also a Jesuit, who gave the prisoners very little consideration. After the end of the Spanish War (March 31th, 1939) Ryan was to have visitors, one of them being Leopold H. Kerney, the Irish Ambassador to Spain who proved to be kind and helpful and who developed a personal friendship with Frank. According to Gerald O'Reilly, he had two other visitors: "one an Irish priest who was very considerate and the other the Duchess of Tetuan. This woman is an ardent Franco supporter but Peadar O'Donnell was responsible for saving a relative of hers, also an O'Donnell, so she is concerned over Frank on that account."*(10) With the Irish priest who visited him, Ryan took up the matter of the behaviour of Father Balinaga, and consequently a new chaplain was appointed who was more satisfactory to the prisoners.

For two years and four months he was in captivity. He did not serve the thirty-year sentence—he was to die not in prison but elsewhere, on June 10th, 1944 at the age of 42 years, as a result of the conditions he had to endure in Franco's prison.

Chapter 12 Notes

*(1)   According to the estimate of U.S. Military Attache, quoted in the U.S. Ambassador's book, "My Mission to Spain," by Claude Bowers, New York, 1954, p. 376.

*(2)   In 1932 there were 100,000 unemployed in Northern Ireland. They were organised—Catholic and Protestant—by the Irish Unemployed Movement which had been launched by the Irish Revolutionary Workers' Group (later the Communist Party of Ireland; see p. 17 of this manuscript). Led by Tommy Geehan, the Unemployed Movement had won the spport of the organised trade union movement through the efforts of James Cater, a shipyard worker who was prominent in the Co-operative Movement, and Betty Sinclair, at present Secretary, Belfast & District Trades Union Council. (Cater was later killed in a Luftwaffe attack on Belfast, 1941). The unemployed, in order to qualify for an "Outdoor Relief" pittance, were compelled to engage on roadwork. On October 3rd, 1932, following a meeting addressed by Betty Sinclair the relief workers went on strike. Violent scenes developed and barricades were erected which were manned by united Catholic and Protestant workless. The armed police, supported by the British soldiers, first used the barricades to prevent food going into the working class areas. In subsequent violence they shot two men, John Geehan and Samuel Baxter. Their funerals made for a demonstration of thousands. At the head of the demonstration was the famous English working class leader, Tom Mann (1856–1941) who was arrested by the police and deported back to Britain. One of the first Internatio4al "Centurias" in Spain was named after him. He was one of the welcoming party which greeted the return of the main bulk of the British Battalion at Victoria Station, London, on December 7th, 1938. (See "Irish Times," Dublin, April 8, 9, 10th, 1974 for profile of Betty Sinclair). Interestingly enough, one of the members of the British Battalion was a Londoner, a former British regular soldier who had served in Belfast in 1932; his experiences there had "turned him political," and he subsequently deserted from the British Army to go to fight in Spain. (Information from John Peet).

*(3)   Landis, p. 450. It should be mentioned that over 400 of the American volunteers were listed as either dead or missing.

*(4)   From a taped interview with Max Parker, 1963, to Arthur H. Landis and published in the latter's book, pp. 491–492.

*(5)   In fact Ryan's rank was higher than that of a Captain. Having been promoted to the position of Adjutant of the XV Brigade, he held the rank of Major at the time of his capture.

*(6)   "Britons in Spain" by William Rust, Lawrence & Wishart, London, 1939, p. 66.

*(7)   Ibid.

*(8)   From a letter written by Gerald O'Reilly, official of the Transport Workers' Union (U.S.A.), who was an old friend of Ryan's. The information quoted came from a message from Ryan to him, which was delivered by Larry Doran and Anthony Kerhlick who were released from Burgos Prison on Eebruary 25th, 1940. Admiral Henry Boyle Townsend Sommerville, County Cork, was shot dead March 24th, 1936 by the I.R.A. because he recruited local young men for the British Navy. Ryan's connection with the I.R.A. had been severed since 1934 when he was publicly expelled for his activities in connection with the formation of the Irish Republican Congress. Therefore he would have had no connection whatsoever with this shooting.

*(9)   This Committee truly represented a cross-section of Irish society. Its members were prominent in the Irish Government party (Fianna Fail), the Trade Union and Labour Movement, literary, cultural and sporting organisations. It contained five leading National-Republican figures of the period of 1916–23; the widow of one of the executed 1916 leaders, John McBride and the sister of another, Padriagh Pearse. The only notable omissions were representatives of the Catholic or Protestant Churches and the Fine Gael party.

*(10)   From the letter mentioned in p. 153 of this book.

THE LAST BATTLE

Chapter 13

... "Si'n troid scuir i, a bhraithre,
Eirighimis chun gnimh
An t-INTERNASIONALE
Snaoidhm—comhair an cine daonn ...

Then comrades, come rally,
And the last fight let us face;
The Internationale
Unites the human race." ...

After the rout on the Aragon Front in March 1938 in which Ryan was captured, the remnants of the XV Brigade, tattered and exhausted hugged the far banks of the River Ebro as a haven. Along with all the other Republican units they had received a terrible hammering. Despite that, they were determined to carry on the fight, making full use of the natural defences offered by the river.

After a period there, the Brigade was withdrawn from the Ebro for a well earned rest, to return later for a further spell of duty there. On May 22nd, it was moved to the Balaguer area where a limited diversionary offensive had been launched by the Republican forces in an effort to recapture the hydro-electric station which supplied Barcelona with current. The XV Brigade was placed in a reserve position but was not called upon to help in the operation which had only a limited success. It returned to the Ebro, to remain there until it was moved to a valley near Falset. This became known as "Chabola Valley" because the volunteers, tipped off that the stay there would not be a short one, constructed somewhat comfortable shelters (chabolas) out of tree trunks, branches and foliage. The period there extended until July. It was utilised for the incorporation of new arrivals; the reorganisation of units; the development of an "Activist" movement in the ranks which laid emphasis on setting emulative standards of discipline, training, better handling and care of weapons, and leadership and involvement in political discussions and classes.

Extensive maneouvers were held. Daily the volunteers practised crossing from one ravine to another, using imaginary boats, perfecting the method of assaults on hills, and learning the technique of infiltration by small groups. The purpose of the training was clear to all in a short time—the Republican forces were going back across the Ebro River!

It was not a comforting time, internationally. The deal of Munich and the sellout of Czechoslovakia were in the air. The British Prime Minister,

123

Chamberlain, foremost champion of the Non-Intervention Pact which deprived the legitimate Republican Government of supplies, had already signed the Anglo-Italian Mediterranean Treaty which allowed the Italian regular troops to remain in Spain until the war was over!

The impending betrayal of Czechoslovakia to Hitler had some limited compensating effects however for the men in "Chabola Valley." Just before the Nazi move-in, a supply of the latest light-machine guns, manufactured at Brno, were got out from there and found their way to the XV Brigade. The training period in the valley was used to master them, to use them at full effectiveness, to be able to strip and assemble them in the dark of the night. Along with this were courses on the Soviet "Dyegtyaryov" light machine-gun, its heavier edition the "Tokarev" and as well the old reliable Maxim gun.

It wasn't all military training and study in the valley. The various national groups took every opportunity to celebrate their appropriate anniversaries, the Americans had their "Fourth of July," and the Canadians feasted their "Dominion Day." In late June the Irish had their celebration to coincide with the Annual Parade in Ireland to the grave of Wolfe Tone at Bodenstown.*(1)

To make it a worthy occasion a special committee was set up. It included four volunteers from Dublin, Liam McGregor, Alec Digges, Tom O'Brien and Eugene Downing; Jimmy Straney and Hugh Hunter from the "green" and "orange" districts of Belfast; the Kerryman, Mick Lehane, and three from Cork, Michael O'Riordan and the two O'Regans (not related), Jim and James F. They were helped in their task by two other Dubliners, Jack Nalty and Paddy Duff from the heavy Machine Gun Company.

Food was very scarce, but the Irish did not draw any rations for two days in order to provide the invited guests from other units with a "banquet" of black rice-bread and mule meat. These were washed down with copious draughts of "vine rojo" which had been collected earlier in the evening in a well scrubbed ash-bin from the nearby vinery at Marsa. Concern was expressed at the overdue arrival of the wine but eventually the two deliverers arrived, none too steady, with the explanation that the bin was found to be too heavy when full, so they had to lighten the load!

The celebration was opened by a speech from Bob Cooney (Scotland), the Battalion Political Commissar. He emphasised the national and internationalist aspects of Tone's life and teachings, and proposed the toast to "The Father of Irish Republicanism." Thereafter many toasts were drunk, and a combined Spanish fiesta, Irish ceildhe and International folk song night developed. Jimmy Straney sang a favourite song of Belfast's Falls Road, "The Four Flags of Ireland," another sang about the "Boys of the County Cork" who "Beat the Black and Tans," there were a number of flamencos, and a noteworthy Cuban song by Domingo Morales who was to be killed the following month.

Tone was honoured well into the night. For the Irish in "Chabola Valley" it was a night of nostalgic memories ... the annual march from the little village of Sallins to Bodenstown Churchyard where lay the remains of a great Irishman and Internationalist ... the wine at this Spanish commemoration was both good and plentiful; but, at the same time, many a pair of Irish lips smacked in the hot night ... there were memories of the pint-glasses of draught stout—their national drink—that the little pubs by the canal served ... which old friends and comrades were marching this year to Tone's tomb? ... did they really understand the reason why the Irish in the International Brigade, instead of marching to Bodenstown were instead marching in "Chabola Valley"? ... that instead of chatting and squatting on the banks of the Royal Canal that flows through Kildare, as they would have wished to, they were instead only a few kilometres from the Ebro River, which they would have to recross under Fascist fire? ... did grasp the fact that here in Catalonia, the banner of Tone and Connolly, of all those who had died for Irish freedom in its internationalist context, was being held aloft by Irish hands; many of which in the short period were to be bloodstained, with not a few of them rigid with death? ... It was a typical warm Spanish summer's night and as the men got tired, drowsy with wine and nostalgic with memories all they had to do was to dig a 'hip-hole' with their bayonets, lie on the hard Spanish earth and snatch a few hours of sleep before "Reveille" sounded for another day of intense training and rehearsal for the fight across the Ebro that everybody knew was coming.

Two days afterwards, some of the Irish were sent which others to a "Cabos" (Corporal's) School in the nearby town of Marsa. There many of them were to meet for the first time a Soviet Volunteer. He was Emil Steinberg, the instructor who lectured on many aspects of warfare. To the combined classes of Spanish and varied English-speaking soldiers he spoke in Russian, being translated into English by a comrade from the "Mac-Paps" (Canadian Battalion) of Ukranian extraction, whose translation in turn was rendered into Spanish by Manuel, Mexican-American officer attached to the "Lincoln-Washingtons." At the conclusion of the course there was a "breaking-up" celebration which developed into an international concert at which the two best vocal renderings were judged to be the traditional ballad, "Kelly From Killane" by an Irish volunteer (naturally) and "Stenka Razin," the song about the famous Russian peasant fighter, by Emil.

In the meantime a welcome visitor to "Chabola Valley" was Pandit Nehru of India, and the Irish here, with thier British comrades, had a full opportunity of exchanging greetings with that famous fellow-fighter against British Imperialism. The British Battalion put on a demonstration of their military skill for him, the highlight being the cutting down of a tree across the valley by a Maxim machine-gun fired by Paddy O'Sullivan (Dublin) who was a Teniente (Lieutenant) in the No. I Company of that Battalion.

On July 24th, 1938, the Brigade was gathered together for a Special Announcement—that everybody had already guessed—the Ebro River was to be crossed again! The meeting took place in the darkness of the night to foil enemy visual observation. The Military Commanders outlined the battle plans, and the Political Commissars explained the political and moral implications of a successful offensive. Following the speeches there was the answering of points raised by the rank-and-file. At the conclusion of the meeting there was the spontaneous singing of revolutionary songs; "Bandera Rossa" (The Scarlet Banner)—the Italian anti-fascist song, as well as many other international songs. In the night there also resounded one that was known to all of the English-speaking volunteers ...

"Soldiers are we, whose lives are pledged to Ireland,
Some have come from a land beyond the wave,
Sworn to be free, no more our ancient sireland
Shall shelter the despot or the slave;
Tonight we man the *Bearna Baoghail*
In Erin's cause, come woe or weal;
Mid cannon's roar and rifle's peal
We'll chant a soldiers song ..."

As well, the Scottish comrades sang a song that they had well preserved, but which at that time had almost disappeared in Ireland; Connolly's "Rebel Song." Its words were also appropriate to the situation, in which in a few hours, the XV Brigade was indeed to man the *"Bearna Baoghail"**(2) ...

"Come, Comrades sing a Rebel Song,
A song of love and hate,
Of love unto the lowly,
And of hatred to the great ...
And we'll sing a Rebel Song,
As we proudly march along,
To end the age-long tyranny
That makes for human tears,
And our march is nearer done
With each setting of the sun,
And the tyrant's might is passing
With the passing of the years ..."

The next morning, under the leadership of Jose Modesto—the ex-wood-cutter—the Republicans crossed the Ebro River. It was indeed an audacious offensive. Everybody thought after the Aragon rout that the Republic had been well and truly beaten, more so since Franco was able to drive down to the east coast and split Republican territory in two. But there on the Ebro was once again a demonstration of the great reserves of morale that the Anti-Fascist fighters possessed.

The night of Monday, July 25th, was a moonless night—as had been calculated for—when small boats left the Republican side of the river, at some minutes after midnight. The boats rowed silently across with muffled oars. Just before they reached the opposite bank their occupants sprang shore, trashing the bank-water, to spring upon the fascist fortifications.

The boats then raced back in a frenzy to bring over other loads, until eventually the entrenched Fascists were overwhelmed. Pontoon bridges that had been semi-assembled in concealment on the Republican banks were quickly laid across the fast flowing river, and more Republican troops rushed over them.

The XV Brigade crossed the river at Asco. The Canadian Battalion was in the vanguard, with the British following them. Before the actual crossing, Sam Wilde, the Battalion Commander, handed a Catalan flag to an Irish Volunteer with the strict instructions that it was to be carried deep into the heart of the Fascist occupied territory of Catalonia. The banner of the "sister country" was indeed carried to the full extent of the Brigade's penetration of that territory, and was emotionally greeted on the way by the liberated peasants.

It was to be an epic fight. To endeavour to stop the advance Franco concentrated his most effective troops, the bulk of his artillery and all his tanks and aircraft. 1,300 Nazi and Italian Fascist planes were hurtled against the Republican river-crossers. In the subsequent bloody battles, the Fascists had a superiority of 15 to 1 in bomber planes, 10 to 1 in fighter planes and 12 to 1 in heavy artillery.*(3)

After crossing the Ebro, the XV Brigade moved forward in the direction of the town of Corbera. On the way up they were subjected to very heavy aerial bombardment, particularly in the vicinity of the crossroads linking Asco and Flix. Late in the day they linked up with the XIII Polish Brigade, (the "Dombrovskis") and captured a hill from the Moors, an operation necessary to clear the way for the XIII Brigade to take Corbera. The XV went on towards Gandesa, the town near which Frank Ryan had been taken prisoner in March. The battleroute the Brigade was taking was almost the same as the one they had been forced to retreat on four months previously; and many landmarks were sadly familiar to them as the scenes where their former comrades had either been killed or where they had last been seen.

The main struggle they were to be engaged in was the attack on "Hill 481" which was highly fortified, and which because of its shape became known as "The Pimple." For five continuous days they were to assault it, many times getting almost to the very top but to be beaten back each time by the rain of machine-gun fire, grenades and trench mortars. One piece of Republican artillery would have made their task of taking the "Pimple" much easier, but there was no such weapon with the Brigade. At dawn they would "go over the top" from the shelter of a hill, rush down the valley through the hail of enemy fire, and begin the hazardous climb up the slopes of the Fascist held hill. Inch by inch they would advance–those who had survived the rush down the valley–until they nearly reached the summit. As dusk fell, they would be withdrawn to the protection of their own hill, until the next morning when the attack began all over again. The heat was fierce, and the Brigaders had neither water nor food. In the day attacks they fought stripped to the waist; but at night shivered in the cold air of the high altitude. The pace of the advance and of the attack in the extreme heat of late July made it necessary to discard everything except one's rifle, and the little coarse twine bag in which one carried ones ammunition–in single rounds. There were neither bandoliers or bullet clips available for them.

Day after day the assault on Hill 481 went on, and day after day volunteers died. After the first day's assault they were not only subjected to fire from the hill itself, but also from severe Fascist flank fire on a valley on their right, and, when in the attacking position, from the town of Gandesa.

On the fifth day–August Monday–they attacked again in the morning and during that day attacked, re-attacked and kept on attacking for twelve hours, and this time the advanced elements had got nearer the top than was the case before when the order was sent to them to withdraw. Hill 481 was considered untakeable by riflemen. The rate of casualities was too high. There fell there; Jimmy Straney; Maurice Ryan of Limerick; Paddy O'Sullivan of Dublin who had developed into an outstanding officer in the No. 1 Company of the British

Battalion. Badly wounded, he lay near the positions of the Fascists for a whole day in the intense heat. His comrades tried many times to rescue him, but were beaten back each time. Also fell: George Gorman (Derry) and James Haughey (Armagh).

By August 2nd, the entire Republican advance was held. Now an even more difficult task than crossing the Ebro had to be undertaken; the territory that had been won had to be held in face of the expected counter-offensive. "Resistance, Vigilance and Fortification" became the slogan of the Army of the Ebro. It began to "dig-in" scooping trenches out of the hard and arid soil with bayonets, some entrenching spades and even fewer picks.

On August 3rd, the Fascist counter-attack began. Using their planes in plenty, the enemy began large-scale and methodical bombing, dive-bombing, low-flying and strafing attacks. Their infantry were reluctant to attack the Republican-held and well-fortified hills; and so the Franco forces used the tactic of concentrating an overwhelming force of planes and artillery on points of the front so as to blast and "blitz" their way through.

The Republican forces fought back with incredible bravery; even drawing a tribute from Mussolini who told his son-in-law to record in his famous diary the following ... "The Reds are fighters, Franco is not" ...*(4)

On August 6th, 1938 the XV Brigade, which had been in continuous action for 13 days, went into a reserve position. This only lasted for a period of eight days, when they were in action again on the 15th in the defence of Hill 666, situated over 2,000 feet up in the Sierra Pandols, south of Gandesa. There the Brigade was subjected to continuous heavy artillery bombing. It fought back, until August 26th when it was brought out of the lines for a rest; that however lasted only until September 6th, when they were called upon again to recapture Hill 356 which the Fascists had taken in a breakthrough near Sandesco.

Captain Radumir Smrčka (the 34 year-old Czechoslovak) XV Brigade Chief of Observers, who had been at Jarama, Brunete and at Aragon and been wounded four times with a total of fourteen separate wounds, gave a description of the fighting that took place in the area of the Sierra Caballs in his diary:

Sept. 6th: We are standing by. A hectic night. The enemy continues its pressure, accompanied by a tremendous concentration of fire. Counted more than a hundred Fascist planes in the air. Front has been boiling since dawn.

Finally our orders. We are to move in immediately to prevent a threatened breach. Within twenty minutes the Brigade is on its way. To get here faster we are using *camions*—eight trucks going back and forth on the shellswept highways, picking up the marching troops and depositing them close to the lines.

The enemy pressure increases. Shells are bursting all over and the Fascist planes are continuously overhead and bombing. There is considerable excitement in the staff. The troops of another unit, unable to hold any longer, gave way, permitting the Fascists to advance. The Lincoln Battalion is rushed into the breach and succeeds in stopping the Fascists. A small advance on a narrow

Haircut in the trenches at the Jarama front.
The victim is Paddy Duff (Dublin),
later an official of the Workers' Union of Ireland,
the barber Steve Troxil (California)

SIGNALEMENT

Taille   1^m 75

Cheveux   *Noir*

Yeux   *Bleu*

Visage   *Ovale*

Menton   *Rond*

Nez   *Moyen*

SIGNES PARTICULIERS

Michael Lehane
(Signature de l'interessé)

Nom: *Lehane*

Prénoms: *Michael*

Date de naissance: *27-9-08*

Lieu de naissance: *Kilgarven*

Nationalité: *Irlandais*

DOMICILE: Pays   *Irlande*

Ville   *Kilgarven. Co. Kerry*

Rue   N.°

Parti Politique: *Antifasciste*

Date d'entrée dans les B. I.:   *14-12-36*

Libre
Célibataire — 2 —

*First page of military identification book of Mick Lehane.
For some months the language of command
of the International Brigades was French;
later all orders, documents etc. were in Spanish*

(top left) Martin Hourihan (New York)

(bottom left) Michael O'Riordan (Cork)

*(top right) Donal O'Reilly (Dublin)
who had been in the General Post Office,
Dublin, in the 1916 Easter Rising.
(see Appendix III)*

(bottom right) Patrick O'Daire (Donegal)

Paddy Duff (Dublin) on the left with Jack Nalty (Dublin).
Nalty fell in action on September 23rd, 1938,
in the last battle of the XV International Brigade

International Brigaders in hospital.
The group includes Bill Scott (centre rear),
Frank Ryan (right rear),
Jim Prendergast (front left)

Paddy Power of Waterford (right)
with an American volunteer and a group of children
during a 48-hour leave to Madrid
from the Jarama front, May 1937

Benisa, September 1937.
Left to right:
Johnnie Power (Waterford);
John Hunt (Waterford);
"Pop" Loughran (Irish-Canadian);
John Henderson (Britain);
Roy Sheehan (Irish-American);
seated centre: a Polish volunteer

(above)

All-Irish group attached to the American Lincoln Battalion. Left to right, front row: Peter O'Connor (Waterford), Michael Kelly (Galway) later killed at battle of Brunete, July 1937; T. Hayes (Dublin); Jim Reagan (Cork); J. Bourke (Liverpool-Irish). Back row: Paul Burns (New York); Joe Rehill (New York); Johnnie Power (Waterford); Charles Coleman (Cork)

Another group from the American Lincoln Battalion. Left to right, front row: Paddy Smith (Dublin); Peter O'Connor (Waterford); J. Bourke (Liverpool-Irish); Paddy Power (Waterford) and his brother Johnnie; Michael Kelly (Ballinasloe, County Galway). Back row: 2nd from left Thomas T. O'Brien (Dublin and Liverpool), killed at Jarama, February 1937; 3rd from left Joe Rehill (Irish-American); 5th from left J. Pickards (Canada); extreme right Steve Troxil (New York)

The Spanish Republican Army launches the Ebro Offensive, July 1938

(below) Republican machine-gunners reach the enemy bank

(above) Republican troops cross the Ebro River on a pontoon bridge

The battle for Gandesa.
Republican machine-gunner
with Soviet-made belt-fed Maxim gun
in the hills south of the Ebro

*(above left) Michael Kelly
(Ballinasloe, County Galway),
killed at the battle of Brunete, July 1937*

*(above right) Liam McGregor (Dublin),
killed on the Ebro front on the last day
of combat of the XV International Brigade,
September 23rd, 1938*

(below right) Peter O'Connor (Waterford)

FOR two years the people of Republican Spain have fought against the combined forces of Mussolini and Hitler.

Barcelona, Madrid, Bilbao, Tortosa and other centres in Spain. have suffered the horrors of air raids. Mussolini openly boasts that he is sending the airplanes, bombs and pilots responsible for the cruel warfare against the women and children af Republican Spain.

This is supposed to be a civil war. It is nothing of the kind. The Spanish people are fighting for liberty against a foreign Fascist invasion.

Frank Ryan, Republican fighter and leader of the Irish Unit, International Brigade, is now a prisoner in a Franco jail. Italian officers control Franco territory and it is they who hold Frank Ryan prisoner. DEMAND HIS RELEASE!

The people of Dublin can extend no welcome to the warships of Mussolini -- the user of poison gas. the betrayer of Austria. the bomber of Spanish women and children and the jailer of Frank Ryan.

Poster protesting against Italian Fascist naval visit to Dublin, and calling for the release of Frank Ryan from a Franco jail

Frank Ryan's grave in Dresden,
German Democratic Republic,
with flowers laid by former
Irish International Brigaders in July 1966

At Frank Ryan's grave in Dresden, 1966
(left to right):
Frank Edwards;
Arno Herring, formerly volunteer
in the XI (German-speaking) International Brigade;
Donal O'Reilly;
Michael O'Riordan;
Anneliese Ichenhauser (interpreter);
behind a representative
of the Socialist Unity Party of Germany

1966: Veterans of the Spanish War pay tribute
at the Soviet War Memorial in Berlin,
German Democratic Republic.
Left to right:
General Enrique Lister;
Ivan Nesterenko;
David Pritsker;
Army General Pavel Batov

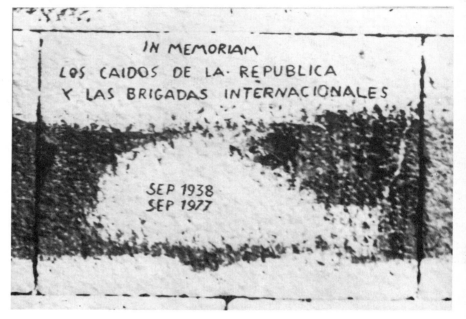

*Fascist war memorials at the scene of the Ebro battle,
given new inscriptions in 1977.*

*(top): memorial on Hill 481 reinscribed
"In memoriam XV International Brigade".*

*(bottom): memorial on the Gandesa–Zaragoza road reinscribed
"In memoriam the fallen of the Republic
and the International Brigades"*

sector—this has been the result so far of the much heralded "decisive" Franco offensive on the Ebro.

Sept. 8th: At 14:00 hours, the enemy starts a new attack following an intense artillery preparation. I go to the lines to lead the Mackenzie-Papineau Battalion into position. I hold a meeting with the Battalion officers while John Gates (then XV Political Commissar) meets with the Commissars. We are under fire. A shell lands near Gates, wounding one of the commissars. The meeting continues. The Mac-Paps go forward in a brilliant attack, reoccupying positions that had been taken by the enemy.

The enemy artillery concentrates on the Mac-Paps but they continue their advance, although the promised flank support fails to materialize. They advance a full kilometre and reoccupy a large commanding hill—one of the most important heights dominating the Gandesa-Corbera road. This Mac-Pap counter assault kept the entire Fascist front from advancing.

The Brigade is doing an excellent job. The Lincolns, the 59th (a Spanish battalion attached to the XV Brigade) and the Map-Paps have all retaken the positions designated in a brilliant manner and are holding fast. The British Battalion is in reserve, one company reinforcing the other troops. The Fascists attack with tanks, but we hold our ground. Four tanks are turned back by rifle fire alone.

Sept. 9th: At 15.5 shell lands right in front of the Brigade staff. Dunbar (the British Brigade Chief of Staff) is wounded, fifteen fragments in face, chest and leg. He refuses to be evacuated and puffs calmly on a cigarette while his wounds are being dressed. Three deserters from the Fascist lines are brought to me for interrogation and they are interesting, different from the usual "we-only-receive-one-can-of-sardines-a-week type."

Their first answer to the routine question "How did you get over here?" is very interesting. They came over through the *Cotas de las viudas, huerfanos y novias* is their answer—through the Hills of the Widows, Orphans, and Sweethearts. This is a new one to us. We have never heard of these hills. They explain. These are the hills where our positions lie. They have lost so many men attacking them that the name has become natural.

Our *avion* works well despite their numerical inferiority. Our troops are used to enemy aviation by now. But they keep coming, 21 to 24 bombing planes at a time, about ten or twelve times a day. Savoia 81, Junkers 52-III, Heinkel III each squad capable of dropping 50,000 kilos of explosives (125,000 lbs). The Fascist bombers on this front have a theoretical capacity of upwards of 750,000 kilos of explosives a day—but our morale is good.*(5).

The Brigade fought under the harshest of combat conditions, but the hardest strain of all was a psychological one. It was common knowledge that the Republican Government had already decided to withdraw the International Brigades altogether from Spain. This decision was taken in an attempt to force the withdrawal of the immense unilateral Nazi-Italian-Portuguese legions from the Franco side.

Each of the international brigaders knew that this was to be the "last fight" and those who had fought at Madrid, bloody Jarama, Pozoblanco, Brunete, Villanueva de la Cañada, Belchite, Quinto, Teruel, and who survived the horrors of the Aragon retreat and who were now fighting in the Catalonian Sierras—could hardy be faulted if the instincts of self-preservation were fully aroused.

On September 13th, a relief for the Brigade arrived and it moved back a short distance from the front. On the 18th another massive Fascist counter-attack began but this did not affect the Brigade who were still retained in reserve.

On September 21st, Dr. Juan Negrin, the Prime Minister of the Republican Government announced at the Assembly of the League of Nations that the International Brigades were to be withdrawn:—

> "In her desire" he said, "to contribute to the pacification and 'restraint' which we all desire, and in order to eliminate all pretexts and possible doubts about the genuinely national character of the cause for which the Republican Army is fighting, the Spanish Government has decided to withdraw immediately and completely all the non-Spanish combatants who are participating in the fight in Spain on the side of the Government" ...

He then asked the Assembly to constitute an International Commission to make all the investigations and verifications necessary to guarantee that the Spanish Government's decision to retire foreign volunteers would be carried out in its totality, and pledged that the Government would give all guarantees, facilities and collaboration that the International Commission would consider necessary for the fulfillment of its mission.

Dr. Negrin then went on to speak about the International Brigades:

> "It is with a feeling of great sorrow that we regard the idea of separating ourselves from this group of brave and selfsacrificing men who, led by a generous impulse that will never be forgotten by the people of Spain, came to our aid in the most critical moments in our history. I want to proclaim here the heroism and the high moral value of the sacrifice they voluntarily undertook, not to safeguard petty selfish interests, but solely to serve and defend the purest ideals of justice and liberty. We are absolutely certain that they will readily undertake this new and painful sacrifice which we are asking at present in order to benefit the cause for which they were ready to give their lives.
>
> "Spain will not forget those who have fallen on her battlefields nor those who are still fighting on her soil; but I feel safe in saying without equivocation that their own countries will feel proud of them and this is the highest moral recompense they can receive."

On September 22nd, the news of Negrin's speech reached the XV Brigades as it lay still in reserve. After the strain of so many battles, the volun-

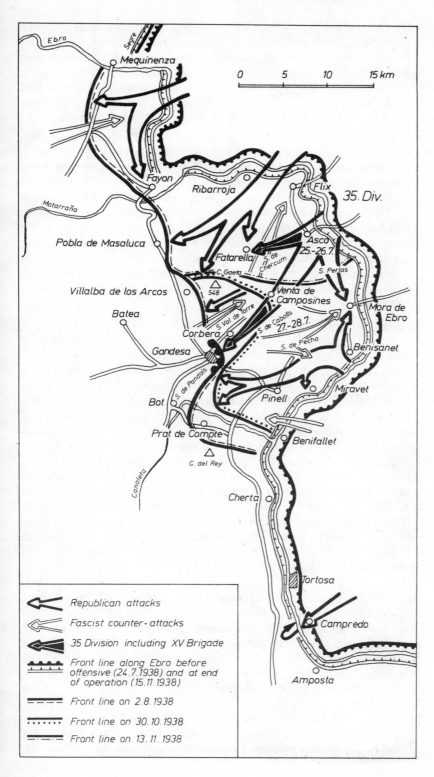

Ebro front,
July–November 1938

Mequinenza

Ebro

Segre

Fayon

Ribarroja

Flix

35. Div.

Matarraña

Pobla de Masaluca

Asco
25.–26.7.

Fatarella

S. de Chercum

S. Perlas

C. Gaeta

548

Villalba de los Arcos

Venta de
Camposines

Mora de
Ebro

Batea

S. Val de Torre

S. de Caballs
27.–28.7.

Corbera

Benisanet

Gandesa

S. de Pecha

S. de Pandols

Bot

Pinell

Miravet

Prat de Compte

Benifallet

C. del Rey

Canaleta

Cherta

Tortosa

Campredo

Amposta

Republican attacks	
Fascist counter-attacks	
35 Division including XV Brigade	
Front line along Ebro before offensive (24.7.1938) and at end of operation (15.11.1938)	
Front line on 2.8.1938	
Front line on 30.10.1938	
Front line on 13.11.1938	

0   5   10   15 km

9*

teers visibly relaxed and jokingly bantered about the first things they would do, and enjoy, when they reached their homes again. The same night came the news of a Fascist breakthrough and of the need to relieve the hardpressed XIII (Polish) Brigade. It was a supreme test for the XV when in the early hours of September 23rd, it moved into battle once more. Those who had been just talking of the joys of home now entered a battle from which they all knew some would not come back. It was a short but fierce battle:

> "What a day it was!" was the entry in the Diary of the British Battalion as it recorded the events of the last day of the last battle, "Such artillery bombardments as I have never seen before. They literally churned up our positions. Under the cover of the artillery the Fascists advanced with infantry and tanks. They were on top of us before we were aware of their advance. Our lads were mown down. We retired in as good order as possible and formed a line on the next ridge. The artillery bombardment continued with continuous bombing added. Somehow or other we managed to hold on till dark when we went out to get our wounded. It took us four hours to evacuate our wounded. That night we were relieved."

In that last fight, amongst those "mown down" were Jack Nalty and Liam McGregor—these two Irish deaths took place exactly two years after the first Irish anti-fascist, Bill Scott, had come to fight in September 1936.

Jack Nalty, one of the first Irish to come to Spain was now one of the last to die in battle. He had risen from the ranks to be second-in-command of the Heavy (Maxim) Machine-Gun Company. In the closing stages of the Irish Civil War he had been a member of Fianna Eireann and afterwards of the South County Dublin Battalion of the I.R.A. He was one of the foundation members of the Irish Republican Congress and later joined the Communist Party of Ireland. A member of the Irish Transport & General Workers' Union he was prominently active in its Oil Workers' Section. Nalty had served two jail sentences in Ireland for his political activities, in Mountjoy in January 1935 and in the Curragh "Glasshouse" in May 1935. As already mentioned he had been wounded at the Cordova Battle in December 1936, after which he returned to Ireland for treatment, but he again—as in the case of Frank Ryan, Mick Lehane and Paddy Duff, all of whom had been also wounded—went back to Spain, crossing the hazardous Pyrenees Mountains, to fight again.

Liam McGregor came from a family long active in the Socialist movement in Dublin. Like two other Irish volunteers—Donal O'Reilly and Jim Prendergast—he had graduated from the Lenin International School in Moscow. An organiser of great ability and the possessor of a keen political mind, he, in the short space of time, had become a Company Political Commissar. The loss of this young comrade was mourned by his fellow-volunteers. In his early twenties he showed considerable promise as a future leader in the Irish Communist movement.

There was a touch of symbolism in the fact that the last two Irishmen to die in Spain should fall in Catalonia, the land which in the text of the Catalan Youth Party's letter to Eamon de Valera, eleven months previously, had put itself "courageously at the side of your country, the noble Ireland to which the Catalan Nationalists gave with veneration the title of sister country, because her misfortunes were ours and her sufferings were felt in our own felsh."

McGregor and Nalty had acknowledged this 'sister country' with their lives ...

Unrisen dawns had dazzled in your eyes,
Your hearts were hungry for the not yet born
In agony of thwarted love and wasted life,
Through all long misery, from countries torn
With savage hands, you did not shrink or bend,
But marched on straighter, prouder to the end.

Not blindly, fighting in another's war,
Lured by cheap promises and drugged with drums,
Striking down brothers in the name of lies,
Slaves of the blackest with all senses numbed—
But clear-eyed, bravely, counting all the cost,
Knowing what might be won, what might be lost.

The rifles you will never hold again
In other hands still speak against the night,
Brothers have filled your places in the ranks
Who will remember how you died for right
The day you took those rifles up, defied
The power of ages, and victorious died.

Comrades, sleep now, for all you loved shall be.
You did not seek for death, but finding it—
And such a death—better than shameful life,
Rest now content. A flame of hope is lit.
The flag of freedom floats again unfurled
And all you loved lives richlier in the world.*(6)

Chapter 13 Notes

*(1)   Wolfe Tone (1763–1798) was the leader of the "Society of United Irishmen" which organised the Rising of 1798. His objective was: "To subvert the tyranny of our execrable government, to break the connection with England, the never-failing source of all our political evils; and to assert the independence of my country." His means to achieve this objective: "To unite the whole people of Ireland, to abolish the memory of past dissensions, and to substitute the common name of Irishman in place of denominations of Protestant, Catholic and Dissenter." An enthusiastic supporter of the French Revolution, he placed its principles of democracy, radicalism and "the rights of man" as the basis for his first Irish Republican movement. Every June since his death his grave in Bodenstown Churchyard, County Kildare, is the centre for a nation-wide radical tribute to his memory. It is a serious political occasion, but at the same time an annual venue for personal and political reunions, and a day for family outings that give it a traditional festive atmosphere.

*(2)   "Bearna Baoghail" in Gaelic, means the "Gap of Danger."

*(3)   "Spain. 1936–1939" by Jose Sandoval & Manuel Azcarate, Lawrence and Wishart, Ltd. London, 1966.

*(4)   "Diaries 1937–1938" by Count Galeazzo Ciano, p. 148

*(5)   "Volunteer for Liberty" (bi-lingual organ of the XV Brigade), Vol. III, No. 32, p. 2.

*(6)   Inspired by, and titled, "Jarama", this poem was written by A.M. Elliot, Headquarters Staff, XV Brigade, and published in "Book of the XV Brigade", p. 112.

THE LEAVING OF SPAIN

"Their deed was as noble as that
of the men of 1916..."*(1)

It was after midnight on September 24th, 1938, that the XV Brigade was relieved for the last time. One, at the Brigade command post, saw them as they passed on the road that was eventually to lead out of Spain. He "heard the marching feet, the shuffling feet, dragging on the road, moving toward the river. It was a low shuffle; there were no voices; there was no singing." *(2)

Though the announcement of the withdrawal had been made on September 21st, and the Brigade withdrawn on the 24th, the actual repatriation of the volunteers did not take place until December 6th, 1938. The delay was due to the hostile attitude of the British and French Governments.

After leaving the Ebro, the Brigade marched first to Marsa, later to Guiamets and then finally to the demobilisation centre at Ripoll. The period of leavetaking actually began when it was coming out of the front lines. A meeting was held with the Spanish comrades who were to continue the fight. The Diary of the British Battalion gives this account:

> "We have had a Battalion meeting to explain the reasons for the withdrawal. Both Spanish and Internationals are sad. We love our homes and our people. We will be glad to see them once again. But it is hard to leave the soil on which we have fought and helped to liberate; the soil under which many of our beloved comrades sleep. It is hard to leave our splendid Spanish comrades. There will be many sad leavetakings. Each of us will leave with the address of a Spanish hermano (brother) to whom we will write and send tobacco, etc. The 57th Battalion of the 15th Brigade will remain and we will follow its struggles with pride. It will always be our Battalion. A pact is to be drawn up between Spanish and Internationals pledging all comrades to fight to the death for the liberation of Spain."

Later there came the news of final promotions for the officers of the Brigade, Milton Wolf of the Americans and Sam Wilde of the British Battalions were raised from Captains to Major, so likewise was Paddy O'Daire of Ireland, and Johnny Power was promoted from the rank of Teniente (lieutenant) to Captain.

On October 16th, the International Brigades paraded for the last time for a review by their commanders. The reviewing officers were Andre Marty, Inspector General of the Brigades; Luigi Gallo (Longo), Commissar General; the two German leaders, Hans Kahle and Ludwig Renn; the young Spanish Commissar Sastre and Major Jose Antonia Valledor*(3) who had taken over command of the XV Brigade in July.

The biggest parade, however, was on October 29th, 1938 when the Brigades made their last appearance before the Spanish people, in Barcelona. It was a fervent and emotional send-off as thousands of the city's citizens lined the footpaths and flung flowers at the 2,000 Brigaders as they marched past. Protective planes flew overhead in case there should be one of the air-raids to which Barcelona was now being frequently subjected. Negrin took the salute and then spoke a few spontaneous works of thanks and farewell.

For the volunteers, however, the most expressive message of appreciation came from Dolores Ibarruri (La Pasionaria). Its text was given to each one of them:—

"It is very hard to say a few words in farewell to the heroes of the International Brigades, both because of what they are and what they represent.

A feeling of sorrow, an infinite grief catches our throats ... Sorrow for those who are going away, for the soldiers of the highest ideal of human redemption, exiles from their countries, persecuted by the tyrants of all peoples ... Grief for those who will stay here forever, mingling with the Spanish soil or in the very depths of our hearts, bathed in the fight of our everlasting gratitude.

You came to us from all peoples, from all races. You came like brothers of ours, like sons of undying Spain; and in the hardest days of the war, when the capital of the Spanish Republic was threatened, it was you, gallant comrades of the International Brigades, who helped to save the city with your fighting enthusiasm, your heroism and your spirit of sacrifice.

In deathless verses Jarama and Guadalajara, Brunete and Belchite, Levante and the Ebro sing the courage, the self-sacrifice the daring, the discipline of the men of the International Brigades.

For the first time in the history of the peoples' struggles, there has been the spectacle, breath-taking in its grandeur, of the formation of International Brigades to help to save a threatened country's freedom and independence, the freedom and independence of our Spanish land.

Communists, Socialists, Anarchists, Republicans—men of different religions, yet all of them fired with a deep love for liberty and justice. And they came and offered themselves to us unconditionally.

They gave us everything: their youth or their maturity; their science or their experience; their blood and their lives; their hopes and aspirations ... And they asked us for nothing at all. That is to say, they did want a post in the struggle, they did aspire to the honour of dying for us ...

Banners of Spain! ... Salute these many heroes! Lower Spain's banners in honor of so many martyrs! ...

Mothers! Women! When the years pass by and the wounds of the war are being staunched; when the cloudy memory of the sorrowful, bloody days returns in a present of freedom, peace and well-being; when the feelings of rancour are dying away and when pride in a free country is felt equally by Spaniards, then speak to your children. Tell them of these men of the International Brigades.

Tell them how, coming over seas and mountains, crossing frontiers bristling with bayonets, and watched for by ravening dogs thirsting to tear at their flesh, these men reached our country as crusaders for freedom, to fight and die for Spain's liberty and independence which were threatened by German and Italian Fascism. They gave up everything: their loves, their countries, home and fortune; fathers, mothers, wives, brothers, sisters, and children, and they came and told us: 'We are here. Your cause, Spain's cause is ours—it is the cause of all advanced and progressive mankind.'

Today they are going away. Many of them, thousands of them, are staying here with the Spanish earth for their shroud, and all Spaniards remember them with the deepest feeling.

Comrades of the International Brigades. Political reasons, reasons of State, the welfare of that same cause for which you offered your blood with boundless generosity, are sending you back, some of you to your own countries and others to forced exile. You can go proudly. You are history. You are legend. You are the heroic example of democracy's solidarity and universality, in face of the shameful, 'accommodating' spirit of those who interpret democratic principles with their eyes on the hoards of wealth or the industrial shares which they want to preserve from any risk.

We shall not forget you, and when the olive tree of peace puts forth its leaves again, entwined with the laurels of the Spanish Republic's victory—come back! ...

Come back to us. With us those of you who have no country will find one, those of you who have to live deprived of friendship will find friends, and all of you will find the love and gratitude of the whole Spanish people who, now and in the future, will cry out with all their hearts:

"Long live the heroes of the International Brigades!"

By December all those of the XV Brigade who survived were gathered at the demobilisation centre of Ripoll. The only Irishman missing was Paddy Duff*(4) who was still in hospital with wounds received at the Ebro. (He had already been wounded at Jarama and Brunete).

On a dry and frosty morning the Irish and British Brigaders set out by train from Ripoll on their last journey in Spain. Again there was a popular send-off. At the station the volunteers in a last gesture handed over to the children present the rations they had been given for their journey to France. They did not know how long they would be travelling without food, but they knew that in France, unlike Spain, there was plenty to eat. They jammed the open doors of the freight-wagons on which they were travelling to wave their last farewells. With Ripoll out of sight they squatted on the floor and chatted. Soon another town came into view. There the station platform was packed with people, the local band struck-up the "Internationale" as the train ground to a halt. The "alcalde" (mayor) stepped forward and another speech was made. Sam Wilde, the Battalion Commander made a reply in which he said, „We shall keep the pledge we made when we came here to fight beside you,

Spanish brothers and sisters! We are not withdrawing from your struggle, once again we are changing our front, to return home this time and there to fight for all-out assistance in your great and heroic fight against International Fascism."

"Vivas!" were shouted, and once again the "Internationale" was played and sung; then there was the final joint chorus of the Spanish Republican anthem, "Hymno de Riego." Station after station en route to the frontier the same kind of parting took place.

There was a count-check and identification process by the French League of Nations International Commission and then a meal on tables in the station buffet which made many of the semi-starved volunteers sick. Then on to a sealed train which went right through to the port of Dieppe. There the French dockers were lined up to present small bouquets of flowers to the Brigaders, and then on the boat to Newhaven and on the train to London's Victoria Station where a tumultuous welcome was given.

The Irish were almost home, after leaving Spain on December 7th, 1938; from the land in which for two years and three months of war they had carried the banner of Connolly.

They had fulfilled their pledge of solidarity and had redeemed the name of the Irish people whose traditions of struggle had been stained by the Blueshirt and Irish Christian Front intervention on the side of the forces that were strangling the creation by a noble people of the Spanish Peoples' Republic.

However, even if O'Duffy's Brigade had never enlisted for Franco, the Irish Unit of the International Brigades would still have come into being, because of the strength of the traditions that bound the Irish struggle for independence with the fight for humanity the world over. Even before Spain, in spite of the difficult conditions, such links had been built. There had been Irish Republican and Communist participation in the World Congress of the Anti-Imperialist League in Brussels in 1927, and in Frankfurt-on-Main in 1929. Peadar O'Donnell had been active in the formation of the European Peasants Committee (the "green" International). There had been delegations to the Soviet Union and the existence of an Irish Committee of solidarity with the Indian struggle against British imperialism.

Once before in history, Irishmen had fought on different sides in a national-revolutionary struggle in Europe. In 1861, the then Irish Cardinal Cullen inspired, and clerical middle class nationalist leasers organised, 1,100 Irishmen to "save the Pope" from Garibaldi who was fighting for the unity and independence of Italy. The Irish "Pope's Brigade" like O'Duffy's later one left Ireland with blessings rained down on them. However, when Garibaldi and his "Red-Shirts" marched from Palermo to the Volturno there were in his ranks John O'Donoghue of Bray, Joseph Nelson, Dunne, Dowling, the artillery-man and eight other Irishmen. 75 years later the "Connolly Column" was to march alongside Italian anti-fascists, who wore distinctive red-neckerchiefs, and who called their International Brigade (the XII) the "Garibaldis."

Ireland had also a tradition of mercenary soldiers, like those pressed into the service of the British Army in the Crimean War. The pressure exacted was the frightful economic and social conditions created by British rule in

Ireland. By the liberal distribution of "The King's Shilling"many joined the forces in order to escape poverty. The country also had the traditions of soldiers who revolted against tyranny like the "Connaught Rangers," an Irish regiment of the British Army in India who mutinied in 1921 against British atrocities in Ireland. There had been the "San Patrico" Company of the American Army who in the U.S. war against Mexico, disassociated themselves from that war of U.S. aggression, and went, under the leadership of John O'Reilly, to fight alongside the Mexicans. Such progressive traditions lived on in Ireland despite all the counter-propaganda.*(5)

Compared numerically with the other national contributions to the International Brigades, that of Ireland was a small one. What it lacked in numbers was made up for in quality, integrity and battle-courage. The contribution was made under the most difficult of internal political circumstances. The total number of Irish volunteers was 145; of that number 61 never came back, which was a proportional casualty rate comparable to the Brigades as a whole.

The Irish newspapers rarely recorded their presence, and their deaths, in Spain. Only in the columns of "The Worker" and in the later weekly, "The Irish Democrat"*(6) were there any accounts of their struggles. All through the war, even after the fiasco of O'Duffy's Brigade and the debacle of the Christian Front, the Irish capitalist and religious press continued to hail the Franco victories.

The Irish, like all others in the Brigades, fought under the most adverse conditions. The "Non-Intervention" countries, under the leadership of Britain and France succeeded in ensuring that the minimum of supplies reached Republican Spain.*(7) Food was scarce, arms were inadequate, and medical supplies even more so.

The armaments available to the Republicans were mainly old and few. In the early days the rifles were the obsolete, straight-bolt, Canadian Ross type, French Lebels and Austrian Steyrs. In 1937, the Soviet Mouisin Nagant rifle was issued. It had a calibre of 7.62 mm, was fitted with a long triangular bayonet, but its magazine held only 5 bullets. It later became the standard weapon of the Brigades in which it was named the "Mexicanski" rifle since it was not established whether it came from Mexico or the Soviet Union. In 1938 a limited number of Czech Mauser rifles became available as well as the first models of the Bren Gun, which augmented the Soviet "Dyegtya-ryov" light machine gun, the "Tokarev" semi-heavy type, and the Maxim heavy gun with its solid carriage and wheels.*(8)

During the progress of the war, the French style steel helmets became so hard to get as to be non-existent. This was also the case with cartridge-belts. (In the Ebro offensive each volunteer was issued with 100 loose rounds, without clips, that had to be carried in small sacks tied around the waist.) Footwear disappeared until the "alpagatas" (rope-sandals) became the general vogue. At this late stage in the war, food often consisted of a slice of bread fried in olive oil and a cup of weak coffee, with the main meal being that of "Garbanzos" (chick-peas). Mess-kits were often an old jam-jar or a tobacco tin, and rudimentary spoons and forks that were self-carved out of wood.

With the withdrawal of the Brigades there took place in reverse the process that had begun in 1936; the Irish went back to where they had come from, home to Ireland, Britain and the U.S.A.

On December 10th, 1938, a small group of the returning volunteers, Johnny Power, James F. O'Regan, Tom O'Brien, Mick Waters, Eugene Dowling John O'Shea and Michael O'Riordan—disembarked at Dun Laoghaire and boarded the train for Dublin's Westland Row Station. There they were greeted by friends and sympathisers, the members of the "Irish Friends of the Spanish Republic" who had fought so well on the "home-front," and by comrades who had previously returned from Spain because of wounds. The seven who came back—minus Paddy Duff—were the last of the Brigade to come home to Ireland.

A curious crowd of onlockers at the station watched as the returning volunteers and the welcoming party formed up in marching order, and led by a single piper, set out for Abbey Street corner, where on a lorry in the midst of a downpour of rain stood Father Michael O'Flanagan. To the small audience he spoke the words of welcome to those back from Spain*(9) The meeting over, the participants adjourned to the Oval Bar to drink, relax and exchange all the news that had built up both in Spain and Ireland.

Many of the Irish stayed on in London not because they were concerned with a possible hostile reception in Ireland, but unemployment was widespread in their native land, and the securing of a job was almost an immediate necessity after returning from Spain. The prospects of an anti-fascist who had been in Spain getting a job were indeed very meagre.*(10)

Nevertheless, quite a number returned, viz.:

— Donal O'Reilly, who after a long spell of unemployment, eventually got back to his trade as a Plasterer and re-commenced his trade union activity.
— Jim Prendergast (1914–74) to his post in the Communist Party of Ireland. Later he had to emigrate to work in Britain. There he was active amongst Irish emigrants. A leading figure in the National Union of Railwaymen he was elected to the post of Executive Committee member in 1970.
— Paddy Duff (1902–72) on his return began to organise agricultural workers and later became a senior official in the Workers Union of Ireland.
— Johnny Power, Paddy Smith and Michael O'Riordan, who spent the years of World War II in the Curragh Internment Camp. There their political task was to explain to the other prisoners of the Irish Republican Movement the anti-national character of Fascism and the relationship between the Anti-Hitler war and the cause of Irish national liberation.
— Hugh Hunter (who died in 1972), to resume his tireless work as an activist in the Communist Party in Belfast.
— Peter O'Connor, to serve as a Labour Councillor of the Corporation of his native Waterford.
— And others, like Frank Edwards, to continue to serve the Irish progressive movement in various capacities.

In the Second World War, five of them fought against Hitler*(11)

— Paddy O'Daire who by sheer military competence broke through to become a Major in the British Army.*(12)

139

— Alec Digges who lost a leg in the fighting in Holland, and who became later a prominent activist in Britain in the solidarity movement with the anti-Franco forces.

— Paddy Roe McLaughlin, of Donegal, who was also in the British forces and Jim Prendergast who served as a rear-gunner in the R.A.F.*(13)

— Michael Lehane, Kilgarvan, County Kerry, who, unable to bring himself to wear a British uniform, but recognising the vital need for the defeat of Hitler in World War II, instead joined the Norwegian Merchant Navy. His contribution was the important one of war transportation and supply. He was killed at sea when his ship was attacked in 1942. Mick Lehane had a distinguished record in Spain, being wounded several times, the last occasion being at the battle of the Ebro, when his close companion, the Londoner Max Nash was killed.

Chapter 14 notes

*(1) From the speech of Father Michael O'Flanagan when he unveiled a Memorial Banner, in 1938, to the Irish dead of the Brigades. This Banner (which is in the custody of the author) does not carry a full list of those killed. Because of the war conditions the deaths of some could not be confirmed until after the painting and unveiling of the Banner, and others were killed later. One volunteer's name, J. O'Shea appears on it, although he "came back from the dead" and survived to return with the last group in December 1938. It also bears the names of two dead who were not Irish, but these were inscribed because they fell in action in the ranks of the Irish Section. They were the young Jewish Londoner, Samuel Lee, and John Scott. The real name of Scott was Inver Marlow, born in South Africa, he received a university education in Britain. "He went to India where he got first hand information of British Imperialism. Though only 29 years of age, Scott had seen the four corners of the globe. He knew the suppression of the masses in India. In Africa he saw the oppression and exploitation of the natives. He had worked in the lumber camps and on the rail-roads." ("The Book of the XV Brigade," p. 110.) Scott, with the rank of Captain, was leading the first battle of the Lincoln Battalion (which consisted of the Irish and Cuban centurias and one American section) at Jarama when "he fell before a stream of machine-gun bullets that was digging up the battle-field like some gigantic machine." (ibid)

*(2) "Men in Battle", by Alvah Bessie, pp. 344–345. First published in New York, 1939, and later republished by Seven Seas Publications, Berlin, G.D.R., 1960.

*(3) Valledor had been sentenced to death for his part in the 1934 Asturian revolt, but was saved by the election of the Popular Front Government. Prominent in the early days of 1936 in the fight against the Generals' Mutiny, he operated as a guerilla leader behind their lines. He was captured but succeeded in escaping from imprisonment in 1938 and rejoined the military struggle.

*(4) Paddy Duff who was too ill to be repatriated with the main body vas later caught up in the final chaos of the defeat of the Republic. He returned to Ireland in 1939 after being held in the French Concentration Camp at St. Cyprien. There the refugees from Spain had to live in made-do shelters built on sand, and the French authorities tried to pressure them into joining their Foreign Legion. For a description of life in that Camp, see "St. Cyprien Concentration Camp" by David Gordon, American Dialog, 130 East 16th Street, New York, Spring 1972.

*(5) Irish International Brigader, Donal O'Reilly, in his article in "1916–1966" (published by Irish Socialist, Dublin) wrote ..." Our home life was always filled with the stories of Myles the Slasher and the Bridge of Finea, John Boyle O'Reilly (a Fenian leader) and the odd mention of the relatives that had crossed the American lines to fight for the independence of Mexico. They were all real people to me." Vid. Appendix III. N.B. For more information on the "San Patrico" Company, see, "Evening Herald" (Dublin), September 5th, 1970.

*(6) The accounts in this journal being written by Sean Nolan.

*(7) Apart from Mexico which sent some military supplies, the Soviet Union was the only country which helped the Spanish Republic. It sent 806 fighter aircraft, 362 tanks, 120 armoured cars, 1,555 pieces of artillery, 500 thousand rifles, 340 mortars, 15,000 machineguns, 500,000 grenades, 862 million rounds of ammunition and other military supplies, as well as anti-aircraft searchlight installations, cars and lorries, fuel etc. Many of their ships bringing such material through the blockade were sunk. The last batch of Soviet military materials sent through France was allowed to cross the French-Spanish frontier only at the end of January 1939 when the greater part of Catalonia was already in the hands of the fascists, and when there was no aerodrome available for assembling planes.

*(8) After the Spanish War, in 1944, an official U.S. Army evaluation gave the Franco forces as having a superiority in arms as 7 to one over the Republican army. See "Lecture Series No. 6-I", War Orientation Course, Lowry Field, Colorado, May 23rd, 1944.

*(9) A few weeks afterwards when Franco had unleashed his last major offensive on Catalonia, Father O'Flanagan went on a visit of solidarity to Barcelona.

*(10) Some of the atmosphere of the time is conveyed in the play, "The Wise have not Spoken" by Paul Vincent Carroll. (Macmillan, London, 1948). In it a small poverty stricken farmer refers to his brother, Francis, as one who *"disgraced us before the whole country fighting with them Red madmen agin the Church in Spain."* At the end of the play, Francis defends, with a gun, the small farm which has been taken over by a local grasping merchant. To him and the armed police who come to carry out the eviction, he shouts: "Come and take what's mine to add to your mountain piles ... But have the price ready! A gallon of pig's blood."

*(11) Many ex-International Brigaders played prominent parts in the events of World War II. Apart from the Soviet volunteers mentioned in note 3, on page 51 and the Polish General Swierszewski, many of them were leaders of the Yugoslav Partisan Army. Colonel Rol Tanguy was the Commander of the Free French forces that liberated Paris. Luigi Longo was a leader of the Italian Partisans. Bob Thompson and Herman Bottcher both won the U.S. Distinguished Service Cross. The brilliant Canadian, Dr. Norman Bethune, who pioneered blood transfusion on the very battlefields of Spain, later died whilst serving with the Chinese Liberation Army. (For Bethune's biography, see, "The Scapel, The Sword," by Syd Gordon and Ted Allen, published by Little, Brown and Company, Boston, 1952.)

*(12) In June 1939, O'Daire, Duff, Larmour and Prendergast volunteered for a unique and dangerous experiment. It was in connection with the loss of the British submarine, "Thetis" with 99 lives in Liverpool a short time before. They spent time in a stimulated compressor in which they were subjected to the same conditions as those trapped in a sunken submarine i.e., lack of oxygen, and induced unconsciousness. They survived the experiment, and their reactions and experiences provided valuable knowledge for the improvement of live-saving techniques. The experiment was conducted by the well-known scientist, Dr. J.B.S. Haldane who had been in Spain himself for a short period as an adviser on antipoison-gas warfare.

*(13) P.R. McLaughlin was incorrectly reported dead in 1937. The following "obituary" appeared in the column "Trailing the Gael" in the December 18th, 1937 issue of the "Irish World and American Industrial Liberator":

> "Paddy McLaughlin is dead—killed in Spain. Paddy McLaughlin? Undoubtedly there are some Gaels outside New York who wonder who Paddy McLaughlin was. However, he needs no introduction to the Irish lovers of freedom around New York City, for he has been with them for many years and was known to be one of the most trustworthy and consistent of all those Irish exiles who served in the 'last war' for Irish freedom.
>
> "Paddy McLaughlin believed and persevered in his beliefs, often to the point of a debate with his most intimate friends, and it is hard to think that he passed on—but he left this world as he always wished—fighting for a principle that was dear to him as life itself ... With Paddy McLaughlin's death A MAN DIED."

N.B. The 'dead man' is still alive and hearty in Liverpool.

RELEASE FRANK RYAN!

> ..."Let cowards mock and tyrants frown,
> Ah, little do we care!
> A felon's cap's the noblest crown
> An Irish head can wear."

The main political task that confronted those who had returned from Spain was to explain what Fascism really meant. This was important not only in relation to the continuing struggle in Spain, but also because of the clearly impending Fascist aggression that eventually swept through Europe in 1939—45.

Many in the Irish national independence movement had been at first confused by the barrage of the Christian Front about the real issues in Spain's war. That there was a growing understanding of the real position was due to the sacrifices of those who went to help the Spanish Republic. Many of them were both well known and well respected. The alignment also of the traditional Irish reactionary forces with Franco, and the role of the British Government in stabbing the Spanish Republic in the back, made clearer the repressive-imperialist character of Fascism.

In the subsequent Second World War, however, the situation became more complex for many because of the involvement of Britain vis-a-vis Nazi Germany. A similar confused position existed in the Indian independence movement. The reaction in Ireland to the issues of the World War would in itself provide the material for another book, but it is mentioned here because it was relevant to the task of the Irish ex-International Brigaders and to the subsequent fate of Frank Ryan.

In July 1938 there was a demonstration in Ireland which indicated that the nature of Fascism was being recognised. It was on the occasion of a courtesy visit of an Italian warship to the Port of Dublin.

An Irish anti-fascist picket was placed on the ship, and as the naval officers went sight-seeing they were followed by a large crowd that were hostile and who were shouting, "Release Frank Ryan" and who sang an Italian anti-fascist song which had been popularised by the returned Irish from Spain:

> ..."Avanti popolo, alla riscossa
> Bandiera Rossa, trionfera!

Dai campi al mare
Alle miniere chi soffre e spera
Rossa bandiera
Avanti popolo alla riscossa
Bandiera rossa, trionfera, ...

The Italian officers had to make a swift return, with a protective police escort, to the safety of the warship.

As the war in Spain continued, Frank Ryan, the sterling and beloved leader of the Irish International Brigaders lay, under the vilest of conditions in Burgos prison.

After the December 1938 homecoming of the Irish survivors of the International Brigade, the Franco forces mounted a massive attack from a line that lay from the Pyrennees Mountains to the Ebro River and the sea. In the period of November—December more and more convoys of German and Italian ships had brought in troops, technicians and hundreds of thousands of tons of war material.

3 Franco Armies, including the Army of Navara and the Army of Morocco; 4 Italian Divisions and a powerful backing force of Italian artillery, aircraft and tanks were assembled to deal the death blow in Catalonia. This mighty superior force was not even under the command of a Spaniard; it was led by the Fascist Italian General Gambara.

Resisting the overwhelming well equipped fascist force of 340,000 strong on the Catalan front were only 120,000 Republicans of whom only 37,000 had rifles—yet a few miles away behind the frontier the French Government had impounded 500 pieces of artillery and 10,000 machine-guns that were destined for the lawful Government of Spain.

The grossly unequal fight began, with the Republican forces grimly and heroically contesting every inch of the fascist advance. The defenders of the Republic were slaughtered.

On January 26th, 1939 the Fascist forces took Barcelona. Thousands of Republican soldiers, and civilian families of men, women, children, who could not live under the Franco rule made the weary trek across the frontier accross the border. With them was Paddy Duff of Dublin. They crossed over the Pyrenees Mountains into France whose Government was to place them in concentration camps.

Catalonia had fallen but Madrid, the symbol of unconquerable Spain still stood. Despite the crushing defeats, resistance was still possible in the large centres like Valencia, Alicante, the naval base of Cartagena and in Almeria. The Spanish Republican forces, in spite of everything, were still intact, and were so on February 27th, 1939 when the British and French Governments— the oldest of the imperialist diplomatic agencies—officially recognised Franco. The British Prime Minister, Chamberlain went to Italy and said "The further prosecution of the war in Spain will only create a dangerous situation ... I think that we ought to be able to establish excellent relations with Franco, who seems well disposed to us." *(1)

Madrid was in a desperate situation; there were few guns, little medical supplies and food was indeed so scarce that the London "Times" could report an February 14th, 1939 that four to five hundred people died each week

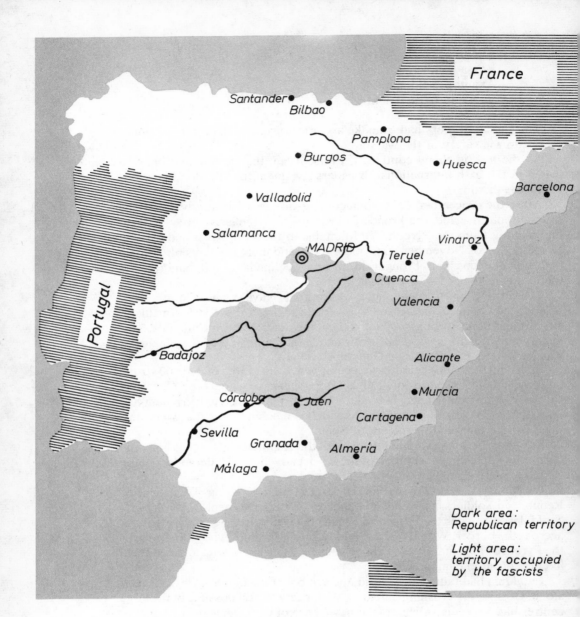

France

Santander · Bilbao ·

Pamplona ·

· Burgos · Huesca

Barcelona ·

· Valladolid

· Salamanca Vinaroz ·

◎ MADRID · Teruel

Portugal · Cuenca

Valencia ·

· Badajoz

Alicante ·

· Murcia

Córdoba · · Jaén Cartagena ·

· Sevilla Granada · · Almería

· Málaga

Dark area:
Republican territory

Light area:
territory occupied
by the fascists

144 *Spain, the front line, January 1939*

in the capital from starvation—but Madrid was as determined to hold out as it did in 1936. "No Pasaran!" was still the slogan of the city.

In the light of the policy of the British Government reinforced as it was by Chamberlain's statement in Italy, the British diplomatic and intelligence forces went to work to sell out Madrid. They succeeded in getting Casado, one of the Commanders in Madrid, to open the gates of the city to the Fascists—but not before the latter had to crush in blood a determined opposition to his policy of surrender.

On March 28th, 1939 theFacist forces marched into the city which they could never take, despite all their superiority. They could only enter it when it was handed over to them.

Two days later—after 986 days of incredible resistance—the Generals' revolt finally triumphed, and all Spain was under Franco rule. The rich, with the massive and ruthless support of the Nazis and the Fascists and the assistance of the ruling class of the "democracies" had vanquished the poor.

With the victory, vengeance was wrought on those who had resisted. The jails were filled. The firing-squads worked overtime. Within nine months, over 100,000 executions took place. Mussolini's son-in-law, Count Ciano, in his diary for July 1939 wrote:

> "There are 200,000 persons in prison. Trials going on everyday at a speed which I would almost call summary ... There are still a great number of shootings. In Madrid alone between 200 and 250 a day, in Barcelona, 150, in Seville." *(2)

By 1942, over 2 million had passed through the jails. The gates remained slammed on thousands for much longer periods; for many it was to be for over 20 years.

Daily executions and inhuman conditions of incarceration. This was the position in which Frank Ryan languished in Franco's prison at Burgos. After he had been sentenced to death he was placed in a cell with eighteen other condemned prisoners. Each morning nine of them were called out and executed, and an equal number of prisoners would file into the cell to take their places, and wait.

Ryan, according to one account, was prepared for the worst:

> "He had no idea that the outer world already knew that he was a prisoner. He scratched his name on a comb. If he were marched off to the firing squad he would throw his comb through the grille of another cell whose occupants had only been sentenced to imprisonment. Perhaps this would be the clue to posterity and his native Ireland as to what had happened to him. Otherwise, he knew he would merely be one of those missing and forgotten as a result of the Civil War." *(3)

As already mentioned, the broad Irish Committee formed to stop his execution was successful. There was a similar group in Britain working for his release which included Michael McInerney who later became Political Correspondent for the "Irish Times" daily newspaper. The work of this committee, based on London, was to organise pressure on Franco, via the

British Government, which was subjected to many petitions and deputations from the British Labour Party and its M.P.s as well as from leading trade union figures and organisations.

In addition, there functioned in the U.S.A. a national committee which had groups in New York, Chicago, San Francisco, Philadelphia, and across the Canadian border, in Montreal. The Chairman of this committee was Gerald O'Reilly; and its Secretary was Joseph Gillespie, who was also secretary of the United Irish Counties association in the U.S. Among the most active people on this committee was Peter MacSwiney (brother of Cork's Mayor who died on hunger-strike in 1920), Paddy Lacken Ryan (a prominent Tipperary I.R.A. leader in the struggle of the 1920s), Connie Neenan (Cork), Paul O'Dwyer (well known jurist and political figure and in 1976 President of the New York City Council) and Michael Quill, President of the Transport Workers Union Of America and member of the New York City Council.

Gerald O'Reilly had also been a prominent I.R.A. leader and had a close personal relationship with Ryan.

All these committees continued, after the commution of the death sentence, to urge his release. Impetus was given by the fact that whilst in 1939 Franco was releasing the International Brigade prisoners, he seemed adamant in still detaining Ryan.

At the 45th Annual Conference of the Irish Trade Union Congress, in Waterford, August 2—4th, 1939, attention was focused on this fact by "Big" Jim Larkin (the famous 1913 Strike leader). He succeeded, with the assistance of Ned Tucker, in getting the Standing Orders suspended to deal with the imprisonment of Frank Ryan as an Irish citizen "and as a trade unionist" (Ryan was a member of the National Union of Journalists).

Larkin said, "I have myself had happiness in past years from unanimous resolutions asking the Government to release me from bondage, British workers, when I was only a humble individual in the Trade Union movement, laid down their tools to demand my release."

"But Frank Ryan was born in this country, and his father was a trade unionist ... this is a man who has been a servant of his people, and a citizen second to none ... I am not given to eulogy of any individual, but knowing the boy since I came back to this country, knowing him as a boy and when he grew into manhood, I know that he has an intellect second to none, that he is a scholar of the best type, with not only intellectual courage but physical courage ... Frank Ryan is unselfish—he never gave himself to anyone for what he would get, he walked the dull ways of the earth, and that is why he is held incommunicado today. The reasons for his imprisonment are apparent ... Because this man stood in the gap, the Government of Spain says: 'Although we have released this man and that and thousands of others, this Irishman—one of the lost legion—we are going to keep in durance vile for 30 years.' That statement was made yesterday, and we should be ashamed of our souls that Englishmen should go to the Duke of Alba, the representative of the Spanish Government in London, to ask for Frank Ryan's release. The Duke said that they were keeping this man because of 'civil crime.' Frank Ryan never in his life could be charged with any offence against the civil law. He is the soul of truth and honesty and honour."

The delegate of the Railway Clerks Association, Mr. F. Geaney, in support, said that whilst Frank Ryan was in jail they should not rest, no trade unionist, no Irishman should rest. It was a crime against our country, against our Labour Movement. "We must take every step in our power to release him, and if this Congress is to mean anything at all in the present or future life of this country, this motion should commend itself to every delegate. I can link Frank Ryan's name with James Connolly's. He would be a defender of Connolly, but now he is languishing in a Spanish jail."

The motion calling for Ryan's release was passed with one dissenting voice. It belonged to R.S. Anthony who throughout his career in the trade union movement had played a consistent opportunistic role*(4) "Frank Ryan," according to him, "might have been a wonderful man—but they were a purely industrial body," and so he therefore opposed the resolution. His fellow delegate from the Typographical Association, A.E. Lloyd (Belfast) disassociated himself from Anthony, saying he had no hesitation in supporting the release of Ryan.*(5)

Twenty seven years later there was a verbal account given of how life in Burgos was when Ryan was there. It was told when former members of the International Brigades gathered in Berlin, capital of the German Democratic Republic, in 1966, to honour the 30th anniversary of the Spanish peoples' national-revolutionary war. There were three former Irish combatants present, Donal O'Reilly, Frank Edwards, and this writer. One evening they returned to the capital from a visit to Dresden, and were introduced to a group of Spanish Republicans which included Fabricano Rojel who had been just released after over 22 years imprisonment in Spain. Meeting the Irish group, he immediately enquired as to how Frank Ryan was. He was profoundly disturbed when he was told that Ryan had been dead for twenty-two years, and that we had only just then returned from paying our respects at his grave.

Rojel plied us with many questions as to the circumstances of his death, and then began to recall how both of them had been imprisoned together, at the beginning of Rojel's own long agony of incarceration, and how Ryan had left an indelible impression on him. He began to express his memories of his "camarada irlandes"*(6) ...

"First," Rojel said, "let me tell you about Frank Ryan in general. I did not know until this evening, when you told me, that he was dead. He was a person who not only in the armed struggle in Spain was an outstanding personality, but who also in the rigorous conditions of prison was a fighter of great integrity." Then he told details of the capture of Ryan, and then continued the story of the trials of Burgos, "Let me tell you," he said, "about his attitude and stance there. This is important as an example for Irish youth. What was it like in Burgos Central Prison? It is Franco's greatest prison and it is comparable with Buchenwald. Ten thousands of Spaniards, especially from the North, were brought to Burgos to be shot. Thousands of men died from beatings and hunger in their cells. There existed the terror of the Fascist 'Falangists' who were the most degenerate of the Franco forces. It was a terrible testing place for men. Frank Ryan did not bow his head; the terror could not break his spirit."

He spoke slowly as he thought back over the period and the man. "He was one of the few foreign prisoners left. There was not one fellow Irishman

10*

beside him. He was a true believer in international solidarity. He developed his Spanish very well and he was able to make contact with all the Spanish comrades. There was an underground committee for all the prisoners. He was in contact with this committee and was an example of discipline. He took part in the work of this committee like a Spaniard and played a great part in creating discipline and restoring morale. He was no sectarian. He was in contact with prisoners who were Communists, Socialists, Anarchists, and with the Basques, who were Catholic, and this point," he emphasised, "is important for Ireland. He got a lot of sympathy and support from the Basques and he got this because of his personality and simplicity."

One of the features of the prison regime, alongside the shootings, beatings and starvation was the compulsion on each prisoner to attend Mass and other religious services at which sermons were preached praising the Franco authority and condemning those who opposed him. Attendance was obligatory under the pain of punishment. "Frank never took part in the prison religious services" said Rojel, going on to explain that "one element of our struggle in prison was the fight for freedom of belief. "This took until September 24th, 1963 for prisoners to gain the right not to go to Mass, if they so wished."

There was an atmosphere of poignancy as he told the story of Ryan, and it attracted others in the vicinity, who listened in silence.

That day we had paid tribute to him in a graveyard in Dresden. (How he came to be buried there will be dealt with anon.) We laid a wreath of red carnations crossed with Irish tri-colour ribbons, and with the inscription, "From his Friends in Ireland." It was a solemn moment that affected not only the Irish but also the German International Brigade veteran, Arno Hering and the representatives of the Socialist Unity Party of Germany who by their presence made it a combined national and international tribute. Beside the grave, that was tended regularly by a local Dresden man who had also been in Spain (but who never met Ryan) there was a sad silence at the last resting place of a man who was loved, who had suffered so much, and who, his Irish comrades knew, had never surrendered.

The talk that night was all about Ryan. Those who listened to Rojel's story of rememberance developed a deep sense of respect for this great Irishman. The interpreter, Anneliese Ichenhauser, felt such a moving reaction that next day she set out to write some verses about him. She was apologetic that she was not a poetess, that she found it difficult to write in English ...

> "There is a grave in Dresden town
> With Ivy growing green,
> And the cross it bears a stranger's name,
> How come? What does it mean?
> Who is it who is lying there
> Under the ivy green?"

> "The man who has been lying there
> for twenty years and more,
> Died a bitter lonesome death
> Far from his Irish shore.
> He was Ireland's fighting son,

And Freedom was his fight,
And Freedom and Humanity and
Every workers's right."

"For every worker everywhere,
No matter what his tongue,
That is why he went
Spain to defend
When the bells of alarm were rung ..."

"And they captured him,
And they tortured him
And he was deaf and and ill,
But the spirit of a man like him
Is something they never could kill."

"There came one day; it was in May,
The saplings were green with life.
When men fatigued with heartbreak and blood,
Victoriously ended the strife.
From the caps of those soldiers of liberty
Gleamed stars as red as he wore,
And wherever their marching steps touched soil,
It was enemy soil no more."

"The earth it was fraternal then
and was a friendly place,
The grave was cared for by a man
Who had never known his face;
He only knew that his brother was he,
And Freedom was his fight,
For Freedom and Humanity and
Every workers's right,
That part of his blood and part of his toil
Is in this friendly fraternal soil."

"Oh, man down in your ivy grave,
See the green, white, orange band!
Your comrades came to visit you
From your beloved land.
See the flowers they put down for you,
and they are crimson red,
Frank Ryan, they say it's twenty years,
But you, lad, have never been dead."

"Your ivy is green and the Shamrock is green,
And there's a fight still to be won,
So Frank, we want to take you home,
Your country's fighting son,
To be near when the ancient Rebel Songs
Will rouse the country wide,
For Freedom and Humanity and
Every worker's right."

"And on your Dresden grave thus empty then,
A stone will tell of you,
Who did in times so very dark
The things you had to do.
And in your name there is a smile,
A smile of certainty,
And in your name there is an oath of solidarity."

Four years after the ceremony in Dresden, the author was to receive another testimony of the impression that Ryan left on those he was imprisoned with. This message took twenty years to be delivered. It came from Josef Schwartz, a member of the XIII (Polish) International Brigade, who had been taken prisoner the same time as Ryan. In 1950, Schwartz lay dying in the Queen Mary Hospital, Roehampton, England, from tuberculosis. To a fellow Polish patient he had recounted his ordeals with Ryan, of how on one occasion they were chained together to a wall, and how "that Irishman" had sustained him by his conduct and example. Knowing that he was dying he requested his companion to tell the first Irish person he would meet of his high regard for Ryan and of what they went through together.

The years went by until the Pole entrusted with this task met in London Joe O'Connor, a prominent Republican of the 1940s in Ireland, and later member of the Communist Party and North London District Council of the National Union of Railwaymen. O'Connor brought him to this writer in 1970 and the Polish messenger—who was non-political—told of the task given to him by Joseph Schwartz. He told his story, expressed pleasure that it would be published, and left us satisfied that he had carried out a last bequest.

Chapter 15 Notes

*(1) Keith Feeling, "The Life of Neville Chamberlain" p. 394.
*(2) "Diplomatic Papers" by Count Ciano, edited by Malcolm Muggeridge, London, 1948, pp. 293–94.
*(3) "Spies in Ireland" by Enno Stephan, Four Square Books Edition, London, 1965, p. 143. (Note: This book was first published in the German language under the title, "Geheimauftrag Irland" in 1961 by Gerhard Stalling Verlag, Oldenburg, Hamburg.)
*(4) Anthony, a Labour Party deputy, was expelled from that Party in 1931 for voting in favour of a military tribunal to replace trial by jury.
*(5) ' Report of the proceedings of the 45th Annual Conference of the Irish Trade Union Congress, 1939. p. 185.
*(6) This author wrote them down in longhand, as his words were translated from Spanish into German and then into English by the Irish group's interpreter, Annaliese Ichenhauser.

FROM BURGOS TO DRESDEN

... "If Ireland was to secure its freedom at the expense of the liberty of other peoples, it would deserve for itself all the execration she herself had poured on tyranny throughout the ages" ...

What trail led from Burgos Prison in Franco Spain to the cemetery in Dresden-Loschwitz in Hitler's Germany? The tracing of this route is a complex one as the only information available is from sources that were involved with the Nazis.

The outbreak of World War II in September 1939, found the then leadership of the I.R.A. in contact with the Nazis. The justification advanced for this reactionary association was that it continued the Irish national tradition of regarding always that, "ENGLAND'S DIFFICULTY WAS IRELAND'S OPPORTUNITY." In other words, any enemy of Britain was automatically an ally of Ireland. As well, it was held in relation to the Nazis that there was the predecent of Roger Casement who had gone to the Kaiser's Germany in order to secure arms, and to try and organise a brigade from Irish prisoners of war, members of the British Army, in the First World War.

The contact with the Nazis was through Sean Russell, the then Chief-of-Staff of the I.R.A. In connection with this, he is quoted as saying:

> "I am not a Nazi. I'm not even pro-German. I am an Irishman fighting for the independence of Ireland. The British have been our enemies for hundreds of years. They are the enemy of Germany today. If it suits Germany to give us help to achieve independence I am willing to accept it, but no more, and there must be no strings attached." *(1)

In view of the Nazi objective to dominate all of Europe, this attitude of Russell's was the extreme in naivety*(2) Far more valid, and certainly more Irish, would have been the viewpoint of the patriot Terence McSwiney who asserted that:

> "If Ireland was to secure its freedom at the expense of the liberty of other peoples, it would deserve for itself all the execration she herself had poured out on tyranny throughout the ages."

The illogical relationship between some leading Irish Republicans and the

151

Hitlerites formed the background to the strange situation in which Frank Ryan found himself in Germany during World War II.

Whilst he lay in Burgos Prison fighting back with the only weapon he had, that of his unconquerable spirit, Ryan was unaware that the Nazi Abwehr—of all organisations—was arranging his "escape!"

Enno Stephan*(3) whose book deals in great detail with I.R.A.—Nazi relations, tells the story of two members of the Abwehr who had spent some time in Ireland in 1930. Dr. Jupp Hoven and Helmut Clissman had been there at a time when they were members of the "Young Prussian League" which was regarded as "Nationalbolshevist." In their sojourn in Ireland they mixed in Republican circles in which Frank Ryan was a leading figure. Clissman, in fact, married Elizabeth ('Budge') Mulcahy, member of a well known Sligo Republican family who were close friends of Ryan. According to Stephan, the Nazis during the early days of the war did not regard them as politically reliable, it was only at a later stage were they accepted into the Abwehr.

Whilst Ryan was in Burgos, Hoven*(4) drew the attention of the Abwehr to his position. He succeeded in convincing that organisation that it would make a good impression in Ireland if Ryan was released because of German efforts and, "also that it might be possible to use him to the advantage of Germany in some way or other."*(5) Eventually Admiral Canaris (head of the Abwehr), who had many personal as well as political contacts in Spain (he had operated from there in his naval capacity during the First World War), came to an agreement with his opposite number in the Franco Secret Service to have Ryan handed over to the Germans.

Stephan, quoting Helmut Clissman, said that the Irish Government was informed of this through Senor Champourcin, a Spanish lawyer who had been engaged by the Dublin Government to appear for Ryan at his courtmartial. The lawyer told the Irish ambassador to Spain, "of this one possibility of obtaining release for Ryan who was already ailing. Kerney (the Ambassador) sent a top secret message to Dublin and Eamon de Valera agreed to Ryan's release through the Germans."*(6)

An "escape" was arranged. Ryan was to be transferred from one prison to another, and be given, en route, the opportunity to regain his liberty. As he was totally unaware of what was afoot, he did not try to escape and was taken to the other jail.

Later, however, he was handed over by the Spanish police to the Germans at the French frontier. There was a witness to this operation:

> "Ambassador Kerney, who trusted neither the Spaniards nor the Germans out of his sight, suspected that Ryan's heralded release was nothing more than an attempt to dispose of him secretly in some convenient way. So he stipulated for Ryan's 'escape' and transfer to the Germans at Irun-Rendaye to be observed by Senor Champourcin. Both sides perforce agreed ..."*(7)

The vigilance shown by the Irish Ambassador was undoubtedly to be an important factor in preserving the life of Ryan during his subsequent stay in Nazi Germany. Kerney had maintained regular contact with him in Burgos Prison and he would have been fully aware of Ryan's unrelenting attitude to Nazism, and he naturally feared for him because of this.

Ryan was first taken to Paris and then to Berlin. There, within a period of three weeks, both Sean Russell and he were brought face-to-face without any previous warning. Russell greeted him most heartily. Despite the fact that they had previous serious differences in the Irish Republican Movement, and held different ideological stands, Russell, nevertheless, shared the general esteem in which Ryan was held.

Russell had gone to the U.S.A. in June 1939, to raise funds for the I.R.A. amongst the Irish emigrants there. These were organised by the "Clan na Gael" organisation which for over eight decades had been a finance-supporting movement for the independence struggle at home.

Russell was in Detroit at the same time as the British Royal family were on a state visit to Canada. His presence in a city close to the Canadian border alarmed the U.S. authorities who took him into custody. His arrest created a furore. The Irish-American political lobbyists waged a campaign for his release, and in the U.S. Congress itself there were strong protests, which succeeded in getting him freed on bail.

Later, when he was served with a deportation order, he went "on the run" to evade expulsion. In the meantime, World War II had broken out, and this created a problem for his returning to Ireland. Shipping to Ireland was limited, and taking the route from New York via Britain would have certainly landed him into the hands of the British police. How to get out of the U.S.A. and back to Ireland?

Gerald O'Reilly, Irish-born leader in the Transport Workers Union of America, in a letter to this author*(8) relates: "Sean Russell arrived here and some of the Clann na Gael officers came to Michael Quill (President of the Union) to know if we could help Russell to get to Ireland. Quill spoke to Joe Curran (President of the American National Maritime Union) and following the talk I took Russell down to see one of the officers of the N.M.U., Blackie Myers. Some days afterwards, I was informed Russell sailed to Europe."

O'Reilly was under the impression that he had sailed to Portugal which was neutral in the war. Instead Russell landed in the Italian port of Genoa. There he made contact with the German Foreign Office and arrived in Berlin on May 3rd, 1940. Following discussions with the Nazis arrangements were made to transport him back to Ireland in a U-Boat. He agreed to take Ryan back with him. On August 8th the submarine left Wilhelmshaven under the command of Naval Lieutenant Hans-Joachim von Stockhausen with its two civilian passengers code named, "Richard I" (Russell) and "Richard II" (Ryan).*(9)

During the voyage, Russell became seriously ill with gastric ulcers which burst causing his death on August 14th, when the craft was only 100 miles off Galway on the west coast of Ireland. Russell was buried at sea, and the U-Boat returned, with Ryan, to Germany.

After his less than one-month freedom from Burgos he was back in Germany again. Four months later the Irish Government was informed by the German Foreign Office that he was in their hands. The de Valera Government did not disclose this fact (and to date still has not), one which would have been an important factor in clearing Ryan from later suspicions that he was at the least voluntarily staying with the Nazis, or at the worst collaborating with them.

Certain credence is given to that suspicion by his return on the U-Boat and by statements concerning him later. Thus, Helmut Clissman is quoted in Stephan's book as recounting that he and Ryan were to be landed in Ireland by seaplane in order to set up a telephone exchange that would come into operation if there was resistance to either a British or American takeover of the Irish ports. Ireland, (apart from Northern Ireland which was part of the United Kingdom) was neutral in the World War, because involvement with either side would have created an Irish civil war situation in itself. Both the British and the U.S. exercised considerable pressure on the Dublin Government to allow the use of Irish ports for the protection of their shipping that was then being severely harrassed by German U-Boats.

Clissman is also reported as describing how both of them were involved in trying to get Irishmen serving in the British Army, who were then prisoners of war in Friesack Camp (in Brandenburg Rhin-Luch), to volunteer for a special unit which in the event of an Anglo-American invasion of Ireland would be sent to that country.*(10)

In face of the rumours, speculations and the statements quoted above, the question arises: Did he collaborate with the Nazis? Did this anti-fascist, in the last analysis, behave just as an Irishman influenced by the long standing proposition "that England's difficulty was Ireland's opportunity"? Was he no different from those Indians, Bretons, Flemings and others who were pro-German, without necessarily being pro-Nazi, in Hitler's bloody and vicious attempt to enslave the peoples of Europe?

As regards Ryan being conditioned by Irish patriotic feelings to working with the Nazis, the reader should remember that he had already made clear his attitude to such influences by his statement: "'The Wild Geese' were honest minded men who went out to fight against their country's enemy" but as he pointed out, "Their fate should have forever killed the slogan, 'England's enemy is Ireland's friend!'"*(11)

It should also be remembered that Ryan did not voluntarily go to Nazi Germany—he was taken there. His U-Boat journey with Russell took place only three weeks after his two-and-a-quarter years in prison under unimaginable conditions. He had emerged sick, emaciated and almost completely deaf.*(12) Because of the short time involved and his phyisical condition he could not be privy to any plans of Russell that had been worked out with the Nazis. It is clear that he naturally availed himself of an opportunity to get back to Ireland, and the Nazis let him go because in the viewpoint of Dr. Hoven his return would make, for the Nazis, "a good impression in Ireland."*(13)

Even if Clissman is absolutely correct about Ryan being involved in 1941 in a proposed operation for the setting up of a telephone exchange in Ireland, or about the Friesack prisoners camp recruitment, they were obviously two schemes that presented him with opportunities of returning to Ireland.

In short, was Ryan in the difficult situation in which he found himself using the Nazis rather than the reverse?

In that period he was clearly conversant with the situation in his own country and the conditions that made the Irish Government's policy of neutrality both inevitable and generally acceptable. Despite his political criticisms of de Valera, he was more than capable of taking a positive position on this aspect of neutrality. An indication of this is recorded in Stephan's book referring to his first interrogation in Berlin: "The Germans were impressed not only with Ryan's alert understanding of political matters, but also and above all with the respectful manner in which this Irish 'Red' spoke about his country's political leader, de Valera." (p. 146)

If Ryan had changed his anti-fascist outlook and had agreed to assist the Nazis, the most useful service he could have rendered would have been in the field of propaganda. The Nazis, in view of the country's political and historical relationship to Britain attached great importance to radio-broadcasting to Ireland. The specific geographical proximity of Ireland to Britain also commanded keen Nazi attention particularly in relation to their proposed invasion of Britain, and later in January 1942 when U.S. troops were based in Northern Ireland preparatory to the subsequent allied invasion of Europe.*(14)

All these factors made it both opportune and necessary to beam special radio propaganda broadcasts to Ireland.

There was a special Irish Section of the German Radio which even broadcast daily programmes in the Gaelic language to Ireland. This was under the command of two Celtic language experts, Professor Ludwig Muehlhausen and Dr. Hans Hartmann. Attached to this station as commentators and news readers in English language broadcasts to Ireland were Francis Stuart, John Francis O'Reilly and other Irishmen. It would have been a major propagandist coup if Ryan could have been used to broadcast talks even if these were limited to anti-British statements without any reference to Nazi ideology. His personal prestige and record as a fighter against British imperialism would have made for a big impression on Irish listeners. A subtle presentation of him as a "friend of Germany" would have had even wider effects in other English-speaking countries, particularly in Britain, U.S.A., Canada and Australia with their large Irish emigrant communities. It is in this respect that the Nazis could have certainly made "use of him to the advantage of Germany" as Dr. Hoven advocated when he first put the proposition to the Abwehr that they should take Ryan from his Spanish prison.

At no time did Ryan allow himself to be used in this way.

Although the Irish Government knew all the time that Ryan was in Nazi Germany, they not only suppressed that information, but also by default contributed to a gross misrepresentation of his political character. Enno Stephan writes: "In Ireland the view stubbornly persists that Ryan had allowed himself whilst in Germany to be drawn into treacherous activities against his native land. It seems astounding that the Irish Government has up to now done nothing to rehabilitate Franco's one-time prisoner." (p. 204).

With reference to this statement, John Peet, editor, "Democratic German Report" in a letter to this author, dated December 14th, 1973, wrote that: "One thing I have done was to compare the English translation of 'Spies in Ireland' with the German original. The most notable fact is that the translation is extremely good, and almost pedantically full, scarcely missing out an adjective. In view of this, one short omission in the English edition may be significant. The original German edition runs as follows:

'It seems astounding that the Irish government has up to now done nothing to rehabilitate Franco's one-time prisoner, *although it (the Irish Government) could have contributed something to this theme.*'

It is not without interest also, as Peet points out, that "Nicklaus Ritter (cover name, Dr. Rantzau) who dealt with Irish affairs in Hamburg has just published a book on his intelligence work but omits all mention of Ryan."

The evidence establishes that Ryan found himself in Germany, neither as a captive anti-fascist nor as an invited voluntary collaborator—but in an unique category. Far from suffering the fate of other opponents of fascism, German and International, who were put into the concentration camps, the gas chambers or before the firing squads, he in fact was allowed to live privately with the Clissmans.

Such exceptional conditions were possible because the Nazis would have been constrained in their treatment of him, wooing, as they did, the Irish Republican movement in which he was regarded as a popular figure and intrepid fighter. There was also the fact that the Irish Government knew of his presence there, and the vigilant concern by the Irish diplomat Kerney created strong protection for his safety. In spite of political differences any action against Ryan would have been considered as a grossly unfriendly act. This would be so not only because he was an Irish citizen, but also because many of the members of the Dublin Government had relations of personal friendship with him. These had been forged in the struggle against the British in 1920, in the fight against the Cosgrave administration in the Irish Civil War and the later broad election alliances of 1932–33. Although he and they had parted politically in the following years his personality was such as to retain many of these former political and personal friendships.

Gerald O'Reilly, who perhaps more than anyone else was able, through Ambassador Kerney, to maintain contact with Ryan in Burgos Prison, recalled in a letter to this writer, (November 21st, 1968) receiving letters from him in December 1940, that is at a time when Ryan was already five months in Berlin. In his own letter, O'Reilly summed up his opinion on his friend's conduct there when he stated: "It has often been implied that the Hitler people must have used him for propaganda, which we know is absolutely untrue."

In the special situation in which he found himself in Germany how did he react? Helmut Clissman relates that: "In Germany Ryan regarded himself as a stranger. He hardly came into contact with the Nazis. In addition, his deafness saved him a good deal. Ryan consistently emphasised his independence ... Like all deaf people, Ryan was extremely suspicious. He was extremely sensitive about German propaganda, and after the outbreak of war with the Soviet Union, sneered at newspaper reports which spoke of hundreds of thousands of prisoners taken in the great encirclement battles. So many prisoners, he thought, could not be taken."*(15)

Francis Stuart (the Irish writer and one-time I.R.A. member in the twenties) who before the war went to Germany to take up an academic post and later to work on the Nazi Radio, had made the acquaintance of Ryan in Dublin years before met him now in Berlin. Stuart in his recollections wrote in 1950: "Although I find it difficult to recall Frank speaking about the war in a general sense certain aspects of it he commented bitterly on. Perhaps it was too close to us, at the time I am telling of, for there to be much room for theorising. It was a horror to be got through from day to day, sometimes from hour to hour. I remember walking down a street with Frank and his giving that characteristic emphatic nod of his towards some headlines on a newsstall: *Terrorangriffe auf deutsche Städte*—Terror raids on German towns. 'Now it's terror attacks,' he said 'when they began it was something different'."*(16)

In January 1943, the toll of the Franco imprisonment caused a serious breakdown in his health. He had an apoplectic fit and endured much pain until his death in Dresden on June 10th 1944. There the Clissmans (who evidently showed much kindness to him during his involuntary stay in Germany) buried him. Over his grave Elizabeth Clissman (Mulcahy) placed a wooden cross with the name Francis Richard and below that his correct name in the Gaelic language—Prionnsias O'Riain.

He had fought a long hard fight. The closing stages of his life would have indeed been brightened if he had known that in a few short years after his death, the grave in which he now lies would be in the territory of a new German state of workers and small farmers. A state in whose construction there participated former comrades of his in the International Brigades, such as Ludwig Renn (Commander of the "Thaelmann Battalion" in Madrid), Franz Dahlem, Hans Kahle and Heinz Hoffman, the present Minister for Defence of the German Democratic Republic.

He lies in friendly and fraternal soil now, but someday he will come back to the Ireland he loved—this patriot and internationalist, gay companion and uncompromising and unconquerable soldier of the wars for human liberation.

His name lives on in Ireland. The years have failed to dim his image in the memories of all who knew him in one way or the other. Indicative of this were the words penned in 1969 by the columnist, W.A. Newman*(17 "There never was a patriot more dedicated than Frank Ryan. There certainly was none of our time more consistent in his vision of a new Ireland, or who joined with that vision a truer sense of democracy ... He was the most likeable person, that big, raw-boned fellow; and over the years since he died I have never met anybody, even among those who heartily damned his Socialist principles, who did not think well of him or rejoice in having made his acquaintance ... His appeal lay, I think, in his great gentleness, contrasting so unusually with his big rugged frame and face. In that quality of gentleness he was of the same order as people who knew both men have told me, with Sean Mac Diarmada*(18)—concerning whom you will doubtless remember Seamus O'Sullivan's lovely poem."

Perhaps the most eloquent tribute paid to Ryan was in August 1973 when an Irish Youth delegation (114 of whom were in Berlin for the 10th World Festival of Youth and Students) went to his grave in Dresden and laid floral tributes as they held a commemorative ceremony at which spoke Arno Hering, formerly of the XI (German) International Brigade.*(19)

Chapter 16 notes

*(1) Reported in the "Irish Times," June 5th, 1958 as having been said by Russell to Lieutenant-Colonel Lahousen, the chief of the Nazi Abwehr (Intelligence Service) section dealing with anti-Allied groups in other countries. Whether this is true or not, it can be taken as a fair reflection of Russell's attitude to the Nazis.

*(2) A similar illusion existed amongst many Indian nationalists. A "Asad Hind" (Free India) legion was formed in Germany. "The unit was sponsored by the Nazi Intelligence service, but many of the Indians who served in the "Asad Hind" wanted to harm British imperialism rather than help German imperialism ... there was an anti-Nazi mutiny in the Legion in Konigsbruck Camp in 1944. More than 50 of the members of the 'Asad Hind' are known to be implicated, of whom ten were immediately shot by the Nazis, and 40 more placed on trial." (from "Democratic German Report" Berlin DDR October 6th, 1971).

*(3) "Spies in Ireland" (Four Square Books Edition) Chpter 12.

*(4) Hoven's real name was Victor Hoven, born in 1909, who became towards the end of his life a Free Democratic Party, M.P. in the West German Bundestag. He died in October 1971.

*(5) "Spies in Ireland" pp. 143—144.

*(6) Ibid.

*(7) Ibid. p. 144.

*(8) November 2lst, 1968.

*(9) Ryan during his subsequent stay in Germany was known as Francis Richard, and it is under this name he was buried in Dresden-Loschwitz.

*(10) "Spies in Ireland" pp. 214—17.

*(11) From his letter quoted on p. 153 of this manuscript.

*(12) "Spies in Ireland" p. 143.

*(13) "Spies in Ireland" p. 143.

*(14) The degree of Nazi interest in Ireland was shown in the appointment by the Foreign Minister, Von Ribbentrop, in 1940 of Dr. Edmund Veesenmayer as his Special Representative for Ireland. It was Veesenmayer who interviewed Ryan on the first day he was brought from Spain, via Paris, to Berlin. Veesenmayer according to Enno Stephan (p. 93), "had the reputation of a shrewd and dangerous man." In 1944 he was appointed Nazi Ambassador to Hungary. On April 14th, 1949 he was sentenced to 20 years imprisonment by a U.S. military court in Nuremberg for war crimes, including the "brutal and inhuman deportation of 150,000 Hungarian Jews." (Keessing's Contemporary Archives, Vol. 1948—50, p. 10759). In December 1951, the U.S. authorities pardoned and released him.

*(15) "Spies in Ireland" p. 204

*(16) "Frank Ryan in Germany" by Francis Stuart, 'The Bell' Vol. XVI. No. 2 November 1950 pp. 37—42.

*(17) "Why not bring Home Frank Ryan?," Irish Press, July 24th, 1969.

*(18) Sean Mac Diarmada, one of the Irish Rising Leaders, was executed with James Connolly on May 12th, 1916.

*(19) This Youth Festival (July 28-August 6th) in Berlin was attended by 25,000 young people from 140 couhtries as well as 300,000 youth from the German Democratic Republic itself. The Irish delegation was comprised of members of the Connolly Youth Movement, Sinn Fein, Communist Party of Ireland, Union of Students in Ireland, Young Liberals, National Federation of Youth Clubs, Irish Union of School Students, St. Gabriel's Youth Club, delegates from the Northern Ireland Civil Rights Association, Amalgamated Transport & General Workers Union, and the Automobile General Engineering and Mechanical Operatives Union. "A highlight of the Festival for us, and a very moving experience, was the visit to Dresden where a wreath was laid on the grave of Frank Ryan, the great Irish Revolutionary and Internationalist ... One great result of our visit was that the local members of the FDJ—Free German Youth—in Dresden have pledged that through their own work they wjll raise the money to build a fitting memorial to this great fighter for the peoples' cause."—from "Forward", organ of the Connolly Youth Movement, 37, Pembroke Lane, Dublin, September 1973.

EPILOGUE

Four decades and one year have passed since Gaelic-speaking Tommy Patton of Achill fell outside Madrid. He died in battle at a time when his own country resounded with a tumult of support for Franço and with opposition to a people who, with inadequate arms, strove to make Madrid, "the tomb of Fascism." Had they performed that stupendous task, and they could have, the world could have been spared the horrors, suffering and mass extermina-tions of the subsequent Fascist-unleashed World War II. They did not suc-ceed. Franco with the help of Hitler and Mussolini triumphed. From 1939 to his death in 1976 he ruled Spain with bloody hands. In the post-war period he was helped by the U.S.A. who propped up the economy in return for war bases.

Franco seized power by brutal force and maintained it in the same fash-ion. The Army was his base with its some 500 Generals and 30,000 Officers in a total complement of 150,000. The armed police, both public and secret, and the para—military Guardia Civil were his main task force against the people. "That the police were organised after the Gestapo model, with Himmler paying a special visit to Madrid to supervise its formation has now been conveniently forgotten."*(1) The jails were always full. There were many others beside Fabricano Rojel, the cell companion of Frank Ryan, who served over 22 years imprisonment. Thirty years after the Generals' Revolt, the Information Agency, "Democratic Spain" (August 24th, 1966) could report that the Franco Government was even refusing to release prisoners who had served their sentences, citing such cases as . . . "Jose Satue, 61 years old who had been in prison for 19 years; Benigno Lorenzo, who had served a total of 26 years, 19 of them without interval."

Some two years after the victorious entry of the Fascist forces into Madrid, the very same type weapons—"Mexicanski" rifles, Dyegtyaryov light machine guns and heavy Maxims—that had been used by the Internatio-nal Brigades were brought into action again by ill-prepared Red Armymen, at the Brest Fortress in 1941, in the attempt to throw back the first stage of the Nazi blitz invasion of their country. This was the harbinger of the eventual crushing of the hitherto invincible army of Hitler Fascism.

From that, at a terrible cost in Soviet lives, came a Europe with new Socialist states, and strengthened movements of the working people in its capitalist countries. The Socialist states included the first workers' and peasants' state in Germany where lies the mortal remains of Frank Ryan. That German Democratic Republic, since its foundation in 1949, carried out consistent solidarity with the anti-fascist fighters in Franco Spain. Prominent in that work were the surviving volunteers of the "Thaelmann Battalion" in the "Komitee der Antifaschistischen Widerstandskämpfer der DDR" (Com-mittee of Anti-Fascist Resistance Fighters of the G.D.R.).

Today after years of heroic underground struggle the inspirer and organiser of the defence of Madrid in 1936, the Communist Party of Spain, is once again a legal political party. Free elections have replaced the dictatorship and Communist deputies sit in the Cortes.

That the change in the world balance of forces initiated by the victory of the 1917 Soviet Revolution (which the Fascists had hoped to "celebrate" in Madrid on the occasion of its 19th anniversary) was indeed further developed by the victory of the Soviet Army in Berlin in May 1945, and has now grown into a world revolutionary process, with ever growing momentum, as has been clearly established in recent years.

38 years after the last surviving International Brigader left Spain the new scope and power of proletarian internationalism was demonstrated by the Soviet Union in the case of new areas of struggle on the African continent. The strengthened force of internationalism was highlighted by the moving and effective actions of volunteers from Cuba in Angola. They continued the internationalist struggle of Pablo de la Torriente Brau (later declared a national hero of Cuba) who fell at Majadahonda, December 19th, 1936 and of whom his fellow Cuban Brigader, Miguel Hernandez, wrote:

"Pass before the noble Cuban/men of his brigade/with furious rifles/irate boots and clenched fists made."

With the passing of time in Ireland the inflamatory speeches of Eoin O'Duffy, Paddy Belton, the Professors Michael Tierney, James Hogan and Alfred O'Rahilly receded hollowly, forgotten by the generation that were incited by them. They are unknown to the youth of today, whilst the representative organisation, the Connolly Youth Movement, has commemorated the dead of "The Connolly Column."

However, the same forces that produced the "Irish Christian Front" and "O'Duffy's Brigade" continued to be a powerful element in Irish politics. From 1973 until 1977, the Fine Gael Party—of which O'Duffy was elected leader in 1933—was the dominant party in a Coalition Government with the Irish Labour Party(!). Fine Gael's 1973 election-victory rally was a heady event with some of the audience giving the old "Blueshirt" fascist salute. Its later—second generation—leadership contains many old familar names, viz. Cosgrave, O'Higgins, Costello, Dockrell. There is even a Paddy Belton. The unnatural political and governmental alliance of the Irish Labour Party with Fine Gael brought out, once again, some of the traits that characterised the weakness of the Labour Party during the pro-Franco campaigns of the thirties ... A later day Roddy Connolly co-chairing a joint Fine Gael meeting in support of the Presidential candidature of Tom O'Higgins, one time "Blueshirt" ... Labour Deputy Sean Tracey in Madrid in 1976 congratulating the Francoists on the occasion of the anniversary of their take-over of Republican Spain's capital.

In September 1971, there occured a significant event in Spain which went almost unnoticed in Ireland. This was the National Assembly of Bishops and Priests, in Madrid, which was attended by 285 clergymen including 80 Bishops and Archbishops. They discussed a motion on the role of the Catholic Church in 1936–1939 which read: "We humbly recognise, and ask pardon for, the fact that at the proper time we did not know how to be true ministers of reconciliation in the heart of our people, when it was divided by a war between brothers." A long debate took place on that motion which received 137 votes with 78 against. As yet there has been no corresponding "recognition" expressed by those Irish ecclesiastical forces who fully supported Franco. Despite the continuation of a strong reactionary strain in Irish politics, nevertheless, there is now, after a gap of so many long years, a growing appreciation of why Irishmen died fighting Francoism. There is now a deeper understanding of the vital connection between the cause of Irish independence and social progress, and the battles that were fought in Spain, Indo-China and Angola, with those being waged in Chile, South Africa, Rhodesia and elsewhere, and the struggles yet to come which, as in the past, will need to be assisted by the appropriate form of internationalist solidarity.

The greatest contribution to the development of such an understanding was made by those Irish patriotic-internationalists whose unmarked graves lie from Boadilla del Monte to the banks of the Rio Ebro and its surrounding sierras.

> ... "Write of the twilight whence we came,
> Of countless battles which we fought,
> Write of the hunter and the game,
> Write of the days that went to nought.
>
> Write of the risings without hope,
> Of Connolly and Ferrer sing,*(2)
> Sing of the bullet and the rope,
> Of Warsaw, Cork and Ottakring.
>
> Sing how, like equinoctial waves
> We fell and rose against the stones,
> How fruitful laps were our graves,
> How fertile dust were our bones.
>
> Write that from every new defeat
> We turned like shadows from the light,
> Until the circle was complete,
> Until the sun was at its height.
> Until we knew how strong we were!
> The laughing locksmith broke the gate ...
>
> Here they come, here they come,
> Without bugle, without drum,
> They have gone as they came,
> I write a new song in their name." *(3)

Michael O'Riordan
Dublin, December 1977.

Chapter 17 notes

*(1)   "The Times," London, August 10th, 1966

*(2)   Francisco Ferrer, a Catalan rationalist-educationalist in the early part of this century, who established the "Escuela Moderna" in Barcelona. A thorn in the side of the Spanish authorities, he was shot in 1909.

*(3)   From the poem, "The Burning River" by David Martin. Fore Publications Ltd. 28/29 Southampton Street, London, March 1944. (David Martin, today a prominent Australian writer, born Ludwig Detsinyi in Hungary, served with the Lincoln Battalion.)

ROLL OF HONOUR OF IRISHMEN WHO FELL IN ACTION IN SPAIN

William Barry (Melbourne-Dublin)	— Boadilla del Monte — December, 1936.
William Beattie (Belfast)	— Brunete — July, 1937.
Michael Blaser-Browne (New York)	— Jarama — February, 1937.
Henry Bonar (Dublin)	— Cordova — December, 1936.
Hugh Bonar (Donegal)	— Jarama — February, 1937.
Danny Boyle (Belfast)	— Jarama — February, 1937.
George Browne (Manchester-Killkenny)	— Brunete — July, 1937.
T. Burke	— Brunete — July, 1937.
Denis Coady (Dublin)	— Las Rosas — January, 1937.
Frank Conroy (Kildare)	— Cordova — December, 1936.
Kit Conway (Tipperary)	— Jarama — February, 1937.
Pat Curley	— Jarama — February, 1937.
Peter Daly (Enniscorthy)	— Quinto — August, 1937.
William Davis (Dublin)	— Brunete — July, 1937.
John Dolan	— Jarama — February, 1937.
Charlie Donnelly (Tyrone)	— Jarama — February, 1937.
Tom Donavan (Skibereen)	— Aragon — March, 1938.
Jim Foley (Dublin)	— Cordova — December, 1936.
Tony Fox (Dublin)	— Cordova — December, 1936.
W.H. Fox (Dublin)	— Bruneta — July, 1937.
P. Glacken (Donegal)	— Teruel — January, 1938.
George Gorman (Derry)	— Ebro — July, 1938.
Leo Green (Dublin)	— Cordova — December, 1936.
Bill Henry (Belfast)	— Jarama — February, 1937.
Robert M. Hilliard (Killarney)	— Jarama — February, 1937.
Jack Jones (Wexford)	— Ebro — July, 1938.
J. Kelly (Roscommon)	— Brunete — July, 1937.

Michael Kelly (Ballinasloe)	— Brunete — July, 1937.
Thomas Kerr (Belfast)	— Barcelona — August, 1938.
Samuel Lee (London-Jewish)	— Jarama — February, 1937.
William Laughran (Belfast)	— Brunete — July, 1937.
Thomas Lynch (Dublin)	— Aragon — March, 1938.
Michael May (Dublin)	— Cordova — December, 1936.
John Meehan (Galway)	— Cordova — December, 1936.
Ben Murray (Belfast)	— Aragon — March, 1938.
Joe Murray (Antrim)	— Aragon — August, 1937.
Thomas Morris (Boston)	— Jarama — February, 1937.
Paddy McDaid (Dublin)	— Jarama — February, 1937.
Bert McElroy	— Jarama — February, 1937.
Liam McGregor (Dublin)	— Ebro — September, 1938.
Eamon McGrotty (Derry)	— Jarama — February, 1937.
Jack Nalty (Dublin)	— Ebro — September, 1938.
Michael Nolan (Dublin)	— Cordova — December, 1936.
Francis (Duffy) O'Brien (Dundalk)	— Teruel — January, 1938.
Thomas T. O'Brien	— Jarama — February, 1937.
Dick O'Neill (Belfast)	— Jarama — February, 1937.
Paddy Stuart O'Neill (Vancouver)	— Brunete — July, 1937.
Johnny Riordan (London)	— Aragon — March, 1938.
Paddy O'Sullivan (Dublin)	— Ebro — August, 1938.
Tommy Patton (Achill)	— Madrid — December, 1936.
Maurice Quinlan (Waterford)	— Jarama — February, 1937.
Charles Regan	— Belchite — August, 1937.
Michael Russell (Ennis)	— Jarama — February, 1937.
Maurice Ryan (Tipperary)	— Ebro — August, 1938.
James Straney (Belfast)	— Ebro — July, 1938.
Liam Tumilson (Belfast)	— Jarama — February, 1937.
David Walshe (Ballina)	— Teruel — January, 1938.
Tommy Woods (Dublin)	— Cordova — December, 1936.
Jim Woulfe (Limerick)	— Aragon — August, 1937.

Michael Lehane (Kilgarvan): Killed at sea with Norwegian Merchant Navy 1942.
Frank Ryan: Died from effects of imprisonment, June 1944.

LIST OF IRISH SURVIVORS OF THE INTERNATIONAL BRIGADES

Victor Barr (Belfast)
Paddy Barry (Mayo)
James J. Beirne (Cavan)
Kevin Blake (Dublin)
Phil Boyle (Donegal)
Peter Brady (Cavan)
Michael Brennan (Killkenny)
Liam Burgess (Mallow)
Paul Burns (Boston)
Paddy Byrne (Dublin)
Jimmy Carroll (Liverpool)
Charles Colman (Cork)
Column Cox (Dublin)
Seamus Cummins (Dublin)
Alec Digges (Dublin)
Gerry Doran (Dublin)
Eugene Dowling (Dublin)
Sean Dowling (Castlecomer)
Bob Doyle (Dublin)
Patrick Duff (Dublin)
Frank Edwards (Waterford)
Andrew Flanagan (Roscommon)
Terence Flanagan (Dublin)
Sean Goff (Dublin)
Pat Hamill (New York)
James Haughey (Lurgan)
P. C. Haydock (New York)
T. Hayes (Dublin)
Tom Heeney (Galway)

James Hillen (Belfast)
Denis Holden (Carlow)
John Hunt (Waterford)
Hugh Hunter (Belfast)
P. Keenan (Dublin)
John Kelley (Waterford)
Steve Kenny (Belfast)
J. Larmour (Belfast)
John Lemon (Waterford)
Maurice Levitas (Dublin)
Pat Long (New York)
Joe Lowry (Antrim)
Chris Martin (Cork)
John McAleenan (Down)
Paddy McIlroy (Dublin)
Alan MacLarnan (Dublin)
Paddy Roe McLaughlin (Donegal)
Joe Monks (Dublin)
Paddy Murphy
Pat Murphy (Liverpool)
Tom Murphy (Liverpool)
Pat Murray (Liverpool)
Tom O'Brien (Dublin)
Peter O'Connor (Waterford)
Patrick O'Daire (Donegal)
H. O'Donnell (Donegal)
Vincent O'Donnell (Donegal)
J. O'Driscoll (Cork)
Pat McGrath (Cork)

Frank O'Flaherty (Boston)
Eddie O'Flaherty (Boston)
Charlie O'Flaherty (Boston)
Liam O'Hanlon (Belfast)
James F. O'Regan (Cork)
Donal O'Reilly (Dublin)
Michael O'Riordan (Cork)
John O'Shea (Kilmeadan)
Sean Penrose (Dublin)
John Power (Waterford)
Paddy Power (Waterford)
Billy Power (Waterford)
Jim Prendergast (Dublin)
Jim Regan (Cork)

Joseph P. Rehill (New York)
Pat Reid (U.S.A.)
John Quigley Robinson (Belfast)
M. Roe (Athlone)
Paddy Scanlan (Cork)
Bill Scott (Dublin)
John Patrick Simms (Tipperary)
Paddy Smith (Dublin)
Patrick Stanley (Dublin)
J. Tierney (Limerick)
Pat Tighe (Mayo)
Michael Waters (Cork)
Joe Whelan (New York)

CHAPTER HEADINGS

Chapter I.

"Los Cuatro Generales" (The Four Generals)—Franco, Mola, Queipo de Llano and Varela—from the song...

...

"Los Cuatro Generales,	The Four Insurgent Generals,
Los Cuatro Generales,	The Four Insurgent Generals,
Los Cuatro Generales,	The Four Insurgent Generals,
Que se han alzado,	They tried to betray us,
Mamita Mia."	Little Mother of mine.
"Para la Nochebuena,	On a holy Christmas evening,
Para la Nochebuena,	On a holy Christmas evening,
Para la Nochebuena,	On a holy Christmas evening,
Seran ahorcados,	They all will be hanging,
Mamita Mia."	Little Mother of mine.
"Madrid, que bien resistes,	Madrid, you wondrous city,
Madrid, que bien resistes,	Madrid, you wondrous city,
Madrid, que bien resistes,	Madrid, you wondrous city,
Los Bombardeos,	They wanted to take you,
Mamita Mia."	Little Mother of mine.

Chapter 2.

The first and fourth verse of the poem, "The Citizen Army" by Liam MacGabhann, Dublin. The second, third and concluding verses are as follows: —

2/ The Citizen Army is out today and if you wonder why,
   Jim Larkin came this way to nail the bosses' lie,
   That the iron gyves on their limbs and lives would crush
      them till they die,
   Those women and kids whose tears are hid as the strikers
      go marching by.
   The docker and carter and heaver of coal, were only the
      backwash then,
   Till Larkin built the union up and the bosses feared again.
   From the old North Wall to Liberty Hall came the deadline
      of unskilled,
   In a new-born fight for the workers' rights, that the bosses
      thought they had killed.

3/ The Citizen Army is out today and if you wonder why,
   Go ask the troops in the master's pay if the blood on their
      guns be dry.

Ah, well, they won, and the baton and gun have swung where
    the dead men lie,
For the women and kids whose tears are hid as the wounded
    go stumbling by.
Jim Connolly watches ships go out through flags at Kingstown Pier,
And starving Dublin sends its toll of Guard and Fusilier,
Food for the guns that over the world have thundered
    murder's peal,
And Dublin's broken union men die first in Flanders fields.

5/ The Citizen Army is out today and if you wonder why,
    Go ask the lords of the banking house if their cash returns
      be high,
    For they are there and we are here, and a fight to the knife
      again,
    The Citizen Army is out today; come, workers, are ye men?

Chapter 3.

The third verse of "BE MODERATE" by James Connolly. The others are:—

1/ Some men, faint-hearted, ever seek
    Our programme to retouch,
    And will insist, when'er they speak
    That we demand too much.
    Tis passing strange, yet I declare
    Such statements cause me mirth,
    For our demands most modest are,
    We only want THE EARTH.

2/ "Be moderate," the trimmers cry,
    Who dread the tyrant's thunder,
   "You ask too much and people fly
    From you aghast in wonder."
   "Tis passing strange, for I declare
    Such statements give me mirth,
    For our demands most modest are,
    We only want THE EARTH.

4/ The "Labour Fakir", full of guile,
    Base doctrine ever preaches,
    And while he bleeds the rank and file
    Tame moderation teaches.
    Yet in his despite, we'll see the day
    When with sword in its girth,
    Labour shall march in war array
    To seize its own, THE EARTH.

5/ For Labour long, with sighs and tears,
    To its oppressors knelt,
    But never yet, to aught save fears,
    Did heart of tyrant melt.
    We need not kneel, our cause is high
    Of true men there's no dearth,
    And our victorious rallying cry
    Shall be "WE WANT THE EARTH."

From "Die THAELMANKOLONNE" (The Thaelmann Column), the song of the first German anti-fascists in Madrid. The text was written by Karl Ernst and the music by Peter Daniel (Paul Dessau).

. . .

1/ Spaniens Himmel breitet seine Sterne,·
   Über unsre Schützengräben aus.
   Und der Morgen grüsst schon aus der Ferne,
   Bald geht es zum neuen Kampf hinaus.

   Spanish heavens spread their brilliant starlight
   High above our trenches in the plain;
   From the distance morning comes to greet us,
   Calling us to battle once again.

   Chorus.

Die Heimat ist weit,	Far off is our land,
Doch wir sind bereit.	Yet ready we stand,
Wir kämpfen und siegen für dich:	We're fighting and winning
Freiheit!	for you—Freedom!

2/ Dem Faschisten werden wir
     nicht weichen,
	We'll not yield a foot to Franco's
	     fascists,

Schickt er auch die Kugeln
     hageldicht
	Even though the bullets fall like
	     sleet.

Mit uns stehn Kameraden
     ohnegleichen
	With us stand those peerless
	     men, our comrades,

Und ein Rückwärts gibt es für uns nicht.	And for us there can be no retreat.

3/ Rührt die Trommel!
     Fällt die Bajonette!
	Beat the drums! Ready!
	     Bayonets, charge!

Vorwärts marsch!
     Der Sieg ist unser Lohn!
	Forward march!
	     Victory our reward!

Mit der roten Fahne!
     Brecht die Kette!
	With our scarlet banner!
	     Smash their column!

Auf zum Kampf
     das Thälmann Bataillon!
	Thaelmann Battalion!
	     Ready, forward march!

Chapter 5.

"An t-Internasionale" the first-ever translation into the Irish (Gaelic) language of the "Internationale." It was done, at this writer's request, by the famous Gaelic scholar, Mairtin O'Cadhain, in the Curragh Internment Camp, Ireland, July, 1941.

Chapter 6.

The poem "The Tolerance of Crows" by Charles Donnelly, published in "Ireland To-day", Vol, No. 2. February 1937. The author was killed in Jarama on February 26th, 1937.

The chorus of the ballad "Man of Men" by Dominic Behan. Sung to the air of "Brennan on the Moor", it was published in the "Irish Workers' Voice," Dublin, June 1955.

1/ There lies a page in history,
   When workers first fought back,
   And the might of exploitation
   At last began to crack.

Chorus
   For Connolly was there,
   Connolly was there,
   Great, brave, undaunted,
   James Connolly was there.

2/ When the bosses tried to sweat the men,
   Away on Glasgow's Clyde,
   A voice like rolling thunder,
   Soon stopped them in their stride.

3/ And then in Belfast city
   The workers lived in hell,
   Until at last they organised,
   And all the world can tell.

4/ To smash the Dublin unions,
   The scabs they did enlist,
   But all their graft was shattered
   By a scarlet iron fist.

5/ They say that he was murdered,
   Shot, dying, in a chair,
   But go, march on to freedom,
   Irish workers don't despair.

   For Connolly will be there,
   Connolly will be there,
   Great, brave, undaunted,
   James Connolly will be there.

Chapter 8 & 9.

From the International Brigade song; VIVA LA QUINCE BRIGADA (Long Live the Fifteenth Brigade):—

. . .

1/ Viva la Quince Brigada,
   Rúmbala, rúmbala, rúm-ba-la,
   Rúmbala, rúmbala, rúm-ba-la.

2/ Que se ha cubierta de gloria,
   Ay Mañuela, ay Mañuela!
   Ay Mañuela, ay Mañuela!

3/ Luchamos contra los Moros,

Rúmbala, rúmbala, rúm-ba-la,
Rúmbala, rúmbala, rúm-ba-la.

4/ Mercenarios y fascistas,
Ay Mañuela, ay Mañuela!
Ay Mañuela, ay Mañuela!

5/ Solo es nuestro deseo
Rúmbala, rúmbala, rúm-ba-la,
Rúmbala, rúmbala, rúm-ba-la.

6/ Acabar con el fascismo,
Ay Mañuela, ay Mañuela!
Ay Mañuela, ay Mañuela!

7/ En los frentes de Jarama,
Rúmbala, rúmbala, rúm-ba-la,
Rúmbala, rúmbala, rúm-ba-la.

8/ No tenemos ni aviones,
Ni tanques, ni cañones, ay Mañuela!
Ni tanques, ni cañones, ay Mañuela!

9/ Ya salimos de España,
Rúmbala, rúmbala, rúm-ba-la,
Rúmbala, rúmbala, rúm-ba-la.

10/ Para luchar en otros frentes,
Ay Mañuela, ay Mañuela!
Ay Mañuela, ay Mañuela!

Chapter 10.

From the Manifesto of the wounded members of the Irish Unit, published in full, pp. 102—104 of this manuscript.

Chapter 12.

From the old Irish national-revolutionary ballad, "The Felons of Our Land." (by Arthur M. Forrester):

1/ Fill up once more, we'll drink a toast
To comrades far away;
No nation upon earth can boast
Of braver hearts than they.
And though they sleep in dungeons deep,
Or flee, outlawed and banned,
We love them yet, we can't forget
The felons of our Land.

2/ In boyhood's bloom and manhood's pride,
Foredoomed by alien laws,
Some on the scaffold proudly died
For holy Ireland's cause.
And, brothers, say, shall we to-day

Unmoved, like cowards stand?
When traitors shame and foes defame
The felons of our land.

3/ Some in the convict's dreary cell
Have found a living tomb,
And some unseen, unfriended fell
Within the dungeon's gloom.
Yet, what care we, although it be
Trod by a ruffian band—
God bless the clay where rest to-day
The felons of our land.

4/ Let cowards mock and tyrants frown,
Ah little do we care!
A felon's cap's the noblest crown
An Irish head can wear.
And every Gael in Inisfail
Who scorns the serf's vile brand,
From Lee to Boyne, would gladly join
The felons of our land.

Chapter 16.

Terence McSwiney; from his book "Principles of Freedom."

INSURRECTIONARY WARFARE

by James Connolly

(These articles were originally published in the "Workers' Republic", Dublin in 1915. They were republished in booklet form by New Books Publications in 1968 with an introduction by Michael O'Riordan. The full text of the booklet is reproduced below.)

INTRODUCTION

When a group of strikers, armed only with hurley-sticks, protectively flanked the Fintan Lalor Pipers' Band in the workers' parades in Dublin during the Great Lock-Out in 1913, they provided not only an effective bodyguard against the vicious "baton-happy" Dublin Metropolitan Police, they also laid the basis for the first Workers' Army in the western area of Europe in this century.

Beginning as a workers' defence corps, the Irish Citizen Army developed with an intensity equal to the fierceness of that great industrial struggle that split the capital city of Ireland into workers and their supporters on one side and, on the other, the combined forces of the Irish capitalist class, the British imperial state machine, and the Church.

The Great Lock-Out imposed a terrible ordeal on the workers, which was endured heroically and militantly by them. The end of the months' long struggle naturally affected the membership of the Citizen Army. After 1913, its parades became less frequent and its roll calls found less responses.

James Connolly, however, had other ideas even at the height of the 1913 struggle about the I.C.A. being just a *defensive* body. In March 1914, he began to reorganise it as an *offensive* force.

On the issue of the use of force he had a very clear attitude: "We believe" he wrote, "in constitutional action in normal times; we believe in revolutionary action in exceptional times." The period in which the meeting was called to revive and develop the I.C.A. was certainly far from normal; ten days previously, there had occurred the revolt of the Carson-led landlords in the North and the reactionary Officers' mutiny at the Curragh of March 12th. An even sharper compelling reason was the clear evidence of an impending war between the imperialist powers, led by Britain on one side and Germany on the other.

In those conditions, Connolly, the working man, with the versatility to be a historian, economist, student of literature, poet and song writer, playwright, municipal candidate, trade union organiser, street corner orator and a journalist, capable of printing his own paper, began to develop another talent as a student of military science. The allround revolutionary had long seen the need to master all forms of struggle. Consequently, he applied himself to what he considered to be a pressing activity in the situation when he published the first of his military articles in the paper, "Workers' Republic," May 1915.

In his articles, he makes it clear that it was not his purpose to deal in detail with the political circumstances of the various armed actions that range from street fighting in Paris, Moscow and Brussels to ambushes in the Tyrol mountains. Emphasising the military factors, he was contented to point out the need for "a knowledge of how brave men and women, have, at other times and in other places, overcome difficulties and achieved something for a cause held to be sacred."

The Great Imperialist War had broken out nine months previous to the publication of the first article. That outbreak was a touchstone for all who called themselves socialists. The majority of the socialist leadership in Europe had failed the test with some noteworthy, honourable exceptions, like Karl Liebknecht, Rosa Luxemburg, Willie Gallacher and the Bolsheviks in Russia.

Connolly, like Lenin, had no ambiguity about his attitude to the imperialist war. Four days after the declaration of war by Britain, he wrote in an article headed, "Our Duty in This Crisis":

"Should the working class of Europe rather than slaughter the benefit of kings and financiers, proceed to-morrow to erect barricades all over Europe, to break up bridges and destroy the transport service that war might be abolished, we should be perfectly justified in following such a glorious example and contributing our aid to the final dethronement of the vulture classes that rob and rule the world." ("Irish Worker," August 8th, 1914.)

To Connolly, the Marxist, it was clear, as it was to Clausewitz, the military theorist, that war whether it was on a national or international scale was simply the continuation of politics by other means. Hence the development of Connolly, in that situation, as a revolutionary military specialist.

How did he succeed in mastering his subject so well?

There is the belief that at the age of 14 years he was driven by economic pressure, like so many others, to join the British Army, and that he enlisted in the King's Liverpool Regiment in 1882. If this was so, his army experience, far from being an asset, would have been more likely to be a disadvantage in the pursuit of revolutionary military knowledge. The British Army training at that period would have laid emphasis on mechanical, foot and arms drill; marching and counter-marching; close formation and frontal assault; the insistence on "spit and polish," and on tactics, based on large scale units of regular battalion and brigade strength—all for the purpose of the production of the robot soldier. In other words, the opposite of the qualities and tactics required in the street and guerrilla warfare that Connolly dealt with in his articles. Such a popular form of warfare, even when large masses of people are involved, is invariably based on small tactical units for a personnel who possess not only passion for their cause, but also qualities of initiative and the creative ability to use the most unorthodox methods of overcoming the superior firepower of a better equipped enemy army.

One cannot, of course, dismiss completely the fact that he gained some useful military knowledge in the British Army, but one must search elsewhere for the reason why he was able to become a proficient military scientist. The answer is simply that he was a complete revolutionary Socialist.

He had displayed his ability to master Scientific Socialism in many spheres, and in connection with his articles, it should be remembered that one of the co-founders of Scientific Socialism, Frederick Engels, had, in his time, also developed a knowledge of the science of warfare, had been an outstanding military critic and writer, as well as an active participant in the 1849 Rising at Baden and Elberfeld. It was in the nature of Connolly's politics that he too should have applied himself to the study of peoples' warfare; it is a measure of his ability as a Scientific Socialist how well he succeeded.

There is no evidence of him ever having had the chance of studying the military writings of Engels; therefore he had independently to develop his own knowledge; likewise, he had no contact with Lenin or his writings on the great issue of the evaluation of the Imperialist War. Again, on an independent basis, he reached essentially the same conclusion as the great leader of the Russian revolutionary movement.

Significantly, the first of Connolly's military articles dealt with an insurrection that had only occurred ten years previously, i.e. the Moscow uprising of 1905. Here, as the article shows, he was dependent for his analysis on the account of the events by the War Correspondent, W.H. Nevinson. How much more valuable the article would have been had he had recourse to Lenin's own articles on that uprising, particularly the one entitled, "The Lessons of the Moscow Uprising," published in the journal, "Proletary," September 11th, 1906.

Amongst the lessons provided by that Rising, according to Lenin, was one referring to tactis and the organisation of forces for the uprising: "Military tactics," wrote Lenin, "depend on the level of military technique. This plain truth was dinned into the ears of Marxists by Engels. Military technique now is not the same as it was in the middle of the nineteenth century. It would be folly for crowds to contend against artillery and defend barricades with revolvers." From the Moscow Rising had come new tactics, "These tactics were the tactics of guerrilla warfare. The organisation which such tactics demanded is that of mobile and exceedingly small detachments; ten, three, or, even two-man detachments." To those who chuckled at the mention of such small units, Lenin pointed out that chuckling was a cheap way of "ignoring the *new* question of tactics and organisation called forth by street fighting under the conditions imposed by modern military technique."

Nine months after he wrote the concluding part of these articles, Connolly applied his theories in practice. How well he had instilled his lessons of street-fighting into the ranks of the Citizen Army is shown in an excerpt from a story by I.C.A. veteran, John O'Keefe, in "1916–1966" (published by the "Irish Socialist" for the Golden Jubilee of the 1916 Uprising):

"We reached our post safely, smashed the windows, climbed in, and waited. The rifles were still spattering at intervals, but it was some time before there was any movement of British troops in our area. Then we saw the khaki-clad figures approaching and prepared to give them a surprise. Stationed at different windows, we pumped the contents of our rifles into them. Then, in order to give the impression of greater strength, we ran to other windows and threw the fuse bombs among them. There was just a roar and a gout of smoke; but it was enough, the enemy broke and scattered back the way they had come."

As I have said, it is not without significance that Connolly's first article dealt with the Moscow uprising of 1905; it was the last armed struggle that had occurred; there was to be none other until Dublin's 1916. Both uprisings, curiously enough, were condemned as 'putsches', and the task of countering this canard, in each case was undertaken by Lenin.

This first-ever reprint of Connolly's military articles is not merely a historical event, on the occasion of the centenary of his birth; they also reveal him still clearer in his role of a revolutionary soldier who approached revolutionary war not as a romantic; he was the least 'militaristic' of the 1916 leaders but he saw it as a serious business, subscribing to Engels' dictum that 'fighting is to war what cash payment is to trade.'

More than half a century has passed since Connolly was executed by the British imperialists. The passage of the years has underlined the great capacity of the people in arms to produce outstanding military leaders from their ranks. This has been proved in the Russian October Revolution, the Liberation of China, the Spanish Peoples Anti-Fascist war, the Anti-Nazi Resistance, in Cuba, and in countless battles in other parts of the world. Nowhere is that ability being more effectively displayed in the Connolly Centenary year than by the revolutionary people of Vietnam in their epic struggle against the powerful, and, in this case, impotent imperialism of America

May 1968   *Michael O'Riordan*

in the "Workers' Republic"
on Insurrectionary Warfare

IRISH CITIZEN ARMY
HQ: Liberty Hall
Commandant: J. Connolly
Chief-of-Staff: M. Mallin

We propose to give under this heading from time to time accounts of such military happenings in the past as may serve to enlighten and instruct our members, in the work they are banded together to perform. A close study of these articles will, we hope, be valuable to all those who desire to acquire a knowledge of how brave men and women have at other times and in other places, overcome difficulties and achieved something for a cause held to be sacred. It is not our place to pass a verdict upon the sacredness or worth of the cause for which they contended: our function is to discuss their achievements from the standpoint of their value to those who desire to see perfected a Citizen Army able to perform whatever duty may be thrust upon it.

We would suggest that these articles be preserved for reference purposes.

May 29th, 1915.

MOSCOW INSURRECTION OF 1905

In the year 1905, the fires of revolution were burning very brightly in Russia. Starting with a parade of unarmed men and women to the Palace of the Czar, the flames of insurrection spread all over the land. The peaceful parades were met with volleys of shrapnel and rifle fire, charged by mounted Cossacks, and cut down remorselessly by cavalry of the line, and in answer to this attack, general strikes broke out all over Russia. From strikes the people proceeded to revolutionary uprisings, soldiers revolted and joined the people in some cases, and in others the sailors of the Navy seized the ironclads of the Czar's fleet and hoisted revolutionary colours. One incident in this outburst was the attempted revolution in Moscow. We take it as our test this week because, in it, the soldiers remained loyal to the Czar, and therefore it resolved itself into a clean cut fight between a revolutionary force and a government force. Thus we are able to study the tactics of (a) A regular Army in attacking a city defended by barricades, and (b) A revolutionary force holding a city against a regular Army.

Fortunately for our task as historians, there was upon the spot an English journalist of unquestioned ability and clearsightedness, as well as of unrivalled experience as a spectator in Warfare. This was H.W. Nevinson, the famous war correspondent. From his book "The Dawn of Russia" as well as from a close intimacy with many refugees who took part in the revolution, this description is built up.

The revolutionists of Moscow, had intended to postpone action until a much later date in the hope of securing the co-operation of the peasantry, but the active measures of the Government precipitated matters. Whilst the question of "Insurrection" or "No Insurrection yet" was being discussed at a certain house in the city, the troops were quietly surrounding the building and the first intimation of their presence received by the revolutionists was the artillery opening fire on the building at point blank range. A large number of the leaders were killed or arrested, but next morning the city was in insurrection.

Of the numbers engaged on the side of the revolutionists, there is considerable conflict of testimony. The government estimate, anxious to applaud the performance

175

of the troops, is 15,000. The revolutionary estimate, on the other hand, is only 500. Mr. Nevinson states that a careful investigator friendly to the revolutionists, and with every facility for knowing, gave the number as approximately 1,500. The deductions we were able to make from the stories of the refugees aforementioned, makes the latter number seem the most probable. The equipment of the revolutionists was miserable in the extreme. Among the 1,500 there was only a total of 80 rifles, and a meagre supply of ammunition for same. The only other weapons were revolvers and automatic pistols, chiefly Brownings. Of these latter a goodly supply seems to have been on hand as at one period of the fighting the revolutionists advertised for volunteers, and named Browning pistols as part of the "pay" for all recruits.

Against this force, so pitifully armed, the government possessed in the city, 18,000 seasoned troops, armed with magazine rifles, and a great number of batteries of field artillery.

The actual fighting which lasted nine days, during which time the government troops made practically no progress, is thus described by the author we have already quoted.

Of the barricades, he says, that they were erected everywhere, even the little boys and girls throwing them up in the most out of the way places, so that it was impossible to tell which was a barricade with insurgents to defend it and which was a mock barricade, a circumstance which greatly hindered the progress of the troops, who had always to spend a considerable period in finding out the real nature of the obstruction before they dared to pass it.

"The very multitude of these barricades (early next morning I counted one hundred and thirty of them, and I had not seen half) made it difficult to understand the main purpose of all the fighting.

"As far as they had any definite plan at all, their idea seems to have been to drive a wedge into the heart of the city, supporting the advance by barricades on each side so as to hamper the approach of troops.

"The four arms of the cross-roads were blocked with double or even treble barricades about ten yards apart. As far as I could see along the curve of the Sadavoya, on both sides barricade succeeded barricade, and the whole road was covered with telegraph wire, some of it lying loose, some tied across like netting. The barricades enclosing the centre of the cross-roads like a fort were careful constructions of telegraph poles or the iron supports to the overhead wires of electric trams, closely covered over with doors, railings, and advertising boards, and lashed together with wire. Here and there a tramcar was built in to give solidity, and on the top of every barricade waved a little red flag.

"Men and women were throwing them (the barricades) up with devoted zeal, sawing telegraph poles, wrenching iron railings from their sockets, and dragging out the planks from builders's yards."

Noteworthy as an illustration of how all things, even popular revolutions, change their character as the conditions change in which they operate, is the fact, that no barricade was defended in the style of the earlier French or Belgian revolutions.

Mr. Nevinson says: "But it was not from the barricades themselves that the real opposition came. From first to last no barricade was 'fought' in the old sense of the word. The revolutionary methods were far more terrible and effective. By the side street barricades and wire entanglements they had rid themselves of the fear of cavalry. By the barricades across the main streets, they had rendered the approach of troops necessarily slow. To the soldiers, the horrible part of the street fighting was that they could never see the real enemy. On coming near a barricade or the entrance to a side street, a few scouts would be advanced a short distance before the guns. As they crept forward, firing as they always did, into the empty barricades in front, they might suddenly find themselves exposed to a terrible revolver fire, at about fifteen paces range, from both sides of the street. It was useless to reply, for there was nothing visible to aim at. All they could do was to fire blindly in almost any direction. Then the revolver fire would suddenly cease, the guns would trundle up and wreck the houses on both sides. Windows fell crashing on the pavement, case shot burst into the bedrooms, and round shot made holes through three or four walls. It was bad for furniture, but the revolutionist had long ago escaped through a labyrinth of courts at the back, and was already preparing a similar attack on another street."

The troops did not succeed in overcoming the resistance of the insurgents, but the insurrection rather melted away as suddenly as it had taken form. The main reason for this sudden dissolution lay in the receipt of discouraging news from St. Petersburg from which quarter help had been expected, and was not forthcoming, and in the rumoured advance of a hostile body of peasantry eager to co-operate with the soldiery against the people who were "hindering the sale of agricultural produce in the Moscow market."

CRITICISM

The action of the soldiery in bringing field guns, or indeed any kind of artillery, into the close quarters of street fighting was against all the teaching of military science, and would infallibly have resulted in the loss of the guns had it not been for the miserable equipment of the insurgents. Had any body of the latter been armed with a reasonable supply of ammunition the government could only have taken Moscow from the insurgents at the cost of an appalling loss of life.

A regular bombardment of the city would only have been possible if the whole loyalist population had withdrawn outside the insurgent lines, and apart from the social reasons against such an abandonment of their business and property, the moral effect of such a desertion of Moscow would have been of immense military value in strengthening the hands of the insurgents and bringing recruits to their ranks. As the military were thus compelled to fight in the city and against a force so badly equipped, not much fault can be found with their tactics.

Of the insurgents also it must be said that they made splendid use of their material. It was a wise policy not to man the barricades and an equally wise policy not to open fire at long range where the superior weapons of the enemy would have been able with impunity to crush them, but to wait, before betraying their whereabouts until the military had come within easy range of their inferior weapons.

Lacking the co-operation of the other Russian cities, and opposed by the ignorant peasantry, the defeat of the insurrection was inevitable, but it succeeded in establishing the fact that even under modern conditions the professional soldier is, in a city, badly handicapped in a fight against really determined civilian revolutionists.

June 5th, 1915.

INSURRECTION IN THE TYROL

In the course of the present war between Italy and the Central States, the Tyrol is likely to come once more into fame as the theatre of military operations. Therefore the story of the insurrection in the Tyrol in 1809 may be doubly interesting to the reader as illustrating alike the lessons of civilian warfare, and the nature of the people and the country in question.

The Tyrol is in reality a section of the Alpine range of mountains—that section which stretches eastward from the Alps of Switzerland, and interposes between the southern frontier of Germany and the northern frontier of Italy. It is part of the territory of Austria; its inhabitants speak the German language, and for the most part are passionately attached to the Catholic religion. They are described by Alison, the English historian, in terms that read strange to-day in view of the English official

177

attitude to all things German. Alison says:—"The inhabitants like all those of German descent, are brave, impetuous, and honest, tenacious of custom, fearless of danger, addicted to intemperance." The latter clause was in itself not sufficient to make any people remarkable, as at that period heavy drinking was the rule all over Europe, and nowhere worse than in these islands. But the Tyrolese were also well accustomed to the use of arms, and frequent target practice in the militia and trained bands as well as in hunting had made excellent shots of a large proportion of the young men of the country.

After the defeat of Austria in 1805 by Napoleon, the Tyrol was taken from that Empire by the Treaty of Pressburg and ceded to Bavaria, the ally of Napoleon. The Tyrolese resented this unceremonious disposal of their country, a resentment that was much increased by the licentious conduct of the French Soldiers sent as garrison into the district. Brooding over their wrongs they planned revolt, and sought and obtained a promise of co-operation from the Austrian Emperor.

In the revolt, alike in its preparation and in its execution, there were three leading figures. These were Andreas Hofer, Spechbacher, and Joseph Haspinger. Hofer, the chief, was an innkeeper, and of great local influence, which he owed alike to his high character and to the opportunities of intercourse given him by his occupation, a more important one before the advent of railroads than now. Spechbacher was a farmer and woodsman, and had been an outlaw and poacher for many years before settling down to married life. Joseph Haspinger was a monk, and from the colour of his beard was familiarly known at Roth-Bart or Redbeard.

It will be observed that none of the three were professional soldiers, yet they individually and collectively defeated the best generals of the French Army—an Army that had defeated the professional militarists of all Europe.

The eighth day of April, 1809 was fixed for the rising, and on that date the signal was given by throwing large heaps of sawdust in to the River Inn, which ran all through the mountains, by lighting fires upon the hill tops, and by women and children who carried from house to house little balls of paper on which were written "es ist Zeit," "it is time."

At one place, St. Lorenzo, the revolt had been precipitated by the action of the soldiers, whose chiefs, hearing of the project, attempted to seize a bridge which commanded communications between the upper part of the valley and Brunecken. Without waiting for the general signal the peasants in the locality rose to prevent the troops getting the bridge. The Bavarian, General Wrede, with 2,000 men and three guns marched to suppress this revolt, but the peasants hid behind rocks and trees, and taking advantage of every kind of natural cover poured in a destructive fire upon the soldiers. The latter suffered great loss from this fire, but pushed forward, and the peasantry were giving way before the disciplined body when they were reinforced by the advanced guard of an Austrian force coming to help the insurrection. The Bavarians gave way. When they reached the bridge at Laditch the pursuit was so hot that they broke in two, one division going up, the other down, the river. The greater part were taken prisoners at Balsano, amongst the prisoners being one general.

At Sterzing Hofer took charge. Here the peasants were attacked by a large force of soldiers, but they took refuge in thickets and behind rocks and drove off the attacks of the infantry. When the artillery was brought up the nature of the ground compelled the guns to come up in musketry range, and then the peasant marksmen picked off the gunners, after which feat the insurgents rushed in and carried all before them in one impetuous charge. Three hundred and ninety prisoners were taken and 240 killed and wounded.

A column of French under Generals Bisson and Wrede made an attempt to force its way up the Brenner. The peasants fell back before it until it reached the narrow defile of Lueg, where it suffered severely as the insurgents had broken down the bridges and barricaded the roads by heaps of fallen trees. The troops were shot down in heaps as they halted before the barricades and bridges whilst a part of their number laboured to open the way.

Meanwhile another large body of peasants had attacked and taken Innsbruck, the capital of the Tyrol, and when Bisson and Wrede eventually forced their way up the Brenner with the insurgents everywhere harrying on their flanks and rear, picking them off from behind cover, and rushing upon and destroying any party unfortunate enough to get isolated, as they advanced into the open it was only to find the city in possession of the insurgents, and vast masses of armed enemies awaiting them at every point of vantage. After a short fight Bisson, caught between two fires, surrendered with nearly 3,000 men.

Sprechbacher took Hall in the Lower Tyrol. A curious evidence of the universality of the insurrection was here given by the circumstance that as none of the men could be spared from the fighting line 400 prisoners had to be marched off under an armed escort of women. In one week the insurgents had defeated 10,000 regular soldiers experienced in a dozen campaigns and taken 6,000 prisoners.

In a battle at Innsbruck on May 28—29th, the woman and children took part, carrying food and water and ammunition. When the insurgents had expended all their lead the women and children collected the bullets fired by the enemy and brought them to the men to fire back at the soldiers. Amongst the number Spechbacher's son, ten years of age, was as active as any, and more daring than most.

After the total defeat of the Austrians and the capture of Vienna by Napoleon, the city of Innsbruck was retaken by a French army of 30,000 men. Hofer was summoned by the French General to appear at Innsbruck. He replied stating that he

"would come but it would be attended by 10,000 sharpshooters."

At first the peasantry had been so discouraged by their abandonment by the Austrians that a great number of them had gone to their homes, but at the earnest solicitation of their leaders they again rallied, and hostilities re-opened on August 4th.

A column of French and Bavarians were crossing the bridge at Laditch where the high road from Balsano to the capital crosses the river Eisach. The Tyrolese under Haspinger occupied the overhanging woods, and when the troops were well in the defile they rained bullets and rocks upon them without showing themselves. Men were falling at every step, and the crushing rocks tore lanes through the ranks. The soldiers pressed on until the narrowest point of the defile was reached when a sudden silence fell upon the mountain side. Awestruck, the column involuntarily halted, and amid the silence a voice rang out—

"Shall I? Shall I? Stephen."

and another answered —

"Not yet, not yet."

Recovering, the troops resumed their march in silence and apprehension, and then as they wound deeper into the path the second voice again rang out—

"Now, in the name of the Father, Son and Holy Ghost, cut loose." And at the word, a huge platform of tree trunks, upon which tons of rocks had been collected, was suddenly cut loose, and the whole mass descended like an avalanche upon the soldiery, sweeping whole companiers away and leaving a trail of mangled bodies behind it. Despite this terrible catastrophe the column pushed its way on towards the bridge, only to find it in flames, and a raging torrent barring their further progress. They retreated to their starting point harassed all the way by the invisible enemy and with a loss of 1,200 men.

On August 10th, Marshal Lefebre, with 20,000 men, attempted to force a passage through and over the Brenner. He was attacked everywhere by small bodies, his progress checked, and his way barred by every obstacle that nature could supply, or ingenuity suggest, and eventually driven back, losing 25 cannon and the whole ammunition of his army.

On August 12th, with 23,000 foot, 2,000 horse, and 40 cannon, he was attacked at Innsbruck by the three insurgent leaders and defeated. Hofer had kept his promise to come to Innsbruck "with 10,000 sharpshooters." The French lost 6,000 killed, wounded and prisoners.

This was the last notable success of the insurgents. The French having made peace with Austria, and having no other war on hand, were able to concentrate upon the Tyrol a force sufficient to make further resistance impossible. The insurgents returned to their homes, and resistance was abandoned.

REMARKS

The nature of the country lent itself to the mode of fighting of the insurgents. But their own genius also counted for much. They used every kind of cover, seldom exposed themselves, and at all times took care not to let bravery degenerate into rashness.

Every effort was made to tempt artillery into close range, the insurgents lying as quiet as possible until such time as their muskets could be brought into play upon the artillery men. To the same end positions were taken up which seemed often to be in direct contravention of military science, since they seemed to abandon every chance of a clear field of fire in front, and enabled the enemy to approach closely without coming under fire. But their seeming mistake was based upon sound judgment as the superior weapons of the enemy would have beaten down opposition from a distance, whereas being compelled to come close in before opening fire the regular soldiery lost their chief advantage over the insurgents and were deprived of the advantages conferred by discipline and efficient control by skilled officers.

June 12th, 1915.

REVOLUTION IN BELGIUM

After the defeat and final deposition of Napoleon the Allied Sovereigns met at Vienna in 1815 and proceeded to settle Europe. All during the war against Napoleon all the Continental Powers in alliance with the British Empire had loudly declared to the world and to their respective peoples that they were fighting for Liberty, for National rights, and against foreign oppression. But when they met at Vienna the Allies proceeded to ride roughshod over all the things for which they were supposed to be fighting. Nations in many instances were ruthlessly partitioned, as in the case of Italy, or were subjected to new foreign rulers without being consulted in any manner. This latter was the case of Belgium. That country was forcibly placed under the rule of Holland. Belgium could not resist as the whole of Europe, except France, was represented at the Vienna Congress, and the armies of all Europe were at the call of the Powers for the enforcement of the decrees of that Congress. In passing, it may be said that this settlement of Europe by the Allied Powers was so utterly at variance with the will of the people, so flagrant a denial and suppression of all that the Allies had pretended to fight for that it led to revolution, subsequently, in every state in Europe.

Holland in its rule over Belgium was accused by the Belgians of a systematic campaign against every expression and manifestation of Belgian national life. It was alleged that it penalised the native language of Belgium, and gave undue official preference to the Dutch, that it sought to place Dutch officials in all posts to the exclusion of equally well qualified Belgians, that it unduly favoured Dutch industries by legislation and retarded Belgian, and that in every possible way Belgium was treated more as a conquered province than as an Allied State.

These grievances were agitated in many ways, and many efforts were made to obtain remedies without avail. Eventually in 1830, fifteen years after the settlement by the Congress of Vienna, revolution broke out in Brussels.

On the August 25th, 1830, a partially armed mob attacked the house and printing establishment of the chief pro-Dutch paper, the *National.* After wrecking these they obtained more arms by sacking gunsmiths's shops. Then the official residence of the Dutch Minister of Justice, M. van Mannen, was attacked, gutted, and burned to the ground.

On the 26th, the troops were called out and fighting took place in the streets. The crowd had got possession of a large amount of arms and ammunition and successfully withstood the soldiery. Eventually the troops withdrew in a body to the Place Royale, the reason for the withdrawal being thus stated in the English Press of the time that—

"in street warfare regular troops, who to be effective must act together, fight at a great disadvantage."

The streets of the city were thus left clear to the people, who proceeded to wreak their vengeance upon the houses and offices of the Government officials. The house of the Public Prosecutor (Procureur du Roi), of the Director of Police, and of the Commandant of the city were sacked, the furniture being taken out, piled up in the street and burned.

Up till this period the middle class Belgians had only looked on passively, but now they organised themselves into a Burgher Guard to defend their property, and took possession of the city partly by force, partly by agreement with the armed workers who up to this time had done all the fighting. Five thousand Burgher Guards were enrolled, the Commandant being one Baron Hoogvorst. All the military posts in the city were occupied by the Guard, the military remaining inactive outside.

A Committee of Public Safety elected by the Burgher Guard issued a Manifesto setting forth the grievances of the Belgian Nation, and instituting reforms. Clause XI of the Manifesto ordered that

"Bread be distributed to all unfortunate workmen to supply their wants until they are able to resume their labour."

On the August 20th, Royal troops marched upon Brussels, but halted outside upon being told that if they attempted to enter they would be resisted, but the Guard would keep order within if the troops remained outside. As yet there had been no talk of separation, but all Royal colours had been torn down, and distinctive Belgian colours hoisted on the buildings, and worn by the armed people.

On the August 30th, the Prince of Orange arrived outside Brussels and sent in word that he was about to enter. He was informed that he could only enter alone or with his own aide-de-camp. He then threatened to storm the city, and the people replied by building barricades in all the leading streets, and occupying the gates in force. Then the Prince issued a proclamation commanding the inhabitants to lay aside their rebellious colours and badges, and that he would enter the city and take over their duties. This was refused, and he then consented to enter the city alone.

A deputation had been sent to the king at the Hague to lay before him the demands of the Belgians. He met the deputation very courteously, as kings always do when in difficulties, promised many reforms, but insisted that his son, the Prince, should enter Brussels at the head of his troops, and that the deputation should confer with the Minister of the Interior. This latter conference took place, and at it the delegates presented a new demand—the separation of Belgium from Holland, and its erection into an independent Kingdom under the same king.

On this point, like Ireland in our day, the country was divided. Antwerp and Ghent petitioned against separation. Tournay, Verviers, Mons and Namur declared for separation, and in each of them the Civic Guard seized the town and proclaimed the revolution. Bruges followed suit. In each of those places, whilst the Civic Guard was hesitating, the working class took the lead and forced the pace, bringing the guard eventually into line.

On the September 19th, the working class of Brussels, tired of the hesitation and inaction of the middle class representatives, took matters in their own hands, rose in rebellion and marched on the Town Hall. There they seized 40 stand of arms. Next day they took possession of the Town Hall, and all the military posts in the city, and were fortunate enough to get possession of a large supply of arms and ammunition. They dissolved the middle class Committee of Public Safety, and established a Provisional Government.

On the September 21st, Prince Frederick advanced upon Brussels and ordered that the guard should surrender their posts, all rebel colours should be taken down, all armed strangers expelled, and threatening to hold responsible personally all members of the Committee of Public Safety, of the Council of Officers of Guards, and of the Municipal Administration. But as all these bodies had been dissolved the Proclamation fell rather flat. The people prepared to fight.

Barricades were thrown up in all the streets and at the gates. Pavements were torn up, stones carried to the top of houses in streets through which the troops would have to pass, and every preparation made, the women being specially busy in the preparations. The attack began on the 22nd, the middle class citizens who had been in the Burgher Guard kept carefully to their houses and out of the fighting. The troops made the attack upon six different points, or districts towards which they opened, Flanders, Auderlecht, Lacken, Schaarbeck, Namur, Louvain. The artillery easily broke through the gates and adjoining barricades but as they advanced, obstacle succeeded obstacle, resistance seemed to multiply itself with every step, and the fighting increased in intensity the farther into the city they penetrated. At the Flanders gate the troops swept at first everything before them with their artillery fire. They advanced with great steadiness until they were met by a strong barricade at a curve in the street which prevented the artillery from being brought to bear. Here they were exposed to a deadly fire from behind the barricade, and overwhelmed from above with showers of paving stones, heavy pieces of furniture, hatchets, fire-irons and every species of missile. Beaten back, they were compelled to retreat. At Auderlecht gate the same fate overtook the soldiery, and at Lacken the insurgents compelled a retreat with great loss.

The division which attacked at Schaarbeck gate fought its way in until it reached an open park in which it took refuge from the close quarters and dreadful hostility of the streets. Then it halted afraid to advance further against the streets. The divisions attacking by Namur and Louvain gates also fought their way in for a short distance and then halted, fearful of attempting a further advance.

On the 24th, the middle class joined the insurgent working class, and the fighting was renewed. After a long day's contest the troops were unable to advance, although they had made themselves masters of one of the main streets. The insurgents were still in possession, but too badly organised to expel the troops from their foothold in the city.

On the 26th, and 27th, volunteers from neighbouring towns joined the insurgents, and, encouraged by their aid, the insurgents began to close in on the troops and drive them back. Eventually, believing their position to be hopeless, the soldiery gave up the struggle and withdrew from the city.

The total insurgent loss from the 22nd, to the 27th, was stated to be 165 killed an 311 wounded.

After the retreat from Brussels the Government had no foothold in Belgium except in its fortresses. The populace rose in the towns, the Belgian regiments declared in favour ot the revolution, and one after another the fortresses fell into the hands of the insurgents.

At Ath and Mons the Dutch garrison was made prisoner. At Namur the garrison surrendered the fortress on condition that it was allowed to depart. At Liege 1,100 men, constituting the garrison, made the same arrangement. Ghent held out against the revolution until October 16th, when it also surrendered on like terms to Namur. By the end of October the Belgians were in possession of all the fortresses except Antwerp, Maestricht and Luxemburg.

On the November 10th, a National Congress established the Kingdom of Belgium, which was afterwards formally acknowledged by all the powers.

REMARKS

The Revolution in Brussels and the successful stand of an insurgent body against regular troops, made such an impression upon Europe that it was long held as an axiom that it was the duty of the officers in command of the army, confronted with such a condition, to refuse to fight in the streets, and content themselves with a regular investment or siege of the city. The official English view has always dissented from this advice.

Two things have to be kept in mind in studying the Brussels Revolution:

First—that, unlike Continental revolutions in general, there were no defections among the troops. It was two nations in conflict. Hence the revolution at Brussels won purely because of its military position and strength.

Second—That the invention of smokeless powder would tend to make such street fighting far more deadly and demoralising to an army which could not see from whence came the shots that decimated the ranks.

June 19th, 1915.

DEFENSE OF THE ALAMO

In 1821 Mexico was separated from the kingdom of Spain and entered upon a turbulent and troubled existence of its own. At that time almost all of the territory comprised in the present American State of Texas was an integral part of the Mexican Republic. It was inhabited largely by Mexicans and other persons of Spanish or mixed Spanish and Indian descent. But along with these there were a large number of immigrants from the United States, some of whom had taken up land under the laws of the Mexican Government, whilst others were hunters, trappers, and adventurers. All these latter were rather disinclined to submit to the laws of the Mexicans, especially when the various changes in the Mexican Government made it at times somewhat problematical what these laws were, and still more of a problem to judge how each fresh incumbent in office would administer the laws. Consequently, the uneasiness grew in volume with each accession of strength in the numbers of the immigrants, and each fresh caprice of the rulers. To add to this uneasy situation the designs of the slaveholders in the United States included an extension of slaveholding territory to the South. Unable to extend the slave belt to the North, and menaced by the continual growth of free states in the West, the slaveholders of the United States were anxious to secure fresh territories which could be erected into slave states whose votes could be counted upon against the pressing danger of the increase of liberationist sentiment in the Congress and Senate. Hence the restless immigrants in Texas received secret encouragement from the United States Government, and having real and genuine grievances of their own their restlessness gradually developed into rebellion.

A Mexican Congress in 1835 adopted a new Constitution for the country, one feature of which was the dissolution of all power in a Congress to meet in Mexico city. This was resented in many parts of the country, and in March 1836, a Texan Congress met at Washington, Texas, and declared Texas to be a free and independent Republic. A provisional Government was organised, and Sam Houston was declared Commander-in-Chief. Hostilities commenced immediately.

Fighting took place at several places, notably at San Antonio de Bexar, where the insurgents after five days battle in the street, compelled the garrison to surrender. On hearing of this disaster to his forces, the Mexican President, Santa Anna, crossed the Rio Grande, the river which forms the boundary line between Texas and Mexico, with an army of 10,000 men, and advanced against the insurgents. In the path of their advance lay an old wooden fort known as the Alamo, into which a Texan officer named Travis threw himself with a garrison of 145 men. The Mexican force laid siege to the place, and Travis sent off the following message for reinforcements:—

"The enemy have demanded me to surrender at discretion, otherwise the garrison is to be put to the sword. I have answered his summons with a cannon shot. Our flag still floats proudly from the walls. We shall never surrender or retreat, Liberty or death!"

The little Texan force of one hundred and forty five insurgents held out for ten days against the Mexican army of 10,000 men. Again and again the Mexicans attempted to storm the place, and as often they were beaten off. The wounded were propped up by their comrades and kept on fighting until death, the rushes of the regular soldiery with bayonets were beaten off by the Texans with clubbed rifles or met with the quick deadly work of bowie knives, and when at last the building was taken and the Mexicans were victorious it was found that the loss they had sustained was without a parallel in history. Fifteen hundred Mexicans had been killed or ten for every Texan engaged.

No quarter was given or asked. All the defenders were killed, their bodies collected in a heap and burned.

But the defence of the Alamo had enabled the insurgents elsewhere to organise their resistance, and General Samuel Houston with twelve hundred men was by this time in the field and in a position to conduct a regular campaign. Houston pursued a retreating and waiting policy refusing to be drawn prematurely into a battle, but patiently biding his time and keeping his men together until he had made them into an army.

Eventually on April 19th, 1836 the two armies met at Buffalo Bayou and the Mexicans were defeated with great slaughter, their General and six hundred men being taken prisoners.

This ended the campaign, the independence of Texas being shortly afterwards formally acknowledged.

REMARKS

The defence of the Alamo was one of those defeats which are often more valuable to a cause than many loudly trumpeted victories. It gave spirit and bitterness to the Texan forces, and more important still gave time to their comrades elsewhere. Fortunately for their cause also they had in Houston a General who recognised that the act of keeping an insurgent force in the field was in itself so valuable an establishment of the revolutionary position that it gave all the functions and prestige of government. Hence he kept his force in the field without fighting as long as possible, despite the murmurs of his men, and only hazarded an engagement when he considered that his army was made.

July 3rd, 1915.

REVOLUTION IN PARIS, 1830

After the deposition of Napoleon by the allied powers the Bourbon family was restored to the throne of France much against the will of the French people. That family at first made some slight concession to the spirit of democracy which the

French revolution had aroused in Europe, but gradually as the people advanced in their claims for enfranchisement the royal family and court became more and more reactionary and opposed to reform.

Eventually the Government took steps to suppress the freedom of the press, and four journals active in the reform movement were proceeded against, their editors sentenced to prison and to pay heavy fines. The Chamber of Deputies took sides against the king, and presented to him an address in favour of reform. He dissolved the Chamber and ordered a general election.

When the election was over it was found that, despite the restricted suffrage and persistent government terrorism, the Reform party out of a total Chamber of 428 members had returned 270, whilst the ministry had only returned 145.

As his answer to the elections the king on the July 25th, 1830, issued a decree destroying at one swoop all the liberties of his subjects.

The new Chamber of Deputies was dissolved before it had even met.

Liberty of the press was suspended. Writings published in violation of the regulations were to be seized, and types and presses used in printing them to be taken into custody, or rendered unfit for their purposes.

The method of election was altered so as to put it completely in the power of the king and his party.

At this time Paris was garrisoned by a force of 4,750 men of the National Guard, 4,400 troops of the line, 1,100 veteran battalions, 1,300 gendarmes or police.

The first sign of resistance came from the press. Four of the principal editors met and issued the following manifesto which was printed in the *National*:

"Legal government is interrupted and the reign of force has commenced. In the situation in which we are placed obedience ceases to be a duty. The citizens first called upon to obey are the writers of journals; they ought to give the first example of resistance to authority which has divested itself of legal character."

On the morning of the 27th, the police began to seize types and break presses. They were resisted in many places. At the offices of the *Temps* and *National* the police were refused admission. Whilst they were attempting to break in the printing of papers went on and copies of the paper were thrown out of the windows as fast as they were printed. Bought up by the crowd these papers were quickly carried all over Paris.

Locksmiths and blacksmiths were brought to break open the door, but they refused to act, and eventually this had to be done by a convict blacksmith brought from the prison. When the police entered they destroyed all the machines.

The example of resistance fired the whole city, and great mobs marched everywhere. The residence of the Premier was protected by a battalion of guards and two pieces of cannon, and a division of lancers patrolled the immediate neighbourhood. Three battalions were in front of the Palais Royal, the Place Louis XI was held by two battalions of guards and two guns, and in the Place Vendôme were detachments of regiments of the line. Thus all the great squares were held by the military.

The police attempted to clear the streets and failed, and soldiers were ordered to assist. As they pushed the people back in the Rue St. Honorè the first shot was fired from a house in that thoroughfare. It came from a shot gun and wounded some of the soldiers.

The troops fired at the house, and the crowd fell away. As the soldiers pursued they were stopped by a barricade made out of an overturned omnibus beside which had been piled all kinds of furniture and other obstructions. But as those behind this barricade were only armed with stones the soldiery after firing several volleys easily stormed it.

In other places fighting took place, in one a police guardhouse was stormed, and the arms carried off.

Next day, the 28th, the people attacked all the gunmakers' shops and took possession of the arms and equipment. Barricades were erected all over the city, and police guardhouses attacked and taken. The working class from the Faubourgs organised and marched upon the City Hall, or Hotel de Ville, and arms were distributed from various centres.

The military planned to enter the barricaded districts in four columns at four tactical points. The first column entering by the richer parts of the city met with little opposition.

The second column entered by Porte St. Martin, and was met by sharp firing. After firing two rounds from the artillery, and a number from the muskets of the infantry it crushed the opposition at this point, but as it advanced into the centre of the city the insurgents built barricades behind it, and the further it advanced the more barricades they built in its rear. It reached its objective the great square of the Place de la Bastille, but when it attempted to return was stopped by the aforementioned barricades, and fired upon from all the intersecting streets. The commanding officer after several fruitless attempts to return by the route marked out for him, at last fearing that he would lose his artillery broke out in another direction, leaving the ground he had occupied in the hands of the insurgents, and reaching a point entirely out of touch with the General in command. This column had passed through the insurgents, but it had left them just as it had found them, except, as one writer remarks, "that they had been taught to meet the royal troops without fear, and to know the value of the method of fighting they had adopted."

The third column reached a huge market place, the Marché des Innocens, but at this point was assailed with a hot fire from the roofs and windows, accompanied by showers of slates, stones, bottles, and scrap iron. One battalion was ordered to march along the Porte St. Denis, clear it, and march back again. In doing so it encountered a barricade in front of a large building, the Cour Batave. Here the insurgents had got inside the courtyard, and fired from behind the iron railing around this building, lying on the ground behind the stones into which the railings were fixed, and keeping up a murderous fire on the troops as the latter body laboured to destroy the barricade. This battalion also was unable to fight its way back, as barricades had been erected behind it as it passed. Its companion battalion at the market place awaiting its return found itself hemmed in, with barricades rising rapidly in all the surrounding streets, and a merciless fire pouring in on it at every opportunity. At last in despair it was resolved to send out a messenger for help.

Ann aide-de-camp shaved off his moustache, got into the clothes of a market porter, and succeeded in getting through the insurgent lines with a message to the commander-in-chief of the Paris district. Help was sent in the shape of another battalion which had to fight its way in. At the market place the forces united, and fought their way out with great loss.

The fourth column was directed to reach the City Hall, the Hotel de Ville. It was divided in two. One part marching across a suspension bridge was attacked by the insurgents, but bringing up artillery and receiving reinforcements of another battalion fought its way through, and reached its objective—the Hotel de Ville and adjacent Place de Grève. The insurgents barricaded all the surrounding side streets, and kept up a fire from all the corners and windows. One writer says:

"The guns attached to the guards were found to occasion only embarrassment."

Eventually finding the place untenable they fought their way out, attacked all the way by the people who closed in like a sea as the troops passed.

The end of the day's fighting found the people everywhere in possession. Next day fresh troops arrived from the country outside Paris, but great preparations had been made to receive them.

Streets had been torn up, and pavements converted into barricades. Great mounds were placed across the streets, barrels filled with earth and stones; planks, poles, and every conceivable kind of obstacle utilised to create barricades.

Carts, carriages, hackney coaches, drays, wheelbarrows had been seized and over-turned, and trees cut down and used to improvise street fortresses.

Then a peculiar thing took place. The troops refused to advance into the streets, and in turn fortified themselves in their positions. This gave the insurgents opportunity to organise themselves and plan their fight more systematically. When they advanced against the troops, after some fighting the soldiery were driven from their central position—the Louvre, some of the regiments of the line surrendered, and the city was abandoned by the troops.

The Revolution had won.

REMARKS

Like the fighting in Brussels narrated in a previous issue the chief characteristic of the Paris fighting in this Revolution was the elusive nature of the insurgent forces. The conquest of a street by the royal troops was not worth the blood it had cost them, for as soon as they passed onwards fresh barricades were erected in their rear on the very ground they had just conquered. No sooner did they fight their way in than it became necessary for them to fight their way out again. They only commanded the ground they occupied, and the surrounding barricades shutting off their supplies and communications made the position untenable. To have successfully resisted the revolution would have required an army sufficient to occupy in force every inch of ground they passed, with another force massed at some tactical point strong enough to assist any part of the long drawn out line at any point where it might have been attacked.

July 12th, 1915.

LEXINGTON

The first blood shed in actual fighting in the American Revolution was shed at Lexington, Massachusetts on April 19th, 1775. Then was fired "the shot heard round the world," the shot whose echoes were as bugle calls summoning a nation to life.

The dispute between the British Parliament and the American colonists had been gradually drawing to a head. The town of Boston which had led in the agitation against the oppressive action of the British Government was filled with British troops intended to intimidate the Americans, and these latter had begun to collect arms and ammunition and to store them in various places inland in order to be prepared for any eventuality. At that time the odds seemed so great against the Americans that few of them dreamt of asserting the independence of the thirteen colonies.

The colonies were but thinly populated, means of communication were very imperfect, roads were bad, and no real bond of cohesion existed. The British had a great fleet dominating the Atlantic sea coast, and able to hurl an army at any point where resistance might be contemplated and crush it before it could attain to any strength. The bad roads, sparse population and almost trackless wilds on the other hand made it difficult to unite the Americans sufficiently to oppose the British expedition. Also large sections of the population were ultra loyal, and resolved to stand by England against their fellow colonists. Owing to all these factors there was still some hope of a peaceful issue of the dispute until the occurrence we are about to describe swept the talkers and doubters aside, and placed the issue in the hands of armed forces.

On the night of the 18th and morning of the April 19th, the British General Gage in command at Boston sent an expedition into the interior for the purpose of destroying certain stores of arms and ammunition the Americans were gathering at the village of Lexington. This expedition embarked secretly on boats at Boston, and were rowed up the Charles River to a landing place known as Phipp's Farm. From there they pushed hurriedly on to the town of Concord, which they reached about five in the morning. Every effort had been made to keep their movements secret, mounted officers and scouts scoured the country and arrested every inhabitant they found upon the roads to keep them from giving the alarm. But the alarm had been given; one mounted citizen, Paul Revere, having ridden ahead of them and spread the alarm far and wide. Bells were rung, fires lighted and guns fired in order to rouse the sleeping inhabitants by those who received the word as Revere passed on his way.

On reaching Lexington the soldiers found the American militia drawn up to receive them. The Officer in command ordered the Americans to disperse; these latter refused, and the soldiers fired, killing eight men and wounding several others.

The Americans fled and the soldiers then proceeded to Concord, sending six companies ahead to seize two bridges beyond the town that they might cut off the retreat of any armed forces opposing them. The American militia at this point retired and the main body of soldiers took possession of the place. At once they set about destroying all stores; three guns, a quantity of carriages, and a large accumulation of powder and ball were thrown into the river. A number of barrels of flour were also thrown in the same place and spoilt. All this time the bells had been summoning the people, bonfires were on every hill, and couriers were speeding along every road with the news that the soldiers were on the warpath. The farmers and townspeople were hurrying from all quarters to the scene.

Upon completion of their work of destruction the army commenced to retire. But here the first real fighting of the day began.

As the Infantry prepared to leave the town they tried to destroy the bridges behind them. A company of militia strove to cross in order to save some of their stores, but the soldiers fired killing two men. The Americans returned the fire, and the regulars were forced to retreat, leaving behind them some killed and wounded, and a lieutenant and a number of soldiers taken prisoners.

As the army retired the whole countryside rose around them. Skirmish followed skirmish, houses, walls, hedges, woods, ditches were lined by riflemen who never ventured into close quarters, but kept up the pursuit, tracking the soldiers as hunters track game. At Lexington the retreating army was reinforced by Lord Percy with 16 companies of infantry, a detachment of marines, and two cannon. From Lexington to Boston is sixteen miles and all the way the troops had to fight. The people closed in to firing distance only, crawled along the ground in their rear, lay in wait behind hillocks, trees, and hedges, firing upon the troops, and never exposing themselves.

For the soldiers it was a terrible experience, as their enemy seemed to rise out of the ground. Front and rear and flanks were alike engaged all the time, and every moment required every sense to be on the alert. Eventually the soldiers reached Charleston, and boats took them off to Boston under the shelter of the fleet.

The British admitted the loss of 273 men killed and wounded, and 2 lieutenants and 20 men taken prisoners. Amongst the seriously wounded were Colonel Smith, the commander of the expedition, a lieutenant-colonel and several other officers.

The total American loss was only 60 killed and wounded.

REMARKS

The battle of Lexington was a victory for the British, inasmuch as they succeeded in their object, viz., to destroy the stores of ammunition at Lexington. But it was also a victory for the rebels, as they held the ground after the battle, compelled the enemy to retreat, and inflicted more loss upon him in the retreat than they had suffered in the battle. In this respect Lexington was like all the battles of the War of the Revolution. In practcally all of those earlier battles the regular soldiers won, but after each

of them the American Army gained in strength and discipline. Lexington destroyed
the belief in the invincibility of the regular soldiers, gave courage to those who
dreaded them because of their perfection in mechanical drill, and gave faith to those
doubters who failed to recognise that no nation can be enslaved if its people think
death less hateful than bondage.

July 17th, 1915.

JUNE 1848

In February 1848, the monarchy of Louis Phillippe was destroyed by an insurrection in the streets of Paris, supported by risings in various parts of the country.
This insurrection, like all previous risings of the same description, owed its success
principally to the determined fighting of the working class. But whereas in previous
insurrections the working class after doing the fighting were content to let the middle
class reap the harvest, it resolved this time to demand certain guarantees for itself.

Education had progressed rapidly, and in addition the relative numbers of the
workers were greater than at any other similar crisis. Hence, after the victory, whilst
arms were still in its hands, it demanded that the new government establish in its social
constitution some provisions making for social well-being. The government consented reluctantly but with great show of zeal for the cause of labour, and established
"National Workshops," guaranteeing work to all comers.

This proposition was, of course, economically unsound and bound to fail, but it
placated the workers for the time. The Republican Government got time to mature
its plans against republicanism, and to organise its military force against labour.
Thousands of workers were taken on in the workshops, and middle class poets talked
enthusiastically and sang ecstatically about the Era of Labour. But all the time the
government was quietly drafting its forces into Paris, removing from Paris all the city
regiments and replacing them with battalions from remote country districts, perfecting its artillery, and calmly preparing to crush the workers should they persist
in their idea that the Republic ought to regard them as its children, not as its slaves.
Eventually when all was ready the government began to dismiss men in thousands
from the National Workshops, and to form brigades of workers to be removed from
Paris ostensibly to work at canal construction in the provinces.

One of these brigades was formed of 14,000 men, almost all of whom were
Parisians, and members of various local Labour clubs. In addition to this wholesale
removal of workers to unfamiliar provinces, the government on the June 22nd, 1848,
summarily dismissed 3,000 more on the pretence that they were not born in Paris,
and ordered them to leave the city at once. Money and tickets were supplied to them
to pay their lodgings along the road to their birthplaces.

Out of this deportation sprung the Insurrection of June 1848.

About 400 of the deported workmen returned to the city that evening and paraded
the streets, calling upon their comrades to resist the plot of the government to destroy
the Labour forces. In the morning the sound of the *generale*, the popular drum beat
to arms, was sounded, and barricades began to be erected in the streets. All the
working class districts rapidly rose, and the insurgents fortified their quarters so
rapidly and skilfully that it was quite evident that astute minds had been busy amongst
them preparing to meet the schemes of the government.

At the Porte St. Denis the fighting began. The barricade here was stormed after
the soldiers had been twice beaten off. At the Porte St. Martin and at several other
points similar fights took place, at each of them the soldiery stormed the barricade.
But at each of them it was found that after the barricade had become untenable the

insurgents were able to fall back behind others that had been prepared for the purpose, and when the troops sought to pursue them they were met by a galling and terrible fire from all the side streets and houses. The insurgents had seized houses which commanded the passage of the streets, but were still so retired that they could not be swept from the front, and had prepared their house in the most scientific manner. The front walls were loopholed, the entrances were barricaded with furniture, boxes, trunks, and obstacles of all kinds, the party walls were cut through so that only one man at a time could pass, and as fast as one house was taken in desperate hand-to-hand fighting they retired through this passage to the next.

Some of the houses were compared to rabbit warrens, full of holes and galleries, and in every corner death was waiting for the soldiers. Windows were blocked with mattresses and sandbags, and marksmen fired from behind them, and women were busy casting bullets, raining slates and stones on the heads of the troops, carrying arms, and tending the wounded.

Before nightfall the troops had been driven back at numerous points, and the roar of artillery was heard all over the city.

Next morning it was found that most of the barricades destroyed during the day had been erected again during the night. To enumerate here the places and districts fortified would be a useless display of names, but sufficient to say that the insurgents had drawn a huge semi-circle around a vast portion of Paris, had erected barricades in a practically continuous line all along their front, had carefully prepared the houses and buildings at tactically strong points, and were now applying to their service everything within their lines that foresight or prudence could suggest.

Two great buildings served as headquarters in the various districts. The headquarters of the North were in the Temple, those of the South in the Pantheon, and in the centre the Hospital of the Hotel Dicu had been seized and held as the strategical bureau of the whole insurrection.

Meanwhile the soldiers in overwhelming numbers were being rushed to Paris from all the provincial centres, and as France was then at peace with all foreign powers the whole force of the army was available. General Cavaignac issued a proclamation that

"if at noon the barricades are not removed, mortars and howitzers will be brought by which shells will be thrown, which will explode behind the barricades and in the apartments of the houses occupied by the insurgents."

No one heeded his threat, and on the next day the fighting re-commenced. But the shortage of ammunition on the part of the insurgents told heavily against them, and in addition, as the government had all along planned, the soldiers brought to Paris outnumbered the armed men in revolt, as well as being possessed of all the advantage of a secure source of supplies.

The first fighting at the Clos St. Lazare was typical of the whole and therefore the following description from the pen of an eye-witness is worth reproducing. He says:—

"The barricades in advance of the barriers were as formidable as regular engineers would have constructed, and were built of paving stones of a hundredweight each, and blocks of building stone cut for building a hospital, and weighing tons. The houses covering them were occupied. The tall houses at the barriers were occupied and the windows removed. The houses on the opposite side of the Boulevard were, moreover, in the possession of the rebels and manned with marksmen. What formed, however, the strength of their position was the perforation of the wall of the city which is twelve or fourteen feet high, at intervals of eight or ten yards for a mile in length, with several hundred loopholes of about six inches in diameter. During all Saturday and Sunday a constant and deadly fire was kept up from these loopholes on troops who could hardly see their opponents.

"The defenders ran from loophole to loophole with the agility of monkeys. They only left the cover of the high wall to seek *ammunition, of which they had only a scanty and precarious supply.*"

It was only when the insurgents' ammunition gave out that the artillery became formidable. Then it was able to pound to ruins the building in which the insurgents were awaiting their attack, and to gradually occupy the district so cleared of its defenders.

By the June 28th, all fighting had ceased in Paris. The isolation of that city from all provincial support, combined with the overwhelming number of the soldiery had won the day.

On the December 10th, 1848, Prince Louis Napoleon was elected President of the Republic, and four years afterwards he destroyed it by the aid of the army which the republican government had turned against the workers of Paris in the fighting just chronicled. When Louis Napoleon was destroying the French Republic its middle class supporters called in vain for the support of the brave men they had betrayed in June 1848.

REMARKS

The insurrection of June 1848 in Paris was the most stubbornly fought, and the most scientifically conducted, of any of the revolutions or attempts at revolutions in Paris. The lessons are invaluable for all students of warfare who wish to understand the defence and attack of cities, towns, villages, or houses. Whatever changes have come about as a result of the development of firearms and the introduction of smokeless powder have operated principally in increasing the power of the defence. In our next week's issue we propose to sum up the military lessons of all the great uprisings dealt with in these notes up to the present.

July 24th, 1915.

STREET FIGHTING—SUMMARY

A complete summary of the lessons to be derived from the military events we have narrated in these chapters during the past few months would involve the writing of a very large volume. Indeed it might truly be urged that the lessons are capable of such infinite expansion that no complete summary is possible.

In the military sense of the term what after all is a *street*? A street is a defile in a city. A defile is a narrow pass through which troops can only move by narrowing their front, and therefore making themselves a good target for the enemy. A defile is also a difficult place for soldiers to manoeuvre in, especially if the flanks of the defile are held by the enemy.

A mountain pass is a defile the sides of which are constituted by the natural slopes of the mountain sides, as at the Scalp. A bridge over a river is a defile the sides of which are constituted by the river. A street is a defile the sides of which are constituted by the houses in the street.

To traverse a mountain pass with any degree of safety the sides of the mountain must be cleared by flanking parties ahead of the main body; to pass over a bridge the banks of the river on each side must be raked with gun or rifle fire whilst the bridge is being rushed; to take a street properly barricaded and held on both sides by forces in the houses, these houses must be broken into and taken by hand-to-hand fighting. A street barricade placed in a position where artillery cannot operate from a distance is impregnable to frontal attack. To bring artillery within a couple of hundred yards—the length of the average street—would mean the loss of the artillery if confronted by even imperfectly drilled troops armed with rifles.

The Moscow revolution, where only 80 rifles were in the possession of the insurgents, would have ended in the annihilation of the artillery had the number of insurgent rifles been 800.

The insurrection of Paris in June, 1848, reveals how districts of towns, or villages, should be held. The streets were barricaded at tactical points *not on the main streets* but commanding them. The houses were broken through so that passages were made inside the houses along the whole length of the streets. The party walls were loopholed, as were also the front walls, the windows were blocked by sandbags, boxes filled with stones and dirt, bricks, chests, and other pieces of furniture with all sorts of odds and ends piled up against them.

Behind such defences the insurgents poured their fire upon the troops through loopholes left for the purpose.

In the attack upon Paris by the allies fighting against Napoleon a village held in this manner repulsed several assaults of the Prussian allies of England. When these Prussians were relieved by the English these latter did not dare attempt a frontal attack, but instead broke into an end house on one side of the village, street, and commenced to take the houses one by one. Thus all the fighting was inside the houses, and musket fire played but a small part. On one side of the street they captured all the houses, on the other they failed, and when a truce was declared the English were in possession of one side of the village, and their French enemies of the other.

The truce led to a peace. When peace was finally proclaimed the two sides of the village street were still held by opposing forces.

The defence of a building in a city, town, or village is governed by the same rules. Such a building left unconquered is a serious danger even if its supports are all defeated. If it had been flanked by barricades, and these barricades were destroyed, no troops could afford to push on and leave the building in the hands of the enemy. If they did so they would be running the danger of perhaps meeting a check further on, which check would be disastrous if they had left a hostile building manned by an unconquered force in their rear. Therefore, the fortifying of a strong building, as a pivot upon which the defence of a town or village should hinge, forms a principal object of the preparations of any defending force, whether regular army or insurrectionary.

In the Franco-Prussian War of 1870 the chateau, or castle, of Geissberg formed such a position in the French lines the August 4th. The Germans drove in all the supports of the French party occupying this country house, and stormed the outer courts, but were driven back by the fire from the windows and loopholed walls. Four batteries of artillery were brought up to within 900 yards of the house and battered away at its walls, and battalion after battalion was hurled against it. The advance of the whole German army was delayed until this one house was taken. To take it caused a loss of 23 officers and 329 men, yet it had only a garrison of 200.

In the same campaign the village of Bazeilles offered a similar lesson of the tactical strength of a well defended line of houses. The German Army drove the French off the field and entered the village without a struggle. But it took a whole army corps seven hours to fight its way through to the other end of the village.

A mountainous country has always been held to the difficult for military operations owing to its passes or glens. A city is a huge maze of passes or glens formed by streets and lanes. Every difficulty that exists for the operation of regular troops in mountains is multiplied a hundredfold in a city. And the difficulty to the commissariat which is likely to be insuperable to an irregular or popular force taking to the mountains, is solved for them by the sympathies of the populace when they take to the streets.

The general principle to be deducted from a study of the example we have been dealing with, is that the defence is of almost overwhelming importance in such warfare as a popular force like the Citizen Army might be called upon to participate in. Not a mere passive defence of a position valueless in itself, but the active defence of a position whose location threatens the supremacy or existence of the enemy. The genius of the commander must find such a position, the skill of his subordinates must prepare and fortify it, the courage of all must defend it. Out of this combination of genius, skill and courage alone can grow the flower of military success.

The Citizen Army and the Irish Volunteers are open for all who wish to qualify for the exercise of these qualities.

DONAL O'REILLY'S MEMORIES OF 1916*

"Eight hours work,
Eight hours play,
Eight hours sleep,
And eight bob a day,
I want to join, I want to join
Jim Larkin's Union."

These were the chants of many of the pupils of Saint Gabriel's National School as we marched and met groups from other schools caught in the fever of Dublin's 1913.

To me it was the crossing of the barrier of the national movement into the working-class movement.

My father, since his arrival in Dublin, had played an active role in each and every development that showed a promise of keeping alive the concept of Irish Nationality. Our home life was always filled with the stories of Myles the Slasher and the Bridge of Finea, John Boyle O'Reilly and the odd mention of the relatives that had crossed the American lines to fight for the independence of Mexico. They were all real people to me.

All those people who fanned the sparks of Nationality in those years in the early 1900s lived in a social and economic unity of their own. They met together and would travel miles to buy even the smallest articles from each other. Their "buy Irish" campaign was a real one; and to buy from a comrade was a law; one that had much to do with the succes of their efforts.

Found a Way In

The Volunteers were founded and the whole speed of life changed. Everyone at home seemed to know at last where they were going. Father, Kevin, Sammie and Dessy were in at the foundation in the Rotunda on November 25th, 1913. Each weekend there were hectic preparations. Each Sunday a busy day as route marches and sham battles kept the older members of the family away from home all day.

As the earnestness of the older people grew more intense, my youth seemed to become more and more a handicap. I was isolated, but sometimes I became the deliverer of an odd message or subscriptions to this fund or that—each Volunteer paid a weekly subscription as well as a weekly amount to the Arms Fund.

Eventually, I found a way in. There could be no objection to joining an Irish class and so I duly enrolled in the Columbcille Hall, in Blackhall Street. This was the centre from which most of the Volunteers and Gaelic Leaguers in the Dublin North West area were directed. They were not then or ever afterwards the same movements; they moved in near watertight compartments and it always seemed strange to me, the small percentage of the Volunteers who were in the Gaelic League, and the small section of the latter who were active in the Volunteers.

The first Great War had started and Dublin was paying a heavy price for its defence of Catholic Belgium. Social and economic pressures helped the recruiting campaign for the British Army. As well, every effort was made to isolate and hold up to contempt the Volunteers with their bandoliers and wooden rifles.

The faith of Fenianism, the closeness of their lives, however, gave them a moral courage which was the one great factor that made, despite diminishing numbers, the Easter Rising a possibility.

Our family were fortunate, as in the Howth gun-running of June 1914, my father and brothers had secured some arms; we always, as well, seemed to have contact with someone who would sell us a gun of some sort.

1916:

> "And in the fierce and bloody fight
>   Let not your courage lag,
> For I'll be there and hovering near
>   Around the dear old Flag."

Monday, Easter Week: In our home it was the ordinary week-end mobilisation. There was the cancellation order by MacNeill in the "Sunday Independent" of course, but somehow we didn't seem to pay much attention to newspapers then. Certainly all the adult members of my family went on parade. At two o'clock, I knew there was a difference. A barricade was up at the Railway Bridge in Phibsboro, which was just a few hundred yards from our home. Houses were occupied and all sorts of guns were in evidence.

Down I went into O'Connell Street. The Proclamation was up. The windows of the G.P.O. were barricaded. The looting had already started and despite efforts by a few Volunteers, shop after shop, was destroyed. How fires were prevented by the few Volunteers that were on the streets seemed a miracle.

Back through the barricades of Phibsboro I went home with wondrous tales to tell! Nobody was home; all were out on their barricades!

Tuesday, Easter Week: There was a silence that I had never known before or since. Nothing moved on the North Circular or Old Cabra Roads. I wanted to go into the city centre again, but how could I get across the barricade on the Railway Bridge? I knew Jim O'Sullivan, the officer in charge, but that would be of little value. I hung around and eventually nobody knew which side of the barricade I should be on. I discovered my own private route into O'Connell Street; down Mountjoy Square, into Hutton's Place, across Summerhill, an area that was then teeming with life, all living in big and small tenement dwellings.

I got to the G.P.O. The looting had ceased and the only movement now was of determined men that came and went. A few groups were gathered around the Post Office trying to get in, but were rejected.

At three o'clock there was a movement at the side door in Henry Street and the "War News" made its appearance. I duly appointed myself as official newsboy to the Garrison. Within an hour-and-a-half, the "War News" was sold and I was back in the G.P.O. with my official status and the money. I got into the main hall. Tom Clarke, whom I had met in his shop and at the lying-in-state of O'Donovan Rossa at the City Hall, saw me and was horrified. I was sent to Jim Ryan and he sent me off to Purcell's with a parcel of bandages. At the Purcell's post I stayed and there I met Cyl MacPartland, a man who was to be very close to me for many years afterwards.

Back at G.P.O.

Wednesday, Easter Week: The silence had gone. The occasional crack of a rifle had given way to the boom af artillery.

Thursday, I returned to the G.P.O.; there was no difficulty in getting in now. The guns were battering away and all the women and youth were being prepared for evacuation. It was proposed that we should go via Princes Street, Abbey Street and Capel Street. I left, crossing O'Connell Street, Marlborough Street and then up by Hutton's Place. Eventually I got to old houses in Berkeley Road, and stayed there until Sunday morning.

Easter Week was over in Dublin but the flame that was started grows ever still brighter. Victory is there for those that will seek and give service.

> "March, march ye toilers, and
> The world shall be free!"

* Ex-International Brigader, Donal O'Reilly wrote this account of how as a boy of 13 years he fellowed his father and three older brothers into the 1916 Rising, in the special issue of the "Irish Socialist," 1916—1966: published March 1966.

PASTORAL LETTER—1922

CARDINAL LOGUE AND THE ARCHBISHOPS AND BISHOPS OF IRELAND TO THE PRIESTS AND PEOPLE OF IRELAND. READ IN ALL CHURCHES AND PUBLIC ORATORIES AT THE PRINCIPAL MASSES ON SUNDAY OCTOBER 22nd, 1922

DEAR REV. FATHER AND BELOVED BRETHREN,

The present state of Ireland is a sorrow and a humiliation to its friends all over the world. To us, Irish Bishops, because of the moral and religious issues at stake, it is a source of the most painful anxiety.

Our country, that but yesterday was so glorious, is now a byword before the nations for a domestic strife, as disgraceful as it is criminal and suicidal. A section of the community, refusing to acknowledge the Government set up by the nation, have chosen to attack their own country as if she were a foreign Power. Forgetting apparently, that a dead nation cannot be free, they have deliberately set out to make our Motherland, as far as they could, a heap of ruins.

They have wrecked Ireland from end to end, burning and destroying national property of enormous value, breaking roads, bridges, and railways; seeking, by an insensate blockade, to starve the people, or bury them in social stagnation. They have caused more damage to Ireland in three months than could be laid to the charge of British rule in so many decades.

They carry on what they call a war, but which, in the absence of any legitimate authority to justify it, is morally only a system of murder and assassination of the National forces—for it must not be forgotten that killing in an unjust war is as much murder before God as if there were no war. They ambush military lorries in the crowded streets, thereby killing and wounding not only the soldiers of the Nation, but peaceful citizens. They have, to our horror, shot bands of these troops on their way to Mass on Sunday; and set mine traps in the public roads, and blown to fragments some of the bravest Irishmen that ever lived.

Side by side with this woeful destruction of life and property there is running a campaign of plunder, raiding banks and private houses, seizing the lands and property of others, burning mansions and country houses, destroying demesnes and slaying cattle.

But even worse and sadder than this physical ruin is the general demoralisation created by this unhappy revolt—demoralisation especially of the young, whose minds are being poisoned by false principles, and their young lives utterly spoiled by early association with cruelty, robbery, falsehood and crime.

Religion itself is not spared. We observe with deepest sorrow that a certain section is engaged in a campaign against the Bishops, whose pastoral office they would silence by calumny and intimidation and they have done the priesthood of Ireland, whose services and sacrifices for their country will be historic, the insult of suggesting a cabal amongst them to browbeat their Bishops and revolt against their authority.

And, in spite of all this sin and crime, they claim to be good Catholics, and demand at the hands of the Church her most sacred privileges, like the Sacraments, reserved for worthy members alone. When we think of what these young men were only a

197

few months ago, so many of them generous, kind-hearted and good, and see them now involved in this network of crime, our hearts are filled with bitterest anguish.

It is almost inconceivable how decent Irish boys could degenerate so tragically, and reconcile such a mass of criminality with their duties to God and to Ireland. The strain on our country for the last few years will account for much of it. Vanity, and perhaps selfconceit, may have blinded some who think that they, and not the nation, must dictate the national policy. Greed for land, love of loot and anarchy, have affected others, and they, we regret to say, are not a few. But the main cause of this demoralisation is to be found in false notions on social morality.

The long struggle of centuries against foreign rule and misrule has weakened respect for civil authority in the national conscience. This is a great misfortune, a great drawback, and a great peril, for a young Government. For no nation can live where the civil sense of obedience to authority and law is not firmly and religiously maintained. And if Ireland is ever to realise anything but a miserable record of anarchy, all classes of her citizens must cultivate respect for and obedience to the Government set up by the nation, whatever shape it takes, while acting within the law of God.

This defect is now being cruelly exploited for the ruin, as we see, of Ireland. The claim is now made that a minority are entitled when they think it right, to take up arms and destroy the National Government. Last April, foreseeing the danger, we raised our voices in the most solemn manner against this disruptive and immoral principle. We pointed out to our young men the conscientious difficulties in which it would involve them, and warned them against it. Disregard of the Divine Law, then laid down by the Bishops, is the chief cause of all our present sorrows and calamities.

We now again authoritatively renew that teaching; and warn our Catholic people that they are conscientiously bound to abide by it, subject, of course, to an appeal to the Holy See.

No one is justified in rebelling against the legitimate Government, whatever it is, set up by the nation, and acting within its rights. The opposite doctrine is false, contrary to Christian morals, and opposed to the constant teaching of the Church. "Let every soul," says St. Paul, "be subject to the higher powers" that is, to the legitimate authority of the State. From St. Paul downwards, the Church has inculcated obedience to authority, as a divine duty as well as a social necessity; and has reprobated unauthorised rebellion as sinful in itself and destructive of sicial stability: as it manifestly is. For if one section of the community has that right, so have other sections the same right, until we end in general anarchy. No one can evade this teaching, in our present case, by asserting that the legitimate authority in Ireland just now is not the Dail or Provisional Government. That Government has been elected by the nation, and is supported by the vast majority of public opinion. There is no other Government, and cannot be, outside the body of the people. A Republic without popular recognition behind it is a contradiction in terms.

Such being the Divine Law, the guerrilla warfare now being carried on by the Irregulars is without moral sanction: and therefore the killing of National soldiers in the course of it is murder before God; the seizing of public or private property is robbery; the breaking of roads, bridges, and railways, is criminal destruction; the invasion of homes and the molestation of citizens a grievous crime.

All those who, in contravention of this teaching, participate in such crimes, are guilty of the gravest sins, and may not be absolved in Confession, nor admitted to Holy Communhon, if they purpose to persevere in such evil courses.

It is said that there are some priests who approve of this Irregular insurrection. If there be any such, they are false to their sacred office, and are guilty of the gravest scandal, and will not be allowed to retain the faculties they hold from us. Furthermore we, each for his own diocese, hereby forbid under pain of suspension, ipso facto, reserved to the Ordinary, any priest to advocate or encourage this revolt, publicly or privately.

Our people will obeserve that in all this there is no question of mere politics, but of what is morally right or wrong according to the Divine Law, in certain principles, and in a certain series of acts, whether carried out for political purposes or otherwise. What we condemn is the armed campaign now being carried on against the Government set up by the nation. If any section in the community have a grievance, or disapprove of the National Government, they have the elections to fall back upon, and such constitutional action as is recognised by God and civilied society. If their political views are founded on wisdom they will succeed sooner or later; but, one thing is certain, the Hand of Providence will not be forced, nor their cause advanced, by irreligion and crime.

It may perhaps be said that in this our teaching we wound the strong feelings of many of our people. That we know, and the thought is an agony to us. But we must teach the Truth in this grave crisis, no matter what the consequences. It is not for want of sympathy with any part of our flock that we interfere, but from a deep and painful sense of our duty to God, to our people, and out of true charity to the young men themselves specially concerned. Let it not be said that this our teaching is due to political bias, and a desire to help one political party. If that were true, we were unworthy of our sacred office. Our religion, in such a supposition, were a mockery and a sham. We issue this Pastoral Letter under the gravest sense of our responsibility, mindful of the charge laid upon us by our Divine Father, to preach His doctrine, and safeguard His sacred rule of faith and morals, at any cost. We must, in the words of St. Peter, "Obey God rather than men."

With all earnestness we appeal to the leaders of this saddest revolt to rise above their own feelings, to remember the claims of God, and the sufferings of the people, on their conscience; and to abandon methods which they now know, beyond the shadow of doubt are un-Catholic and immoral, and look to the realisation of their ideals along lines sanctioned by Divine Law and the usages of wellordered society. Let them not think that we are insensible to their feelings. We think of them with compassion, carrying as they do on their shoulders the heavy responsibility for what is now happening in Ireland. Once more we beg and implore the young men of this movement, in the name of God, to return to their innocent homes, and make, if necessary, the big sacrifice of their own feelings for the common good. And surely it is no humiliation, having done their best, to abide by the verdict of Ireland.

We know that some of them are troubled and held back by the oath they took. A lawful oath is indeed a sacred bond between God and man; but no oath can bind any man to carry on a warfare against his own country, in circumstances forbidden by the law of God. It would be an offence to God and to the very nature of an oath to say so.

We, therefore, hope and pray that they will take advantage of the Government's present offer, and make peace with their own country; a peace which will bring both happiness and honour to themselves, and joy to Ireland generally, and to the friends of Ireland all over the world.

In this lamentable upheaval, the moral sense of the people has, we fear, been badly shaken. We read with horror of the many murders recorded in the Press. With feelings of shame we observe, that when country houses and public buildings were destroyed, the furniture and other fittings were seized and carried away by people in the neighbourhood. We remind them that all such property belongs in justice to the original owners, and now must be preserved for and restored to them by those who hold it.

We desire to impress on the people the duty of supporting the National Government, whatever it is; to set their faces resolutely against disorder; to pay their taxes, rents, and annuities; and to assist the Government, in every possible way, to restore order and establish peace. Unless they learn to do so, they can have no Government; and, if they have no Government, they can have no nation.

As human effort is fruitless without God's blessing, we exhort our priests and people to continue the prayers already ordered, and we direct that the remaining October devotions be offered up for peace. We also direct that a Novena to the Irish Saints, for the same end, be said in all public churches and oratories, and in semi-public oratories, to begin on the 28th of October and end on November the 5th, in preparation for the Feast of all the Irish Saints. These Novena devotions, in addition to the Rosary and Benediction, may include a special prayer for Ireland and the Litany of the Irish Saints.

Excerpt from Lian Mellowes'
"NOTES FROM MOUNTJOY"

"We are forced to recognise that the commercial interests and the merchants are on the side of the Treaty. We are back to Tone and it is just as well—relying on the men of no property."

"The stake-in-the-country people were never with the Republic—they will always be against it until it wins."

Referring to the attitude of the Irish Hierarchy, his notes recorded: "Invariably wrong in Ireland in their political outlook—against the people in '98. Fr. Murphy, Roche, Kearns excommunicated by the then Bishop of Ferns—against Emmett, 'condemning outrage'—against Young Ireland, 'Godless young men,' support of Sadlier and Keogh—against Fenians; Dr. Cullen, Bishop Moriarty; 'Hell not hot enough or eternity long enough.'—against 'Plan of Campaign'—against Sinn Fein (early days, when it was mild and water)—against Irish Volunteers—support for England in European War, 1914—morally to blame for deaths of thousands of Irish youths in France, Flanders, Mespotamia, Gallipoli, Macedonia, etc. Nothing can condone this. European war was a hideous holocaust on altar of Mammon; a struggle between Europe for power—Irish hierarchy blood—guilty."

"Hierarchy against Easter Rising, 1916, denunciation of Pearse, etc. (Pearse, the great example of Christian idealism). Hierarchy only opposed Conscription when forced to do so by the attitude of people. Against I.R.A. during Terror. Bishop Cohalan's excommunication degree of December 1920. Hierarchy's abandonment of principle, justice and honour by support of Treaty. Danger to Catholicism in Ireland from their bad example—their exaltation of deceit and hypocrisy, their attempt to turn the noble aspect of the Irish struggle and bring it to the level of putrid politics, their admission that religion is something to be preached about from pulpits on Sundays but never put into practice in the affairs of the Nation, their desertion of Ulster etc."

PASTORAL LETTER—1931

In the Pastoral Letter read at all the Masses in every Catholic church throughout Ireland on October 18th, 1931, Cardinal MacRory, and the Archbishops and Bishops of Ireland, expressed the grave anxiety with which they viewed the progress made by anti-social and anti-Christian organisations, and called for a great Crusade of Prayer to stay the peril which threatened Ireland.

The Pastoral was as follows:—

DEARLY BELOVED IN CHRIST,

Assembled in Maynooth for our annual October Meeting, and deeply conscious of our responsibility for the Faith and Morals of our people, we cannot remain silent in face of the growing evidence of a campaign of Revolution and Communism, which, if allowed to run its course unchecked, must end in the ruin of Ireland, both soul and body.

You have no need to be told that there is in active operation amongst us a society of a militarist character, whose avowed object is to overthrow the State by force of arms. In pursuit of this aim they arrogate to themselves the right to terrorise public officials and conscientious jurymen, to intimidate decent citizens into silence or acquiescence, and even to take human life itself.

Such methods and principles of action are in direct opposition to the Law of God, and come clearly under the definite condemnation of the Catholic Church; nor can the deeds of bloodshed to which they lead be made legitimate by any motives of patriotism.

To guard against misrepresentation, it is to be clearly understood that this statement, which we feel called upon to issue, has reference only to the religious and moral aspect of affairs, and involves no judgment from us on any question of public policy, so far as it is purely political. The political issue is a matter for the country at large, and is to be decided by the votes of the people as a whole. But no policy, however good, may be prosecuted by methods and means like those we have referred to, which are contrary to Divine Law and subversive of social order.

The existing Government in Saorstat Eireann is composed of our own countrymen and has been entrusted with office by the votes of the people. If the majority of the electors are not in agreement with its policy or its work they can set it aside by their votes, and return another to take its place. But so long as the Government holds office, it is the only lawful civil authority, a proposition that would be equally true if the Government were defeated to-morrow and if any of the opposition parties assumed responsibility. From this it follows that no individuals or combination of individuals are free to resist its decrees or its officials by armed force, violence or intimidation. If such things were lawful, if any body of people who felt that they were aggrieved, were free to set up a rival executive and a rival army, the inevitable result must be anarchy, the destruction of personal liberty, and the material as well as the spiritual ruin of the country.

Side by side with the Society referred to, is a new organisation entitled "Saor Eire", which is frankly Communistic in its aims. Its published programme, as reported in the press, when reduced to simple language, is, amongst other things, to mobilise the workers and working farmers of Ireland behind a revolutionary movement to set up a Communistic State. That is, to impose upon the Catholic soil of Ireland the same materialistic regime, with its fanatical hatred of God, as now dominates Russia, and threatens to dominate Spain.

This organisation, which is but a translation into Irish life, under Bolshevistic tuition, of a similar scheme in use in Russia, proposes to attain its object by starting throughout the country districts wherever it can, and in towns and amongst industrial workers, what they call "Working Peasant Clubs," or "Cells," disguised for the moment in terms of Nationality and zeal for Farmers and Workmen, but which are to serve as revolutionary units to infect their disciples with the virus of Communism, and create social disruption by organised opposition to the Law of the Land.

Thus are we to see, if their efforts are successful, the ruin of all that is dear to us in history, religion, and country, brought about in the name of Patriotism and Humanity. For materialistic Communism, in its principles and action, wherever it appears, means a blasphemous denial of God and the overthrow of Christian civilisation. It means also class warfare, the abolition of private property, and the destruction of family life.

We cannot contemplate without sorrow the heedlessness of those who seem to make light of these imminent dangers, and, with stolid indifference, allow the propagation, far and wide, of those doctrines, which seek by violence and bloodshed the destruction of all Society. It is our duty to tell our people plainly that the two Organisations to which we have referred, whether separate or in alliance, are sinful and irreligious, and that no Catholic can lawfully be a member of thêm.

We appeal most earnestly, and with deepest anxiety, to all our people, and especially the young, who, through misguided counsels or mistaken love of country, have been caught in the meshes of these evil associations, to abandon them at once, and at any price. Surely the ranks of Communistic revolution are no place for an Irish boy of Catholic instincts. You cannot be a Catholic and a Communist. One stands for Christ, the other for Anti-Christ. Neither can you, and for the same reason, be an auxiliary of Communism.

Furthermore, we appeal, and with all the earnestness we can command to men of all political parties who love their religion and country, to forget their differences for the time being, and join their forces in an endeavour to find a solution, for our social and economic economic problems, that shall be in accordance with the traditions of Catholic Ireland.

With anxious hearts we turn to God, who has mercifully watched over our country through the ages, to extend His protecting arm to her now; to save her from the horrors of civil strife and religious ruin; to open all eyes to the danger impending over us; and to strengthen all hearts to resist the forces of evil with unflinching Faith.

We know, and it is a consolation to us, how sincerely Catholic our people are as a body; but, in view of the peculiar enemies that are now assailing Divine Faith, our very feeling of security may become a source of danger.

As an act of expiation, and to invoke the Divine aid and the blessing of peace, we hereby direct that a Triduum of Prayer be opened in every Parish Church, and in all religious Houses, on Tuesday, 3rd, November, in preparation for the Feast of All the Irish Saints; the devotions to consist of the Rosary, and the Litany of of the Irish Saints, in presence of the Blessed Sacrament exposed. We call upon our people to join in these devotions with the utmost zeal and fervour.

The Religious behind their Convent walls will, we know, give Ireland, in her hour of trial, the benefit of their prayers. And we expect all our teachers to urge the children under their care, both boys and girls, to join in the same Crusade of Prayer.

Finally, we direct our priests to exert every effort to keep young people from secret societies, and diligently instruct them on the malice of murder, and the Satanic tendencies of Communism.

Praying for the mercy and blessing of God upon our country, we remain, your faithful Servants in Christ.

LABOUR&TRADE UNION MANIFESTO

(Manifesto issued jointly by the Administrative Council of the Irish Labour Party and the National Executive of the Irish Trade Union Congress and distributed at the Connolly Memorial Parades, May 6th, 1934)

FASCIST DANGER ·

The Irish Trade Union Congress and the Irish Labour Party take a serious view of the growth of Fascism in this country; and the pronouncements of Fascist advocates regarding the Trade Union and Labour Movement. These pronouncements, representing the opinions of prominent men in the political life of the country, cannot be ignored.

> *They constitute a grave danger to the free existence of trade unions as well as pointing to the overthrow of democratic government.*

DEMOCRACY AND TRADE UNIONISM IN PERIL.

The present world economic situation is considered by the Fascists in this country to have created a suitable setting and environment to push forward the violent principles of Fascist reaction. Through the exploitation of economic distress the disappointed remnants of the Cumann na nGaedheal Party, by coalescing with other reactionary political elements, adopting new theories and party cries, and promoting a semi-military political organisation, hope to disguise their past, and rehabilitate themselves once more as a Government.

In this aim and objective these disappointed politicians have the support of every reactionary element which sees in the national and social advance of the people the loss of a privileged class position that has been enjoyed since the Conquest. These anti-National elements are centring their hostility to the people under the banner of Fascism. In this attack on the principles of democracy and trade unionism the forces of landlordism and reaction, linked with disappointed party politicians avaricious for power, are massing themselves under Fascist leadership. These Fascist preparations portend the gravest menace the workers of Ireland have ever been called on to face.

> *On the issue of this struggle will depend whether the people of Ireland, and the workers in particular, will maintain the political and social advancement secured through centuries of sacrifice.*

CONTINENTAL IMITATIONS

The Fascist Movement is developing this country on lines similar to those followed in continental countries—inflammatory oratory, spectacular parades, the glamour of uniforms, appeals to youthful enthusiasm, political gasconading, promises of material reward—and behind it all the backing of a private political army. The advocates of Fascism by such means emulate their confreres on the Continent and hope thereby to secure power and control of the State.

Once seated in the saddle of Government the mask will be thrown aside, and by the suppression of democratic organisations and popular rights, Fascism will reveal itself here as elsewhere—the oppressor of liberty and the effective instrument of heartless capitalism.

Largely because the mass of the people failed to appreciate the significance of its aims, Fascism in continental countries succeeded in gaining control of the State by means of specious promises, the savage suppression of opposition and, to an extent, the apathy of public opinion. To-day in the Fascist countries the trade unions and other popular organisations are destroyed, their buildings stolen, their funds confiscated, and their leaders in gaol or in their graves. Such are the methods by which Fascism alone can succeed. These are its approved methods in all countries where it has obtained control of the State machine.

Anyone who has studied the growth of the Fascist Movement elsewhere will recognise the same methods, phrases, and party slogans; the salutes, uniforms and badges of its counterpart in the Blue Shirt Movement here.

"CORPORATE STATE" OR CORPORATE SLAVERY.

That Movement, like Fascism in other European countries, adopts an "Economic" code, and sets out to advocate the so-called "Corporate State" in furtherance of which trade unionism must be destroyed.

> *To replace the Trade Unions, puppet organisations will be established with constitutions and rules drafted by the Government, who will appoint the officers and control their policy.*

Let us see what the chief exponent of this policy has to say; we are told the Corporate plan is to mobilise

> "all the workers and all the employers in a particular industry ... in a federation ... If the two sections cannot agree the difference between them will ... be settled by an Industrial Court, the decision of which will be enforceable with all the authority of the State. The worker or employer who fails to comply with it will be prosecuted ... Further, there will be machinery for the transference of workmen from factory to factory" ... *While strikes are to be illegal.*

Here is the graveyard of civil liberty.

"FORCED LABOUR GANGS."

The able-bodied unemployed are to be further degraded by the Managers of the "Corporate State". They are to be disciplined, engaged on task work and allowed home at week-ends, if possible. This organisation of the unemployed is dignified with the title "Reconstruction Groups." These groups are better recognised as the "Forced Labour Gangs" of the Fascist countries. Thus, bound in absolute bondage, the unemployed worker can be driven hither and thither at the mercy of the "Corporative" dictators. Any protest will be met by stopping any food ration or pittance which may be allowed; and should these methods prove ineffective, then the Fascist terror chamber. Such is the programme the Fascists are outlining week by week.

> *Fascism has, therefore, nothing to recommend it to the people. Its trail across the face of civilised Europa has been one of violent upheaval, bloodshed and terrorism.*

Cognisant of the dangers which confront the workers of Ireland, we urge the masses of the people to distinguish between spurious promises and the realities of Fascism as expressed by the Blue Shirt Movement. *The issue is one of life and death for democracy and trade unionism.*

To crystallise the hostility of the Trade Union and Labour Movement to the realities of Fascism, public meeting are to be organised throughout the country, commencing on the 6th May, 1934. Trades' Councils and Labour Party branches are, therefore, called upon to make the requisite arrangements for holding demonstrations in their areas.

This call for action is issued to the Irish workers, confident in the knowledge that now, as in the past, they will heartily respond and resist the attack aimed at their liberties.

This call is addressed not alone to the working-class, but to every hater of arrogance and lover of liberty.

For the Irish Labour Party—   William Norton
   (Administrative Council)   L. J. Duffy
                                   William O'Brien.

For the Irish Trade Union Congress—   Michael Duffy
   (National Executive)   Eamon Lynch

Report of the National Executive for year 1933–34, published by the Irish Trade Union Congress, 32, Nassau Street, Dublin, 1934 pp. 38–43.

LABOUR PARTY REPORT

(Report of the Administrative Council of the Irish Labour Party for the year 1933–34)
THE MENACE OF FASCISM

Towards the end of last year the League of Youth Section of the United Ireland Party (generally known as the "Blueshirts") assumed the mannerisms, the uniforms, the salutes, the slogans and the aggressive militarism of Continental Fascism. Military titles were conferred on its leaders and officials, and a campaign was inaugurated to paralyse local government and to render impotent the whole machinery of State administration. The leaders of the Blue Shirt movement did not disguise their purpose; they proposed to inaugurate the Fascist corporate State—the peculiar device for destroying personal liberty invented by Continental Fascism. "The Dail was not suitable for modern Government," said Mr. Blythe. "This miscellaneous assembly is not a suitable assembly for discussing the business of the Nation," and the Assistant General Secretary of the Blueshirt Organisation speaking at Kilmurry south an May 6th said: "Looking at Italy, they saw there was good in the (Fascist) System as against the present rotten system in this country." The same strain ran through all the speeches delivered at hundreds of meetings organised by the Blueshirts throughout the country. At times the speakers were at pains to disavow any affinity between their organisation and Continental Fascism; at times they were enthusiastic in their support to the savage regime imposed on Italy and Germany by Mussolini and Hitler. Emulating the terrorist tactics of German Fascism General O'Duffy told an audience of 4,000 in Kinsale: "We must make life intolerable for those who will not yield to our demands."(11/4/34).

Speaking in Ballaghaderreen on May 6th, General O'Duffy announced that the Blueshirt movement was not "designed on Italian lines, or on German lines, but on Irish lines"; and in Blackrock on June 18th Mr. J. A. Costello, ex-Attorney-General, stated "they would offer the people a Corporate Statd—not as an Italian or a German policy, but as an Irish policy." But some months later—on September 3rd—General O'Duffy abandoned his antagonism to the German and Italian model. Speaking in Fethard he said: "When in Germany recently he noticed that every workman wore Hitler's badge. Under Hitler and Mussolini those workmen were getting their daily wage, and were not depending on doles. No power in the world could induce the people of Germany or Italy to change. Hitler had done more for Germany than any other leader in the world had done for his country." (Tipperary Star, 8/9/34). This tribute to the Fascism of Hitler and Mussolini that survives only because it is a tyranny and an oppression which tramples on liberty and denies to its critics even the right to criticise, fairly indicates the path which the Blueshirt organisation has mapped out for itself. And this admiration for the methods of Hitlerism is not an isolated indiscretion nor of recent growth. In the Dail on February 28th, Mr. Costello gave expression to an equally enthusiastic tribute. He said: "The Blackshirts were victorious in Italy, and Hitler's Shirts were victorious in Germany, as, assuredly . . . the Blueshirts will be victorious in the Irish Free State." There is not even room for doubt but that it is the intention of the Blueshirt organisation to emulate their Continental model down to the smallest detail of Fascist tyranny. For instance we find the Assistant General Secretary of the Organisation (Mr. T.P. Gunning) telling his audience in Ballindaggin on May 21st that when they got into office as a Government, "they will exile De Valers" and other political opponents; ex-Comdt. Cronin told an audience of Blueshirts in Clane (8/5/34) "we are determined to have an eye for an eye, a tooth for a tooth," and later, in the white heat of hhs enthusiasm he announced: "When we are a Government—By God we will govern." The same speaker, by way of encouragement, told a Kilkenny Blueshirt audience: "The next time a policeman endeavours to take a baton off a Blueshirt he will first have to know himself a better man" (13/5/34). A week earlier General O'Duffy had issued a command to his followers: "If you are attacked," he said, "defend yourself . . . with your fists, or even with a stick."

Blueshirts' Economic Policy.

Nor does the economic policy of the Blueshirts differ materially from the rampant capitalism of Hitler and Mussolini. Evidently General O'Duffy is opposed to doles; that is, the unemployment benefit which a workman pays for when he is in employment to sustain himself and his family when he is out of work. The system is bad for the national morale, we are told. Evidently the denunciation of doles does not however extend to the pensions provided by the taxpayers for ex-police officers, ex-army officers, etc. On May 6th, General O'Duffy said: "This country is losing its national pride and its morale. There was a time when people would starve sooner than take free meat." Of course it is historically true that thousands of our people did starve although at the time there was in the country more than sufficient food to maintain twice its population, but, apparently unknown to the Blueshirts, there has been an advance since then-the Irish people in the present generation will not starve in the midst of plenty. But the standard of wages contemplated by the Blueshirt leaders makes it incumbent on their organisation to discourage doles; they realise that if an unemployed workman can obtain benefit of any kind he will not accept the wages which a Blueshirt employer is willing to offer him. We have not been left in doubt as to what is the wage policy of their movement; in April a member of the Executive of the United Ireland Party announced it in these terms:—

> "the organisation which was so well represented that day had the decent labourers with them, was who were willing to work for 6/— or 8/— a week ..."

A few months earlier it was announced when the Labour Policy of the Blueshirts was published that the rates of pay a workman was entitled to receive would be fixed for him by law; strikes would be illegal, and his wages would be determined by an official of the Corporate State. No body of workmen has voluntarily embraced that policy so far.

Resistance to Fascism.

Regarding it as a duty to the Nation to expose the danger lurking behind the Blueshirt propaganda in favour of a Fascist State from which individual liberty and representative Government will have disappeared, the Administrative Council in conjunction with the National Executive of the Trade Union Congress organised meetings in all the important centres in the Saorstat, at which the subject was very fully discussed and issued a statement concerning the development of Fascism which had a wide circulation. Developments of various kinds, at home and abroad, gave point to the accusations directed against the Blueshirt movement and emphasised its resemblance to Continental Fascism. For instance, in May their official organ instructed Blueshirt officers to prepare "a black list" of individuals who opposed their policy, so that when they get into power, disciplinary action may be taken against those listed, and it was indicated that the appearance of a name in the Black List might be regarded as prima facie evidence of culpability entitling a Blueshirt Government to inflict whatever punishment it thought fit. A campaign of boycotting directed against people who refused publicly to identify themselves with the Blueshirts was organised on approved Fascist lines, and openly encouraged by responsible members of the organisation including certain Deputies. Workmen were told specifically that they would be deprived of their employment unless they attired themselves in the semi-military uniform of the Blueshirt organisation and paraded at meetings, fairs and cattle sales.

Events abroad were not less disconcerting to the apostles of Fascist philosophy. In Germany particularly, terrorism and crime became a synonym for Fascism. The Nazis' attacks on religion—indeed, on Christianity—alarmed many of the pseudo-constitutional and wealthy supporters of the Blueshirts in this country who were conscious of the admiration which General O'Duffy entertained for Hitlerism. In May the Irish Times wrote:

> "Cardinal Faulhaber in Bavaria, like Pastor Niemoeller in Berlin, is fighting the battle of revealed religion against the philosophy of paganism." (Irish Times, 14/5/34).

"A Regular Rabble."

Again, another organ friendly to the Blueshirts (Cork Examiner, 18/9/34) announced that, as an act of revenge, Nazi doctors had boycotted a Catholic Hospital. In this instance, there is a striking similarity between the language used in the Nazi circular and the language invariably used in public pronouncements by, say, General O'Duffy or ex-Comdt. Cronin. "I give strictest instructions," says the President of the Dusseldorf Nazi Doctors' Association, "that no patients are to be sent to St. Mary's Hospital. I shall publish the names of any doctors who disobey this order." There, we find the same idea, the same terrorist methods, and almost the same language as was noticed in the official Blueshirt newspaper when it instructed the officers of the organisation to compile a "Black List" of persons marked down for future punishment and exile. As the facts became generally appreciated in the country, it is not difficult to understand the uneasiness created by declarations such as that made in Fethard by General O'Duffy.

Although the large crop of political assassinations in Germany at the end of June created a profound sensation in this country, it is unnecessary to consider to what extent they emphasised the relevance of the Anti-Fascist campaign in the Saorstat. By that time the people perceived in the Fascism of the Blueshirt movement germs of lawlessness, the existence of which threatened the whole social structure. At an early stage in his campaign, General O'Duffy frequently boasted of the discipline of his organisation. On May 6th he said: "I am proud to say the the Blueshirt organisation has maintained a self-sacrificing discipline that is wholly admirable." But he seems to have tired of the monotony of that discipline, and on May 27th we find him telling his followers: "If they do attack you, you can give them ten blows for every one you receive."

The effect of that encouragement was not lost on his followers. Blows were struck, railway lines were ripped up, telegraph wires were cut, trees were felled and thrown across the public roads. A striking commentary on the character of certain sections of the Blueshirt organisation and the absence of discipline amongst them is provided in a statement made by the District Justice at Ballymote (Co. Sligo) at the termination of a case in which a number of Blueshirts appeared before him. "It is quite clear," he said, "that a big proportion of the ... were a regular rabble." Subsequently the Blueshirt organisation split into warring sections. Evidently the astute politicians behind the organisation, watching the public reaction to O'Duffy's campaign, were alarmed by the devastating results of his indiscretions, and in the hope of preserving the remnants of their Party, resolved that if its Fascist character is to remain, its advocacy must be less flamboyant. O'Duffy was removed from the Dictator's chair, not because the U.I.P. renounced their former objective, but to enable them to pursue new tactics to which their Leader was unwilling to adapt himself.

Labour Party Programme.

As opposed to the Fascism of the United Ireland Party, the Labour Party pursues a policy of ordered development having as its objective the Workers' Republic envisaged by James Connolly. So long as one Section or one class in the community is exploited by another section or another class, there is neither individual liberty nor political freedom. To end that exploitation and to stamp out the evils in which Fascism is bred, the Labour Movement must rescue the mass of the people from want, unemployment, casual labour, wage-slavery and place them firmly on the land of this country, masters of its destinies, the makers of its laws and the defenders of its liberties. Industrial development, improved farming methods, the breaking up of estates, encouragement of agriculture, extension of tillage in the existing organisation of society will create more opportunities of employment no doubt, but will tend to widen the gulf between the owners of property, the financiers and the rentiers at one end of scale, and the wage earning and small farming class at the other. Every new machine invented will be an added menace to the security of the latter and an added source of wealth to the former.

Fascism is the negation of liberty erected into a system of government. Born out of the post-war confusion in Western Europe, it is in essence a savage dictatorship. Wherever it has manifested itself its adherents used their power to suppress by violence all other parties. Murder, torture, confiscation of property and the jailing of its opponents were, and still are its weapons. Fascism is capitalism in its most decadent form. To gain power it seeks the support of the masses; to those who are employed in a period of depression it will promise work, to those who have low wages it will promise betterment, to those who are patriotic it will promise deeds of heroism, but it is merely the last attempt to prevent the downfall of a system which has completely failed, and even if it tried, it could not fulfil these specious promises.

After twelve years of Fascist rule in Italy, on May 25th, Mussolini confessed:

> "Two things only can happen, either we shall stay for a long time in the depths, or else little by little we shall begin to live again. But, in my opinion, we must abandon the idea that the days of what we called prosperity can ever return."

Irish Labour Party, Fourth Annual Report, pp. 9—14.

A DIARY
OF PULPIT-PROPAGANDA

1936

August 30th,—An appeal for prayers for the Catholics of Spain, that the shocking outrages against them might cease, was made by three Irish Bishops to-day. *Most Rev. Dr. Mageean, Bishop of Down and Connor,* in a letter read at all masses in the diocese urged a crusade of prayer for the persecuted Spanish Catholics.

He directed that next Sunday be observed as a day of atonement and expiation for the sacrileges of the past few weeks. There will be Exposition of the Blessed Sacrament from the last Mass until the evening Devotions in every parochial church and convent chapel.

"The account of the atrocities committed in Spain, as reported in the daily press," said Dr. Mageean in his letter, "have filled the Catholic world with dismay, and by many it is feared that the Spanish disturbance may upset the fabric of European peace. At the moment Christian civilisation is passing through a crisis. The war in Spain is between Christianity and Communism, and it is through prayer—the atonement for past crimes and a feeling for further security—that we can render the greatest help to our afflicted brethen and the cause of Christian civilisation in general.

"Accordingly, I ask the priests of the diocese to urge the faithful in their churches to join in a crusade of Prayer, say the Family Rosary, to hear Mass, and receive Holy Communion for the blessing of peace and the welfare of Spain, a country to which our Irish nation owes much for many favours in the past."

Most Rev. Dr. Wall, Bishop of Thasos, after he had blessed the new school of St. Saviour's in Little Denmark St. Dublin, said that day by day, as they took up the papers, they found in one part of Ireland or another new churches and new schools were being erected. It was very pleasing to see this, especially when they turned to the other side of the paper and saw another Catholic land—Spain—to which Irishmen owed a great deal, and which had been described as "Noble Spain," which came to their help in the days when education was being penalised—when they saw what was going on there today. In Spain churches had been destroyed and schools had been pulled down; nuns and priests were outraged and murdered—all the result of Bolshevist proclivities and because the children had come to maturity who had been taught that there was no God and no restraint on their morality. The only help that the nations of the world could give Spain was to stand aloof, because if one nation entered another would follow, and there would be war in Europe.

"But surely," his Lordship added, "we need not stand aloof in our sympathy and, especially in our prayers. We can pray that this shocking revolution and these shocking outrages might cease, and that Almighty God would help the Spanish people."

Most Rev. Dr. McKenna, Bishop of Clogher, addressing pilgrims to the shrine of Blessed Oliver Plunket, in St. Peter's Church, Drogheda, said:—"To-day Catholics are suffering terrible persecution in Spain. It has not been easy for us to learn from history what our people suffered in the past for the faith, but the persecution to-day towards Catholics in Spain by the enemies of Christ, will help us to realise what our forefathers suffered.

"The Spanish Catholics had shown great courage and great heroism in their terrible suffering at the hands of the enemies of their faith."

September 13th—To-day was observed in St. Mel's Cathedral, Longford, as a day of reparation for the outrages in Spain and of supplication for the Church in Spain.

Most Rev. Dr. McNamee, Bishop of Ardagh and Clonmacnoise, delivered a striking denunciation of the persecution of the Church by the Spanish Reds.

The Cathedral was visited by groups of parish Sodalities, and there was Exposition of the Blessed Sacrament. The devotions were brought to a close in the evening by the singing of "The Miserere," the chanting of the Litany of the Saints, and a procession and Benediction of the Blessed Sacrament. The Cathedral was crowded for these ceremonies.

Most Rev. Dr. McNamee, Bishop of Ardagh and Clonmacnoise, presided at High Mass at noon, and in an address to a large congregration said that the day was to be observed in the Cathedral as a special day of reparation and of supplication for the hideous outrages recently perpetuated in Spain against religion and supplication for the sorely tried Church of Spain in her hour of affliction and of desperate need. There was no need, His Lordship said, to recount the unspeakable barbarities perpetuated in that unhappy land by Communist energuments against Bishops, priests and nuns in their hell-inspired hatred of God and of His Church.

It was impossible to speak or even to think, of these abominations without loathing, so utterly shameful and inhuman were they in their unmitigated beastliness. The orgies of the Roman amphitheatre in the pagan days of Nero, the bloodiest massacres of the French Revolution, had nothing more atrocious to show.

September 20th—The following letter from *Most Rev. Dr. Mulhern, Bishop of Dromore* was read at all Masses throughout the diocese to-day.

"The sufferings of our brethren in Spain, and the deeds of horror with which this persecution is carried out, call for prayers and good works of the faithful that God may stay the hand of the persecutors, and solace and strengthen the victims of their cruelty.

"The campaign of outrages, at present carried on in Spain, is but part of a well-organised movement for the destruction of the Church and religion and civilisation throughout the world.

"As events have shown the mask is off, and the contest in Spain is not a struggle between political parties as to who should rule, but between God and His enemies. As to the ultimate result, there cannot be any doubt. But, in the meantime, unspeakable outrages are being perpetrated against the Infinite Majesty of God and the blasphemies uttered against Him; churches are desecrated; God's ministers and religious, men and women, are being done to death under the most revolting circumstances.

"It is the plain duty of all Christians, as far as it is possible for them, to make reparation to Almighty God for the insults offered to Him, and to beg Him to take pity on a sinful world, to bestow on it that peace which He alone can give, and to bring to naught the schemes of His enemies.

"For this end, and to carry out the desire of the Holy Father, you will please ask your people to assist at Holy Mass, to offer their Communions, and to visit the Most Holy Sacrament as often as possible, and on Sunday, the 27th, let there be Exposition of the Blessed Sacrament from last Mass until the Evening Devotions, at which the Act of Reparation to the Sacred Heart will be read."

October 13th—His Eminence, Cardinal Mac Rory presided at a meeting of the Irish Hierarchy in St. Patrick's College, Maynooth to-day. The following statement was issued:—

"Assembled for the October meeting in Maynooth College, we, the Bishops of Ireland, avail of the opportunity of expressing our profound regret at the sufferings inflicted on the unhappy Catholics of Spain.

"We know how shocked and how horrified our people have been by the brutal outrages on religion and humanity perpetrated by Communist factions there; and how deeply they sympathise with that great nation on the tragedy of ruin and shame it has been made to endure at the hands of an infamous minority under foreign direction.

"Spain at this moment is fighting the battle of Christendom against the subversive powers of Communism.

"In that fateful struggle it has, we believe, the prayers and good wishes of the great body of Christians throughout the world, and nowhere more than in Ireland, which is not unmindful of Spain's kindness to our ancestors.

"We feel that we are but satisfying a general desire amongst our people when we authorise, as we do now, collections to be made at all Masses in the various churches of each parish on Sunday, October 25th, the Feast of Christ the King.

"When these collections have been taken up in the parishes of each diocese they are to be sent to the Bishop, who will pass them on to Cardinal Mac Rory, to be transmitted by His Eminence to the Cardinal Primate of Spain for the relief of her suffering Catholics.

"In authorising these collections we in no way wish to discourage similar collections that are being made for the same purpose with laudable zeal by other organisations, such as the Christian Front. On the contrary, our desire is to enlarge and support them.

"In times of affliction and stress it has been the fruitful practice of the Church to turn the thoughts of her children to prayer and supplication. Society all over the world is beset with difficulties and dangers of the extreme kind, and the Holy Father, in grievous anxiety, appeals to the faithful everywhere for the assistance of their prayers before the Throne of God.

"Accordingly, to make atonement for the sacrileges and outrages committed against Christ and in supplication for the victory of Christianity over anarchy and Communism, we direct that on the Feast of Christ the King, at least in the principal churches of each parish, the Most Holy Sacrament should be publicly exposed wherever possible for some few hours after last Mass, during which the Rosary of the Blessed Virgin and the Litany of the Holy Name and other suitable prayers should be solemnly recited.

"And we also order that the *Orato Imperata Pro Pace* (italics added) should be said in the Mass, when permitted by the Rubrics, *tanquam pro re gravi* (italics also) till the end of the year. The priests concerned will kindly regard this notification as sufficient without further instructions."

December 5—His Eminence, Cardinal Mac Rory has received from the dioceses of Ireland, and other sources, subscriptions amounting to the magnificent total of £ 43,331 for the suffering Catholics of Spain.

1937

January 13th—Most Rev. Dr. Wall, Bishop of Thasos representing His Grace, the Archbishop of Dublin, blessed the first ambulance being sent to Spain by the Irish Christian Front. The ceremony took place at the North Wall before the ambulance was placed on board the Liverpool steamer.

*February 7th—*The Lenten Pastoral letters of the Bishops of Ireland were read in the churches throughout the country to-day. They deal for the most part with the modern world evils which threaten to sap faith and against which all must needs be on guard. Communism is undoubtedly the greatest of these evils and the Cardinal Archbishop of Armagh devotes practically the whole of his Pastoral to the subject. He appeals particularly to the young men to set their faces against it. In most of the Pastorals the lesson of events in Spain is emphasised.

The following are brief passages from the Pastoral Letters:

His Eminence, Cardinal MacRory—And what is the condition of the rank and file, the great mass of the Russian people? They are reduced to a dead level little above slavery, held down under an iron discipline, treated as so many State machines, and afraid at the peril of their lives to utter a word of criticism of these circumstances.

The Archbishop of Dublin—During his prolonged and painful illness, borne with exquisite patience and characteristic fortitude, the Holy Father has offered his sufferings particularly for Spain, Mexico, Russia and other countries where religion is now being persecuted. It will be our privilege to join with the Supreme Pontiff in his prayer, by offering up our Lenten penance and prayer in reparation for the shocking outrages which are credibly reported to have happened in these unhappy countries.

The Bishop of Achonry—In a Catholic country such as ours it should not be in the power of any individual to proclaim from the housetops doctrines that imply the overthrow of the existing order, and destroy sentiments dearer to those who cherish them than any other possesion on earth.

The Bishop of Derry—We have a group in our midst who are making every effort to draw off the sympathy of the people for the Insurgent forces and the Spanish Church. They appear to be able to combine profession of Catholic Faith with Communism, a combination which Pius XI declares impossible.

The Bishop of Elphin—Everyone now knows that the war being fought in Spain is not a war between royalists and republicans, it is not a war between rich and poor; it is a war between Christ and anti-Christ.

The Bishop of Limerick—How is it that the Christian nations of Europe are not united as one man against the spirit that emanates from Moscow and Madrid? The answer is that though Europe has long been the home of Christianity, the days, as foretold, have come when faith has grown dim and charity grown cold.

The Bishop of Waterford—The Catholics of Spain still need your aid; the struggle is by no means over.

February 25th—The following letter addressed to His Eminence Cardinal Pacelli, Papal Secretary of State was handed to-day to His Excellency the Apostolic Nuncio, the Most Rev. Paschal Robinson, Archbishop of Tiana, by William Norton, T.D., Leader of the Irish Labour Party in Dail Eireann:

> His Eminence, Cardinal Pacelli,
> Cardinal Secretary of State,
> Vatican City.

Your Eminence,
I have the honour of bringing to the notice of your Eminence a copy of a news paragraph published in the Dublin daily press of the 18 inst. which, as your Eminence will observe, calls attention to the terms of an article published in *Osservatore Romano* under date 13 inst. I beg the opportunity of assuring you that there is no foundation for the allegations contained in the *Osservatore Romano* article as far as they reflect on the working class movements in this country, and I think it regrettable that any responsible organ should publish statements as obviously lacking in truth.

The article in *Osservatore Romano* to which I take the liberty of directing the attention of your Eminence asserts, inter alia, that the 204,000 Irish workers who are members of trade unions affilated to the Irish Trade Union and to the Irish Labour

Party tacitly support Communism, and that the Irish Trade Union Congress Congress circulated an article in which the Catholic Church was described as an enemy of the workers. As a Catholic and the accepted Leader of the Irish Labour Movement, I desire most emphatically to repudiate both statements.

Your Eminence will observe that in making these assertions *Osservatore Romano* purports to summarise a rather lengthy article published on the 4 inst. in a Dublin newspaper describing itself as the "Irish Catholic."

I would like to suggest to your Eminence, if I may, that *Osservatore Romano*, if it desired to publish reliable information on the religious beliefs and economic viewpoint of Irish workers would, in the first instance, have recourse to the distinguished Churchman who occupies the position of Rector of the Irish College in Rome, or to the other Irish ecclesiastics in that city.

In my humble judgement the absence of any suggestion in the public pronouncements of the Cardinal Primate of Ireland or of the Irish Bishops that the industrially and politically organised workers of this country tacitly support Communism should have suggested to those responsible for the article of which I complain the necessity of checking the information on which the article was based by reference to a recognised Catholic authority qualified to interpet the tendencies of political movements in Ireland. ...

(Here Norton goes on to give a lengthy account of his work against the introduction of Communist ideas into the Irish Labour Movement—*but makes no reference to the struggle in Spain.*)

... May I express the hope that with these assurances to assist you in appraising the damage that statements of the kind of which I complained are capable of doing when used for unworthy purposes in this country, your Eminence will take such action as you may deem expedient to prevent a repetion of the baseless allegations to which I have refered.

May 16th—The delegates of the C.Y.M.S. (Catholic Young Mens Society) attended a Special Mass celebrated by Mrg. Waters in St. Kevin's Chapel, Pro-Cathedral and offered Holy Communion for the success of the convention. Among the main matters on which resolutions were adopted were exposition of the dangers of Communism, and of the insidious campaign of Communist agents, a recommendation to the Irish Trade Union Congress on the question of affilation with an international body, a decision to work for the establishment of vocational groups as outlined in the Papal Encyclicals, and immediate provision of machinery to safeguard the faith of Irish emigrants to Great Britain.

A striking paper was read by Rev. D. Fahey, C.S.Sp., D.D., Blackrock College on "Will Ireland remain faithful to Christ the King?"

June 21st—The members of the Irish Brigade who served under General O'Duffy in Spain were given a reception in the Mansion House, Dublin, this afternoon after a march from the Alexandria Basin where they disembarked.

They were greeted and addressed from the steps of the Mansion House on arrival by the Lord Mayor who was thanked by General O'Duffy.

A reception held in the Round Room was presided over by the Right Rev. Magr. Waters, P.P., V.G., who said his sole purpose in taking the chair was to honour them as soldiers of the Cross.

October 12th—A statement on the situation in Spain was issued by the Irish Hierarchy at the conclusion of the October meeting in Maynooth to-day, at which His Eminence, Cardinal MacRory, Archbishop of Armagh and Primate of All Ireland presided.

1938

January 1st–An important New Year's Message to the Irish people was contained in a striking sermon by His Eminence, Cardinal MacRory, Archbishop of Armagh and Primate of All Ireland, in St. Patrick's Cathedral, Armagh, when he presided at Solemn High Mass.

Reviewing events of the past year abroad and at home, he began by referring to the persecution of Christians in Russia, the struggle for God and Christian civilisation waged by General Franco and youth of Spain, and the outlook in Germany where, he said, the danger to Christian Faith might be greater even in Russia.

1939

April 24th;A Solemn High Mass, in thanksgiving for the victory of the Catholic cause in Spain, was celebrated in the Pro—Cathedral, Dublin, and was followed by the singing of the *TE DEUM*. His Grace, the Archbishop of Dublin presided.

The large congregation included members of the Diplomatic Corps, men prominent in various Catholic organisations, and members of the Irish Brigade who fought in Spain.

At the conclusion of the service, messages were sent to Cardinal Goma Y Tomas, Primate of Spain, and General Franco by a Committee representative of 12 Catholic societies.

Extracted from the "Record of Irish Ecclesiastical Events", IRISH CATHOLIC DIRECTORY AND ALMANAC, 1937–38–39–40: published by James Duffy & Co., Ltd. 38 Westmoreland Street, Dublin

DECREE OF THE SPANISH GOVERNMENT REGARDING THE INTERNATIONAL BRIGADE

The units constituted by Spanish and foreign volunteers were organised by the decree of August 31st, 1920 ("Diario Oficial" No. 195) developed in the circular order of September 4th of the same year. Neither of these orders is, however, fully applicable to the forces similarly recruited, which are at present fighting heroically as part of the Republican Army.

Even though the Units now existing under the name of International Brigades are legally those which the Spanish State, using its sovereign rights has constituted to take the place of the Units which revolted in July 1936, and are analogous to those which under different names exist in the armies of almost all countries, it is necessary to lay down fresh norms which should regulate their recruitment, organisation, administration etc. To meet with this necessity I have determined:

1. To take the place of the Tercio de Extranjeros (Foreign Legion), formed under the decree of August 31st, 1920 ("Diario Oficial" No. 195) the International Brigades are formed as Units in the Spanish Army. At the present time five of the above-mentioned Brigades should be constituted on the basis of those formed spontaneously in the course of the present war, adapting their constitution to the norms indicated in the present order.

2. Tactically the International Brigades will be used as front-line troops and in all the services of peace and war, with no restriction other than that of their military utility.

3. Their organisation will follow the model assigned to the Mixed Brigades in the Spanish Army. The troops forming these Brigades will be subject to the Code of Military Justice and to the Army Statutes, in the same way as Spanish soldiers.

4. The training of the International Brigades will be adjusted to the same regulations and instructions as those which are in force in the other Units of the Army.

5. The uniforms and equipment will be the same as those of the other forces in the Spanish Army with no difference other than that of wearing on the right side of the shirt or jacket, two centimetres above the pocket the emblem which will be published in the Diario Oficial and which only those incorporated in these Units, whatever their military rank will be entitled to use.

6. In Albacete the International Brigades will have their Base, the fundamental mission of which will be to receive the volunteers, both Spanish subjects and foreigners who present themselves to swell the ranks of the Brigades, to train them and send them to the Brigades as circumstances demand. Once the recruits are incorporated in the Brigades, they will cease to be subordinate to the Base, whenever the Brigades

are tactically subordinate to the corresponding administrative units in an analagous manner to the other Mixed Brigades in the Army.

Nevertheless the International Brigades will depend on their Base for the following:

a) In addition to their reports to their own military commanders, the Brigades will report to the Base all their movements from one place to another, their losses, leaves granted for the interior of Spain and in general all that supposes a change of any importance in the life of the Brigades.

(b) Petitions for leave abroad will be noted by the Brigade Commanders and forwarded to the Base. In no case will the applicant be authorised to absent himself from the ranks of his unit before the leave has been granted.

(c) All proposal for promotion to whatever rank, beginning with promotion from corporal to sergeant, will be forwarded to the Base by the Brigade Commanders.

(d) When any Brigade has a soldier who, after previous medical examination in the Unit is declared to be unfit, the Brigade, without removing him from its list of effectives will send him to the Base where his case will receive final medical examination. When his unfitness is confirmed this will be communcated to the Brigade so that the latter can remove him from the list of effectives. In cases where unfitness is not confirmed, the person concerned will return to his Unit.

(e) The Brigades should send to the Base all particular statements and reports for which they are asked.

7. In addition to the organs necessary to execute the above functions, the Base of the International Brigades will have the organs corresponding to the following:

(a) To collecting and distributing among the Brigades, all the gifts which international solidarity may send expressly to the Brigades.

(b) To take the first steps in matters of pensions for death or incapacity, collecting the documents and antecedents demanded by the legislation in force and then forwarding them to this Ministry for decision.

(c) To forward to this Ministry, after investigating them, the petitions for permission to leave Spanish territory made by Members of the International Brigades of whatever rank.

(d) To report to the Ministry on the incorporation of recruits and their departure for the Brigades.

(e) To keep a file, which will contain all the relevant particulars, concerning the members of the Brigades.

(f) To propose the formation, and when necessary to undertake the direction of centres for re-education necessary for members of the Brigade who stand in need of this, as a result of injuries received in war service.

(g) To propose the formation, and when necessary to undertake the direction of rest homes in which those combatants who have their families abroad, and who have no residence here, can spend their leave in Spain.

8. In no case will the Base intervene in the functioning of the Supply and Medical Services relating to the International Brigades. The Brigades will make use of the general services of the Army in the same way as the other Mixed Brigades. Nevertheless on the basis of a proposition which the Base will make to this Ministry, the General Medical Inspectorate will be able to organise, under the Inspectorate's control, the installation of special hospitals with the qualified staff and assistants necessary for the wounded and convalescent members of the International Brigades, who are in need of lengthy hospital treatment. Entrance to the said hospitals will be regulated at all times by the General Medical Inspectorate.

9. The relation between this Ministry and the Base of the International Brigades will be effected through the Foreigner's Bureau, attached to the Section of Services of the Under Secretariat of the Army.

10. The International Brigades will be formed of Spanish and foreign volunteers.

Nevertheless this Ministry reserve the right to send directly to the Brigades the soldiers, non-commissioned and commissioned officers, and commanders whom it deems desirable. The personal at the Base will consist preferably of members of the Brigades who are unfit for service at the front, and in any case it will be indispensable for the members of the personnel of the Foreigner's Bureau will be appointed by the Ministry.

11. The foreign personnel of the Brigades will consist of those, who of their own accord, present themselves at the Foreigner's Bureau or before its delegates and who, after admission, will be sent to the Base for registration. The Spanish personnel will consist of those who apply for admission to the Brigades to this Ministry, either directly if they are not subject to military service, or through the regulation channels if they are in the Army. The petitions will be dealt with as a matter of urgency, and in the event of their being answered in the affirmative by this Ministry, the order will be given for the person concerned to be removed from the list of the effectives of the Unit from which be proceeds his entry at the Base of the International Brigades and his immediate enrolment in the Brigades.

12. The Spanish or foreign soldiers of the International Brigades will fill by promotion fifty per cent of the vacancies in the Brigades for sergeants, officers and commanders. With this object the Brigades, when reporting to the Base that such posts are vacant, will propose those members in the Brigades whom they regard as deserving of promotion. To pass from one post to another, it will be necessary to have held the lower post for a minimum period of two months. If the Brigade does not posses sufficient personnel to fill the vacancies, they will be filled by the nominees of other International Brigades, and in the event of there being none, they will be filled by the Ministry by direct nominations of military personnel. A vacancy will not be considered to have been created, except in cases of death, or when the base communicates that the post is vacant through unfitness, a change in post or removal from the Army. Absences due to wounds, illness or leave will not be considered as vacancies, and when necessary the posts concerned will be filled temporarily by men from lower posts, without this supposing any promotion. Those who are promoted, will receive the corresponding rank of sergeant, officer or commander of the International Brigades, and when the present campaign is ended they will constitute the permanent commanding cadres is the said Units. The sergeants, officers and commanders of the International Brigades cannot be sent outside these units. They can be isolated, expelled or reduced in rank for obious incompetence or impropriety in the execution of their duty, after a report has been made by the Commander of the corresponding Brigade and by the Commander of the Base.

13. The other fifty per cent of the vacancies of sergeants, officers and commanders will be filled with men sent directly by the Ministry of Defence, from among those who are already recognised in those posts in the Army. These men will remain subject as far as promotions are concerned to the general existing norms in the matter of recompenses.

The commanders, officers and sergeants who desire to be sent into the International Brigades should send in the appropriate application to the Personnel Section of the Under Secretariat of the Army.

14. Soldiers, non-commissioned and commissioned officers and commanders both Spanish and foreign, belonging to the International Brigades will in cases of incapacity or death have the same rights as those in the rest of the Army.

15. All members of the Brigades will have the right to thirteen days' leave, for every six months at the front, always providing that the necessities of service permit it, and providing that the conduct of the soldiers concerned make them deserving of this in the Commanders' opinion. For this purpose the corresponding turns, two a month, will be fixed in each Brigade, so that each month leaves can be begun once they have been passed in review by the Commissar. Those who wish to spend their

leave outside Spain should apply in advance, abiding by the decision which is taken. The Commander of the Base of the International Brigades, will communicate to each of the Brigades, the number of places at their disposal in the rest homes which may be installed in virtue of the provisions of Section (G) of the seventh article of this order.

16. The measures laid down in this order, will be put rapidly into operation by the soldiers and officers, now constituting the International Brigades, and their Base as they receive the appropriate instructions from the Foreigner's Bureau of the Under Secretariat of the Army.

17. The commanders of the International Brigades will send to the Base of the Brigades with all possible speed, a statement of the leading forces specifying their nationality, date of birth, date of entry into the International Brigades, and date at which they were given their present posts, so that the Ministry can proceed to confirm them in those posts when it considers this fitting.

18. The necessarily variable condition of the organisation of the personnel constituting the Base of the International Brigades makes it impossible, at least for the moment, to assign to it a fixed organisation. For the purpose of the review by the Commissar, the numerical account will be sent monthly to the Foreigner's Bureau, and in relation to this the review should be made.

19. To those foreigners who have served for more than a year in the Army with a clean record, and very deserving conduct, a certificate will be forwarded which will serve as the basis for according them Spanish nationality should they so desire.

20. All those who voluntarily enter the International Brigades undertake to remain in them until the end of the present campaign. When this campaign is finished, the norms will be laid down in accordance with which these Units should be organised in the future.

Published in "Volunteer for Liberty" (Organ of the International Brigades). Vol. 1. No. 21.

DECLARATION BY THE COMMISSAR INSPECTOR OF THE INTERNATIONAL BRIGADES ON THE DECREE OF THE SPANISH GOVERNMENT

We are publishing the Decree which lays down the position of the International Brigades in the Spanish People's Army, and the rights and duties of all Volunteers for Liberty.

This is the first document which determines in an official manner this position and these rights and duties.

It determines these in a way which is complety satisfactory to our soldiers.

It is clearly emphasised in the Decree, that our brave Brigades have nothing to do with the "Tercio" which revolted against the Republic in 1936, and is composed of the dregs of all countries.

In our Brigades are gathered together the best sons of all peoples. The Brigades are the World People's Front fighting by the side of Spain to defend the people's liberty and independence.

It is to express this highly political significance that the Decree determines that all the Volunteers for Liberty should wear as their distinguishing mark, the three-pointed star, which is the symbol of the World People's Front.

The Decres also lays it down that our Brigades form an integral part of the Spanish People's Army.

We have always asked for this and have always affirmed it. We have come here with one single purpose: to defend the liberty and independence of Spain. We have always obeyed the orders of the Government and its General Staff. We only ask for the honour of serving the common cause of liberty on the same terms as the Spanish fighters.

A regular army and a unified command: these are the essential conditions for victory in the armed struggle against fascism.

Because of this we receive with enthusiasm all those measures in the Decree, which tend to make our Brigades more and more integral parts of the Spanish People's Army.

The needs of the first days, the lack of organisation which still existed at that time, made it necessary to have a rather special organisation of our services.

Now our army has developed. All our services function remarkably well, and all the services of the International Brigades should be organised on the basis of the services of the Regular Spanish Army.

Our postal, supply and medical services should therefore form an integral part of the respective Spanish services.

As a token of the services rendered by the Brigades, the Decree grants the recognition of some advantages to the combatants. This is the significance of the points concerning the nomination of officers and the International Volunteer's right to thirteen days' leave abroad for every six months's service at the front.

The last point in the Decree, which lays it down that all the volunteers enroll until the end of the war, emphasises even more strongly that our Brigades are not formed of mercenaries, but of volunteers ready to fight to the finish to secure the defeat of Spanish and international fascism.

They are fighters, who know all the hardships of the struggle, and who never flinch, and never will flinch before the fascist butchers, either in their own countries or in the trenches of freedom.

Victory or death is their slogan, just as it is the slogan of all the Spaniards.

L. GALLO.

Commissar Inspector of the International Brigades.

BRIGADE COMMISSARIAT OF WAR

Political Commissars, or "Commissar Delegates of War"—as they are officially termed in the Spanish Republican Army—arose out of the same historical necessity that gave birth to the first Political Commissars on record—the Commissars of the French Revolution.

Faced with the task of defending their newly-won freedom against the armed combination of reactionary powers of Europe, beset with treachery on all sides, forced to rely on military leadership whose loyalty was often doubtful, the members of the Paris Convention hit upon the expedient of sending to the Army units their own delegates—tried and trusted adherents of the Revolution. The experiment justified itself; these Commissars guided the army, established discipline, built up morale, spread education among the men and carried the revolution into the enemy camp.

The creation of Political Commissars in Spain closely parallels the French historical example. At the outbreak of the military revolt the Spanish People's Government had only untrained men to oppose the military units of the Fascist officers. Victory for the Government demanded the mastering of military technique, an efficient military organisation and discipline resting on political education, and comradeship between the command and the militia. These unmistakably political problems demanded a political solution; for that purpose, the Commissariat of War was established four months after the outbreak of the revolt.

The Commissars are an integral part of the Army. Primarily their role is to inspire their unit with the highest spirit of discipline and loyalty to the Republican cause and establish a feeling of mutual confidence and good comradeship between Commanders and men. In the People's Army discipline is not based on militarism but on the conscious realisation that the interests of the people and of its Government are the same. The Commissar teaches the recruit that victory depends on carrying out unquestioningly and unwaveringly whatever order the military Command may issue. In an Imperialist Army soldiers are kept forward in the attack by another file of soldiers who will shoot them if they retreat; the Commissar aims at keeping the soldiers forward in the attack by their own passionate devotion to the cause for which they fight.

The Commissar is an educator in the broadest sense of the word. He does not lecture or teach (although he may when the necessity arises) but uses every opportunity to clarify all political issues that arise. He strives to increase the store of knowledge of both officers and men. In Imperialist Armies the rule is to keep the men in ignorance; in a revolutionary Army the Commissars keep the men fully informed of the aims of the war, and also of the immediate objectives of the Command. A soldier who knows the importance of the military objective and also the reason for it can be trusted to put up a much better fight for it. The Commissar knows how to impart military knowledge and yet keep the military secrecy so essential to successful operations.

The Commissar's work extends to the smallest details that contribute to the material well-being and comfort of the men. He is not a cook, but he sees that the food is prepared as well as possible; he is not Quartermaster, but he worries about clothes and supplies; he is not a doctor but he worries about health, hygiene and sanitation; he works indefatigably so that the men may have maximum comfort, leisure, rest and recreation.

The Commissar never forgets that the interests of the soldiers and civilians are the same; he strives to develop the most fraternal relationships between the troops and the population. The Army is there to help the people—as every soldier will readily affirm; the Commissar ensures that this is translated into practice. Troops relieved from front-line duty are often seen spending their rest-period helping the peasants with an enthusiasm that only the most profound feeling of mutual interest could arouse. The Commissar strives to ensure that the same feeling of fraternity is shown to the population in territory redeemed from Fascist control, and he exerts his propagandist skill to the utmost to win over apathetic—and even hostile—elements.

The Commissar co-operates closely with the military Commander at whose side he is appointed. He participates, in an advisory capacity, in the decisions of the military Command, bringing his intimate knowledge of men and his political understanding to bear on military problems. As a mark of complete agreement between military and political leadership, orders and reports are signed jointly by the Commander and the Commissar.

Propaganda directed against the enemy plays an important part in the Commissar's activity. Here again, the military and political leaders work hand in hand, undermining the morale of the enemy, destroying his will to fight and thus helping the People's Army to more speedy victory.

The Commissar is always on the alert to promote and popularise education, especially in military subjects, and to help to promotion from the ranks those who deserve it. At all times, the Commissar sets a personal example to the Volunteers of the rank and file. In action, he is found where his personal example and influence is the most decisive. "First to advance and last to retreat"—the slogan of the Commissars—has been sealed in the blood of many of the ablest and best men of the Spanish Republican Army.

The Brigade Commissariat, office of the Brigade Commissar, was established by Batthel, first Commissar of the Brigade after Copic took over military command. Aitken, Nelson and Doran in turn have contributed to its further development and brought it to its present state of efficiency. The Brigade Commissariat publishes daily a mimeographed bulletin *Our Fight*, giving a news-digest in English and Spanish, and articles of special interest to the Brigade. When time and opportunity permit, it also publishes a printed journal under the same title.

The Commissariat has a special department of propaganda directed towards the enemy and also a Sound-Truck for that purpose. It maintains a library, a photographic department, and recently, it has begun the organisation of musical and drama groups. Special effort is given by the Commissariat towards eradicating illiteracy among Spanish soldiers.

The Commissariat co-operates with the civilian population and maintains the most harmonious relationship with them. When occasion permits, joint fiestas are organised in the villages. The Sound-Wagon is often put to use to give concerts. It is worthy of mention that the Brigade distributed over 22,000 pesetas worth of gifts to the children, last Christmas, with money raised through voluntary contributions by the men.

It is impossible to give within this limited space a full description of the manifold function of the Commissariat. Its work never ceases; in action or at rest, the political, physical, cultural, educational and recreational needs of the men are always provided for—factors that are all-important in maintaining the morale of the troops at their maximum military efficiency.   *S.M.*

"The Book of the XV Brigade," pp. 217–220.

INDEX

226